World education report 1998

Teachers and teaching in a changing world

UNESCO Publishing

The designations employed and the presentation
of the material in this publication do not imply
the expression of any opinion whatsoever on the part
of UNESCO concerning the legal status of any country,
territory, city or area, or of its authorities, or concerning
the delimitation of its frontiers or boundaries.

Published in 1998 by the United Nations
Educational, Scientific and Cultural Organization
7, Place de Fontenoy, 75352 Paris 07 SP

Graphics by Visit-Graph, Boulogne-Billancourt
Printed by Darantiere
ISBN 92-3-103450-2

©UNESCO 1998
Printed in France

Foreword

The world we leave to our children depends in large measure on the children we leave to our world. The world's hopes for the future rest with today's young people and their readiness to take up the challenges of the coming century. On the threshold of the twenty-first century, the education of the young has never been more in need of our commitment and resources. Our teachers have never been more crucial to our collective future.

The communication and information revolution currently underway reinforces this need. New technologies are bringing the different peoples of the world closer together, helping them to become more aware of their common humanity and shared concerns and hopes for the future. At the same time, these technologies accentuate divisions both within and between societies, between those who are able to utilize them for the enrichment of their cultural, social, economic and political lives and those who are unable to do so because of poverty or lack of the necessary knowledge and skills. Without a greater commitment to education on the part of governments and society at large, these divisions will widen further.

While progress is being made towards the goal of Education for All, renewed efforts are needed to ensure that the education provided is of high quality and relevant to social needs. This is essential if the young are to acquire the knowledge, skills, attitudes and values needed to lead active and productive lives in the knowledge-based societies of the future. More resources for education will be required not only to provide greater access to education but also to make that access meaningful. Teachers must be well prepared and appropriately rewarded for their work; adequate supplies of educational materials should be made available, and school conditions need to be healthy, comfortable and conducive to effective teaching and learning.

Teachers in particular require our encouragement and support. In that connection, the *Recommendation concerning the Status of Teachers,* prepared jointly by the International Labour Organization (ILO) and UNESCO, and adopted by a special intergovernmental conference in 1966, is especially relevant today.

This report, the fourth in UNESCO's series of *World Education Reports,* reviews recent trends and developments in education and educational policy affecting the world's 57 million teachers. Teachers have a pivotal role to play in preparing the young generation to help realize our hopes that the coming century will see a more socially just, more tolerant and more peaceful world. The situation of teachers merits the closest attention of all who wish to leave such a world to our children.

Federico Mayor
Director-General of UNESCO

Contents

List of boxes, figures and tables

Figures and tables for which no source is indicated have been drawn from the database of UNESCO's Division of Statistics. In these figures and tables, where a regional breakdown is shown, there is an overlap between the two regions of sub-Saharan Africa and the Arab States (see Explanatory Notes to Appendix II on page 104).

Boxes

Figures

Tables

Text tables

Regional tables

World Education Indicators

Acknowledgements

THE INFORMATION presented in this report is drawn selectively from the range of information available to UNESCO from both official and unofficial sources, including in particular the national reports of Member States presented at the 45th session of the International Conference on Education (Geneva, 1996), the replies of Member States to a questionnaire survey administered by the International Bureau of Education in preparation for the Conference, and the database of the Organization's Division of Statistics.

The report has been prepared by the World Education Report Unit of the Secretariat's Education Sector, under the general direction of Colin N. Power, Assistant Director-General for Education, in collaboration with the Division of Statistics. The staff of both the Education Sector and the Division of Statistics provided advice and suggestions as well as background material.

A number of individuals and organizations outside UNESCO also contributed advice and suggestions and/or background material. A preliminary draft of the report was reviewed by members of an external editorial advisory group comprising Jean-Pierre Boyer, Michael J. Dunkin, Ulf Fredricksson (Education International), Gilbert de Landsheere, P. Obanya, J. S. Rajput, William Ratteree (International Labour Organization) and Peter R. C. Williams. Specific advice and suggestions were also provided by Meng Hong-wei and Tim O'Shea. Background papers were provided by Peter Blatchford and Harvey Goldstein, Michael J. Dunkin, Education International, the National Commission of the People's Republic of China for UNESCO, J. S. Rajput, and Robert Wood. A UNESCO-sponsored International Colloquium on 'Virtual Learning Environments and the Role of the Teacher' was organized at the Open University, United Kingdom, in April 1997 as part of the background preparation for Chapter 4; the report on the Colloquium was prepared by Tim O'Shea and Eileen Scanlon. Unpublished statistical data were provided by the Statistical Office of the European Communities (EUROSTAT), the International Association for the Evaluation of Educational Achievement (IEA), the International Labour Organization (ILO) and the Organisation for Economic Co-operation and Development (OECD). The kind co-operation of all these individuals and organizations is gratefully acknowledged. None of them necessarily agrees with the views expressed in the report.

World Education Report team

Chief editor:	John Smyth
Programme specialist:	Ranwa Safadi
Statistics Division co-ordination for the Report	Vittoria Cavicchioni
Consultant:	John Ryan
Data and documentation preparation:	Roser Cusso and Sophia Gazza
Secretary:	Micheline Gingras-Kovatcheva
Camera-ready preparation of the Report:	Josette Pentcheff and Marina Rubio
Publications officer:	Wenda McNevin

1
Introduction

As THE PRESENT CENTURY draws to a close, education has emerged at the forefront of the world's concern over its own future. The challenges of the coming century to eliminate poverty and ensure sustainable development and lasting peace will fall to today's young people. Educating the young to meet these challenges has become a priority objective for every society.

The young generation is entering a world which is changing in all spheres: scientific and technological, political, economic, social and cultural. The outlines of the 'knowledge-based' society of the future are forming. The status of education is changing: once seen as a factor of unity and integration within societies, capable of overcoming social and economic differences and distinctions, it is increasingly becoming a source of such differences and distinctions between societies in a global economy which rewards those who possess more advanced skills and limits the opportunities of those who do not. Perceptions of the scope of education also are changing as societies come to recognize that, in the words of the International Commission on Education for the Twenty-first Century, 'the time to learn is now the whole lifetime', not just during the period of childhood and youth.

In the Commission's vision of the coming century, 'much will be expected, and much demanded, of teachers' (Box 1.1). 'Teachers', the Commission has insisted, 'have crucial roles to play in preparing young people not only to face the future with confidence but to build it with purpose and responsibility'.

This report considers the situation of the world's teachers. It reviews recent trends and developments in education and educational policies affecting their status, the contexts in which they work and the pressures they face, and their education and training. It considers too the emerging challenges for teachers and teaching posed by the introduction into education of the new information and communication technologies. The discussion is necessarily broad in scope and selective in the details chosen for emphasis.

UNESCO since its earliest days has monitored trends and developments in education and educational policies affecting teachers. For more than thirty years, the main inspiration for the Organization's activity in this area has been the *Recommendation concerning the Status of Teachers,*

Box 1.1
'Much will be expected,
and much demanded, of teachers'

Our vision of the coming century is of one in which the pursuit of learning is valued by individuals and by authorities all over the world not only as a means to an end, but also as an end in itself. Each person will be encouraged and enabled to take up learning opportunities throughout life. Hence, much will be expected, and much demanded, of teachers, for it largely depends on them whether this vision can come true. Teachers have crucial roles to play in preparing young people not only to face the future with confidence but to build it with purpose and responsibility. The new challenges facing education – to contribute to development, to help people understand and to some extent come to terms with the phenomenon of globalization, and to foster social cohesion – must be met from primary and secondary school onwards. ...

The importance of the role of the teacher as an agent of change, promoting understanding and tolerance, has never been more obvious than today. It is likely to become even more critical in the twenty-first century. The need for change, from narrow nationalism to universalism, from ethnic and cultural prejudice to tolerance, understanding and pluralism, from autocracy to democracy in its various manifestations, and from a technologically divided world where high technology is the privilege of the few to a technologically united world, places enormous responsibilities on teachers who participate in the moulding of the characters and minds of the new generation.

Source: J. Delors et al., *Learning: The Treasure Within. Report to UNESCO of the International Commission on Education for the Twenty-first Century,* pp. 141–2, Paris, UNESCO, 1996.

which was adopted by a special Intergovernmental Conference convened jointly by UNESCO and the International Labour Organization (ILO) in Paris in 1966. Aimed at improving the status of teachers, the *Recommendation* provides guidelines for countries to follow in regard to the professional preparation, employment and conditions of service of teachers.

As in the case of the *Recommendation*, the focus of the report is broadly on teachers in the formal education system at the pre-primary, primary and secondary levels; teachers at these levels currently account for nearly nine out of ten teachers in the world's formal education systems (Figure 1.1). Teachers at the tertiary level are not considered in the report except in passing; an international recommendation concerning their status was recently adopted by the General Conference of UNESCO at its 29th Session in Paris in November 1997.

At the time when the *1966 Recommendation* was adopted, there were fears in many countries that the status of teachers could be affected by the recruitment of large numbers of unqualified teachers to meet current teacher shortages. On the other hand, the long-term prospects of an improvement in the status of teachers appeared to be favourable, provided that appropriate measures were taken. Education was being given increasing priority in national development policies and was receiving an increasing share of national resources. However, from the late 1970s onwards and especially during the 1980s after the second oil crisis (1979), as more and more countries experienced economic difficulties and policies towards expenditure on education became more restrictive, teachers became increasingly regarded as a cost as much as a resource for educational development. Their position in a majority of countries as the largest single category of public sector employees meant that they rarely escaped from the impact of policies of economic restructuring and adjustment. The connection between the status of teachers and attitudes

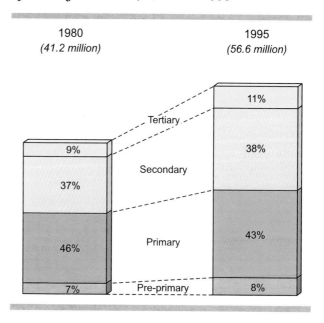

Figure 1.1

Percentage breakdown of teachers in the world's formal education systems, by level of education, 1980 and 1995

towards education was noted at that time by the Joint ILO-UNESCO Committee of Experts on the Application of the Recommendation concerning the Status of Teachers (Box 1.2).

Taking the guiding principles and provisions of the 1966 *Recommendation* as points of reference, the main trends and developments in education and educational policies affecting the status of teachers over the past decade are reviewed in Chapter 2. In anticipation of the discussion, two trends may be noted in advance. First, in response to the continuing pressures of student enrolments and the still large backlog of out-of-school youth (Figure 1.2), a growing percentage of the world's teachers are employed in the world's less developed regions (Figure 1.3). Forty-six out of every hundred teachers in the world today live in Asia (see Appendix II, Table 9).

Second, the economic restructuring and adjustment which most countries underwent in varying degree in the 1980s, and which some countries still are engaged in, has left what appears to be a

Thus, although the World Conference on Education for All (Jomtien, Thailand, 1990) ushered in a decade of growing recognition of education's vital role in national development and the preparation of young people for active and productive lives in the knowledge-based societies of the twenty-first century, many governments have continued to regard public expenditure on education as an area of potential savings rather than as an investment in the future. In consequence, improvement in the material rewards for teaching and in teachers' status generally have not been priority concerns of educational policy. In most regions of the world, few (if any) informed observers believe that the status of teachers has improved in recent years; the majority believe it has declined.

Moreover, it has not just been teachers' salaries and status which have failed to benefit in recent years from policies towards public expenditure on education. Teaching and learning conditions and the material situation of the schools generally, in

Figure 1.2
Estimated numbers (millions) of out-of-school youth in the world, 1995 and 2010

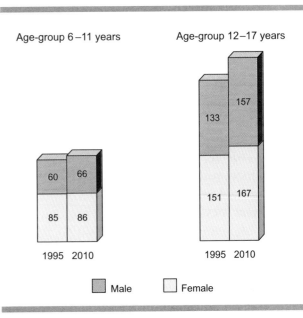

lasting imprint on national policies towards expenditure on education. At least, the education sector has not up to now managed to establish a claim for special treatment or exemption from policies designed to control public expenditure generally.

Figure 1.3
Regional distribution of teachers
in the world's formal education systems,[1]
1980 and 1995

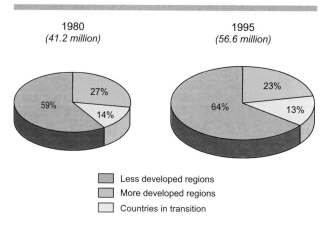

1980
(41.2 million)

1995
(56.6 million)

- Less developed regions
- More developed regions
- Countries in transition

1. The country-composition of the regions is indicated in Appendix II, p. 104.

communication technologies for the achievement of 'Education for All' goals need to be revised today in the light of the experience gained so far in applying the new technologies for educational purposes (Box 1.3), there are signs that these technologies could eventually have radical implications for conventional teaching and learning processes. In reconfiguring how teachers and learners can gain access to knowledge and information, the new technologies challenge conventional conceptions of both teaching and learning materials, and teaching and learning methods and approaches. How to utilize the new technologies for educational purposes is itself a growing new field of knowledge.

As in the case of other sectors of the wider economy and society, education will need to come to terms with the new technologies. This

probably a majority of countries, have also failed to benefit. Yet at the same time – as is discussed in Chapter 3 – national policy-makers and society in general increasingly desire improved educational quality and relevance, in particular improved 'learning outcomes'.

The immediate prospects of resolving the contradictions that are now embedded in educational policies over the question of resources appear to be limited, but a development is gathering momentum that could in time greatly change matters: the introduction into education of new information and communication technologies. These technologies are costly, at least compared with conventional teaching and learning materials, but they have become more and more present in the schools – up to now mainly in the industrial countries – as educational authorities, students and parents become increasingly aware of the growing number of jobs that require computer literacy skills. This development is discussed in Chapter 4.

Although the hopes raised at the beginning of the decade of readily harnessing information and

Box 1.3
Harnessing information and communication technology to meet basic learning needs

New possibilities are emerging which already show a powerful impact on meeting basic learning needs, and it is clear that the educational potential of these new possibilities has barely been tapped. These new possibilities exist largely as a result of two converging forces, both recent by-products of the general development process. First, the quantity of information available in the world – much of it relevant to survival and basic well-being – is exponentially greater than that available only a few years ago, and the rate of its growth is accelerating. A synergistic effect occurs when important information is coupled with a second modern advance – the new capacity to communicate among the people of the world. The opportunity exists to harness this force and use it positively, consciously, and with design, in order to contribute to meeting defined learning needs.

Source: World Conference on Education for All. Meeting Basic Learning Needs, Jomtien, Thailand, 1990, *Framework for Action to Meet Basic Learning Needs*, para. 27, New York, Inter-Agency Commission for the World Conference on Education for All, 1990.

Box 1.4
'What Makes a Good Teacher? Children Speak Their Minds'

A good teacher is a friend . . .
'You need to be kind, trusting and friendly to me . . . you must listen and understand us all . . . never lose your temper . . .'
Rose, 9 years old, from New Zealand.
'. . . treat us equally and understand the feelings, aspirations and moods of each one of us'.
Le Nhu Anh, 9 years old, from Viet Nam.

A good teacher listens . . .
'To become a good teacher, you not only teach the children but you also learn from them'.
Tasha-Leigh, 12 years old, from Jamaica.
'I like a teacher who helps me think and get answers for myself'.
Bongani Sicelo, 9 years old, from Zimbabwe.

A good teacher is a role model . . .
'A good teacher is someone who transmits to the future generation what is the most precious to her: her culture and her education'.
Nawal, 12 years old, from Morocco.
'The teacher should behave well since children copy them'.
Julietta, 12 years old, from Ghana.

. . . helps us grow and develop.
'The teacher should know how to make the pupils autonomous and help them to become adults'.
Anabella, 12 years old, from Italy.
'A good teacher guides us through the right way to achieve our goals'.
Analia, 12 years old, from Mexico.

Source: What Makes a Good Teacher? Children Speak their Minds. Brochure of the International Children's Contest organized by UNESCO through the Associated Schools Project, Paris, UNESCO, 1996.

---

could require substantial public and private sector investments in software research and development, purchase of hardware and refurbishing of schools. It will be difficult for national policy-makers to resist finding the necessary resources, whatever their sensitivities over expenditure on education, although without international co-operation and assistance the poorest countries could fall still further behind. Parents and the public at large, in the industrial countries at least, are unlikely to accept for too long that education should be less well equipped with the new technologies than other areas of social and economic activity.

Paradoxically, therefore, it is possible that technology will cause attitudes towards expenditure on education to change. If children need technology, they need good teachers too (Box 1.4).

2
The changing status and profile of teachers

THERE WERE 16 million teachers in the world's formal education systems when the *Recommendation concerning the Status of Teachers* was adopted, and their number was increasing rapidly. The 1960s was a period of considerable expansion of education in most regions of the world and there were widespread shortages of teachers, especially in the newly independent developing countries. Many countries adopted temporary, ad hoc measures to meet the shortages, notably by employing untrained teachers, while at the same time postponing the investment needed for long-term solutions. In consequence, questions concerning the status of teachers were very much in the air.

In retrospect, the growth and sheer size of the teaching profession in most countries have been handicaps in obtaining improvements in the status of teachers, which was the overall aim of the *Recommendation*. The 57 million teachers employed in the world's formal education systems today constitute the largest single distinctive category of people engaged in professional and technical occupations; this fact alone makes it difficult for society to accord teachers a status similar to that of smaller professional and technical groups such as physicians, lawyers and engineers.

In any case, the status of teachers is affected by the characteristics of teachers considered in the aggregate. From this standpoint, the teaching profession is notable for the diversity of its members' backgrounds and the multiplicity of their occupational functions, ranging from managing kindergarten classes to giving university lectures, training industrial technicians and running adult education courses. Many of its members are quite modestly trained before they begin their first job, while others undergo a lengthy preparation. Other characteristics too are relevant, notably the fact that in most countries a majority of teachers work in the public sector where they normally are not highly paid in comparison with persons in other occupations with similar or even less training, and long tenure in the job usually does not bring very large increases in salary. Also, a majority of teachers at the lower levels of education often are women, which has probably in the past helped to keep salaries low. Moreover, although the teaching profession attracts large numbers of academically able graduates from secondary or higher education institutions, it must also recruit large numbers of less able graduates in order to meet the enormous human resource needs of the education system as a whole. Taken together, all these factors account in large measure for the teaching profession's uncertain status.

In practice, therefore, the challenge for teachers has mostly been to ensure that their status is at least broadly comparable with that of other major professional and technical groups, while not foregoing the prospect of improvement when conditions are favourable. This challenge is a continuing one. The situation of teachers today is different from that of thirty years ago when the *Recommendation concerning the Status of Teachers* was adopted: there are more of them, the national education systems in which they work are very much bigger, the pupil/student populations are more diverse, and the global economic, social and cultural context has changed.

What these changes have broadly implied for the status of teachers is the main concern of this chapter. There are four sections. In the first, with a view to clarifying the nature of the continuing quest for improved status, key elements of the *Recommendation concerning the Status of Teachers,* in particular its Guiding Principles (Box 2.1), are recalled. In the second section, the pressures driving the growth of the world's education systems – and hence growth in the number of teachers – are considered. In the third section, major trends and developments in educational policy and expenditure in different parts of the world that have had implications for the status of teachers are examined. In the fourth and final section, a broad assessment of the emerging status and profile of the world's teachers is made.

Box 2.1
The Guiding Principles of the *Recommendation concerning the Status of Teachers*[1]

1. Education from the earliest school years should be directed to the all-round development of the human personality and to the spiritual, moral, social, cultural and economic progress of the community, as well as to the inculcation of deep respect for human rights and fundamental freedoms; within the framework of these values the utmost importance should be attached to the contribution to be made by education to peace and to understanding, tolerance and friendship among all nations and among racial or religious groups.

2. It should be recognized that advance in education depends largely on the qualifications and ability of the teaching staff in general and on the human, pedagogical and technical qualities of the individual teachers.

3. The status of teachers should be commensurate with the needs of education as assessed in the light of educational aims and objectives; it should be recognized that the proper status of teachers and due public regard for the profession of teaching are of major importance for the full realization of these aims and objectives.

4. Teaching should be regarded as a profession: it is a form of public service which requires of teachers expert knowledge and specialized skills, acquired and maintained through rigorous and continuing study; it calls also for a sense of personal and corporate responsibility for the education and welfare of the pupils in their charge.

5. All aspects of the preparation and employment of teachers should be free from any form of discrimination on grounds of race, colour, sex, religion, political opinion, national or social origin, or economic condition.

6. Working conditions for teachers should be such as will best promote effective learning and enable teachers to concentrate on their professional tasks.

7. Teachers' organizations should be recognized as a force which can contribute greatly to educational advance and which therefore should be associated with the determination of educational policy.

1. Paragraphs 1–7 in this box correspond to paragraphs 3–9 of the *Recommendation*.

Source: Recommendation concerning the Status of Teachers adopted by the Special Intergovernmental Conference on the Status of Teachers, convened by UNESCO in co-operation with ILO, Paris, 5 October 1966.

The *Recommendation concerning the Status of Teachers* (1966)

The status of teachers, as in the case of other professional groups, is generally understood in most societies to have an affective as well as a material dimension. Both dimensions are recognized in the *Recommendation concerning the Status of Teachers*: 'The expression "status" as used in relation to teachers means both the standing or regard accorded them, as evidenced by the level of appreciation of the importance of their function and of their competence in performing it, and the working conditions, remuneration and other material benefits accorded them relative to other professional groups' (Section I).

At the time when the *Recommendation* was adopted, the critical role of teachers in the development of education was becoming increasingly recognized. There was too a growing international consensus that temporary measures to cope with the widespread shortages of teachers should not be such as to undermine the status of teachers and the quality of education generally. This provided the immediate context for the preparation of the *Recommendation*.

As finally adopted at a Special Intergovernmental Conference convened for that purpose, the *Recommendation* has eleven sections, which basically contain various common standards and measures relating to educational policy, preparation for the teaching profession, the further (continuing) education of teachers, and teachers' employment and terms of service, that states are invited to apply 'in order to ensure that teachers enjoy a status commensurate with their essential role' in 'the advancement of education' (Preamble). It differs from an international convention in that the latter legally binds the ratifying states to apply its provisions.

Neither before nor since have so many states agreed in principle on a set of common standards and measures designed to support the status of such a large body of people. Broadly speaking, by setting out such standards and measures, e.g. that teachers should have at least completed secondary education (Section V), and 'should be adequately protected against arbitrary action affecting their professional standing or career' (Section VII), the overall strategy of the *Recommendation* was to try to reduce the temptation for teachers' employers to provide, at both students' and teachers' expense, a pale shadow of education rather than the real thing.

While it would be misleading to single out any one of the *Recommendation*'s Guiding Principles for special mention, since all are to some extent interrelated, the third merits attention in the context of the present report because of the connection it draws between the status of teachers and educational aims and objectives, and hence educational policy. This connection was noted in the preceding chapter. It implies that what the authorities who direct the education system expect from teachers, and hence what measures they are ready to take regarding their status, must inevitably reflect to some extent the nature of the educational aims and objectives, or in general the policy purposes, for which the teachers are hired. In the first of its Guiding Principles, the *Recommendation* affirms that the aims and objectives of educational policy should be noble ones. That in day-to-day practice they are usually quite mundane – often having more to do with saving money for other purposes outside of education altogether – is essentially where the difficulty in applying the *Recommendation* has arisen.

The fourth paragraph of the Guiding Principles, which affirms that 'Teaching should be regarded as a profession', also merits attention, especially

in the light of the recent efforts of teachers' leaders in a number of countries to induce the educational authorities to consider teachers as responsible partners in the educational process rather than as mere passive implementers of official policies.

A mechanism for monitoring the application of the *Recommendation* was not foreseen in the *Recommendation* itself, but was set up subsequently in 1968 by the governing bodies of UNESCO and ILO in the form of a Joint ILO-UNESCO Committee of Experts on the Application of the Recommendation concerning the Status of Teachers. The Committee was originally mandated to receive and consider reports from governments on the application of the *Recommendation,* but later was also authorized to consider information from national and international organizations representing teachers. As was (and still is) the usual practice of bodies set up in the United Nations system to monitor the application of normative instruments such as the *Recommendation,* the Committee initially based its work on a broad-ranging questionnaire sent out every three to four years to governments. Eventually, however, experience showed that this practice was unsatisfactory; many governments did not complete the questionnaire and the information provided by those that did respond was often inadequate (e.g. Box 2.2).

Accordingly, at a special session convened in 1991 to consider its methods of work, the Committee decided to adopt instead a more focused approach, following a methodology combining case studies, comparative analysis and specifically directed statistical questionnaires, and concentrating on selected topics or issues concerning the status of teachers that it considered to be of major importance, e.g. the initial and continuing education of teachers; participation, consultation and collective bargaining in the teaching profession; stress and burn-out of teachers; and gender issues in the teaching profession. In 1994, the Committee moved a step further in calling upon UNESCO

Box 2.2
**Reports by states on the application
of the *Recommendation concerning
the Status of Teachers***

The mandate of the Committee of Experts invites
it to supervise periodically, the application of
the *Recommendation concerning the Status of
Teachers* in all the Member States of UNESCO and
of the ILO. This mandate cannot be fully carried
out unless the greatest possible number of states
provide reports, covering the period under examination, and giving the development trends during
this period and unless these reports provide as
exact information as possible on law and practice
with regard to all the provisions of the *Recommendation*. Yet only 72 states out of 144 replied to the
questionnaire as compared with 77 out of 126 in
the Committee's previous survey [in 1969] and the
replies provided for each of the two periods under
examination did not always come from identical
states. As a result, it is very difficult to make useful
comparisons of reported changes over this period
and to make meaningful judgements on the way
in which the situation has developed. Moreover,
while the questionnaire invited the different states
to provide elements of information both in a general part, on the application of all the various sections of the *Recommendation*, and secondly more
thoroughly on various specific problems, the information given in the general part of the govern-
mental reports was so inadequate that the Committee found itself unable to draw any really useful conclusion from it. The Committee is, on this
account, unable to fulfill the main part of its mandate.

*Source: Conclusions of the Final Report adopted by the Joint ILO-
UNESCO Committee of Experts on the Application of the Rec-
ommendation concerning the Status of Teachers (Third Session,
Geneva, 8–19 March 1976) and Relevant Decisions Taken by
UNESCO General Conference at its Nineteenth Session (Nairobi,
October–November 1976), para. 16, Paris, UNESCO, 1977. (Doc-
ument ED-77/WS/61.)*

the Committee's work has not dispensed with the
need for UNESCO itself to monitor the major
trends and developments in education and educational policies that are likely to affect the status
of teachers, since these constitute the context for
any analysis of specific topics of immediate concern. The analysis of developments in teacher
education, for example, depends in part on how
teacher demand-supply balances are interpreted
and on how these relate to both the growth of
educational enrolments and the policies of
governments concerning this growth.

Before turning to consider the pressures driving
the growth in the number of teachers in the world,
one further aspect of the work of the joint ILO-
UNESCO Committee may be noted, namely, its
position with respect to teachers in adult and
non-formal education. The question of whether
to extend the scope of the *Recommendation* to
cover such teachers was raised on several oc-
casions in the 1970s and 1980s, but at a special
session in 1985, convened to consider the possible updating of the *Recommendation,* the Committee rejected this idea, fearing that it 'might
weaken' the impact of the *Recommendation* and
also 'introduce a degree of doubt as to the relevance of its existing provisions to some situations'.
It is likely that the Committee was also impressed
by the practical difficulties which would be created by such a broadening, particularly so in light
of the problems already encountered in monitoring the situation of teachers in the formal system.
When the idea surfaced again in 1991, the Committee acknowledged that 'non-formal education
was rapidly expanding' and that this was 'a trend
that may require more attention in the future'.

and ILO to develop a set of reliable, internationally comparable statistical indicators that
could facilitate monitoring the status of teachers;
this development is now under way in the two
organizations.

The more focused, topic-oriented approach in

The global pressures
of student enrolments

While the growth in the total number of teachers
in the world's formal education systems can be
basically regarded as a response to the pressure of

Figure 2.1
*Estimated trends in population
of the 6–14 age-group, by region, 1975–2015*

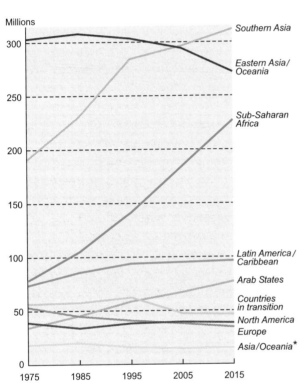

Millions

Southern Asia
Eastern Asia/
Oceania
Sub-Saharan
Africa
Latin America/
Caribbean
Arab States
Countries
in transition
North America
Europe
Asia/Oceania*

★ Those countries in Asia/Oceania that are classified under 'more developed regions'.

Source: United Nations Population Division database (1996 revision).

students already in the education system to continue their education to higher levels.

As noted earlier, the teacher shortages of the 1960s and the 1970s, especially in the less developed regions of the world, were met to some extent by employing large numbers of unqualified, untrained teachers; in many cases they were simply primary-school graduates. This did not accord with the provisions of the *Recommendation,* which required that prospective teachers should have completed secondary education and that their teaching preparation should be at the post-secondary level. In 1976, the Joint ILO-UNESCO Committee observed that these conditions were not yet attained in a third or more of the countries that replied to its questionnaire.

A measure of the tremendous efforts exerted by countries in the less developed regions to provide teachers to meet the challenge of the explosive growth in their school-age populations is that they managed to achieve an improvement in their enrolment ratios, i.e. the percentages of the relevant age-groups enrolled at the various levels of education (Figure 2.2). Even so, sub-Saharan Africa was an exception: the gross enrolment ratio in primary education fell back between 1980 and 1995.

The special difficulties faced in recent years by the countries in transition in maintaining the growth momentum of previous decades in secondary and tertiary education are indicated by the stagnation and/or fall in the overall gross enrolment ratios for these levels between 1980 and 1995. In the more developed regions, the falling birth rates and declining population pressures on school enrolments – and hence softening of the demand for teachers – provided an opportunity for reducing student-teacher ratios and class sizes at the middle and lower levels of the education system, although this was offset by an increasing need for teachers to meet the expansion of enrolments at the upper and lower ends of the education system in higher education and pre-primary education respectively.

Still, over time, as the outputs of the education

increasing student enrolments, the global pattern of student enrolments by region and level of education has changed considerably over the last thirty years, and continues to evolve.

Taking the size of the population in the 6–14 age-group as a broad indicator of the overall demand for education, recent decades have witnessed strong pressures on teacher demand-supply balances in Southern Asia, sub-Saharan Africa and the Arab States (Figure 2.1). These pressures are projected to continue well into the next century. In the other major regions, the pressures have levelled off or even declined, except in so far as there has been increasing demand from

systems in the less developed regions of the world increased and teacher-training capacities expanded, the levels of recruitment improved and growing numbers of qualified, trained teachers entered employment. The consequence of this trend, though, was that by the late 1970s and early 1980s, the primary-level teaching force in many countries was made up of groups of teachers with often very different educational and training backgrounds, ranging from teachers who in some cases (mainly older teachers) had not received much more than a primary education themselves to others who had received a full secondary education and teacher training in addition. The whole issue of the status of teachers was thus extremely complex, since in all these countries there was really no such body as a 'typical' primary-school teacher, at least in the same sense that this term could be applied in countries with a stable primary-level teaching force, most of whose members had received a similar education and training. The situation in respect to secondary-school teachers was not much different.

These developments helped to bring to the fore, among other things, the question of the in-service education and training of teachers, to which a section of the *Recommendation* was specifically devoted. Several other developments pointed in the same direction. Initiatives to reform school curricula, for example, could not be followed up successfully in many countries without taking into account the very heterogenous composition of the teaching force which would have to implement the new curricula in the schools. From the late 1970s onwards, therefore, the objectives, organization and management of the in-service education and training of teachers gained increasing attention from national educational policy-makers; recent trends and developments in this area are considered in Chapter 3.

One further aspect of the demographic background that needs to be noted with respect to global teacher demand-supply balances is the gradual ageing of the world's population.

The world's population is living longer and birth rates, despite their high levels in some

Figure 2.2
Gross enrolment ratios, by level of education and region, 1980 and 1995

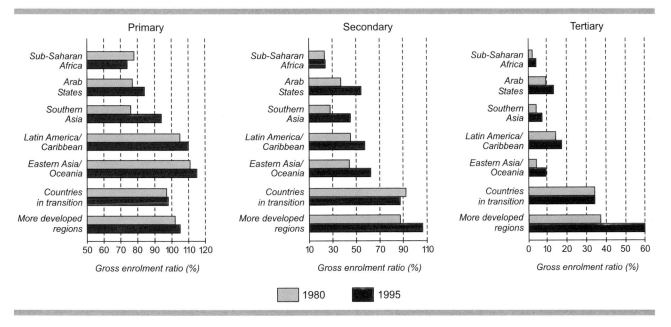

Table 2.1
Early childhood, school-age and old-age
dependency ratios (percentages),[1]
by region, 1995 and 2015

	1995			2015		
	0–5	*6–14*	*65+*	*0–5*	*6–14*	*65+*
WORLD TOTAL	20.8	29.6	10.5	16.2	23.3	12.1
More developed regions of which:	11.2	17.3	20.9	10.3	15.3	27.2
North America	13.7	19.8	19.1	12.1	17.0	22.1
Asia/Oceania	9.5	15.8	19.8	9.9	15.8	34.5
Europe	10.0	15.9	22.8	8.9	13.6	28.9
Countries in transition	12.7	23.0	16.9	10.9	16.2	18.1
Less developed regions of which:	23.6	32.8	7.7	17.5	25.1	9.4
Sub-Saharan Africa	40.4	46.5	5.7	32.0	40.8	5.7
Arab States	30.8	41.2	6.2	22.0	31.4	7.0
Latin America/Caribbean	22.3	32.5	8.3	15.9	23.4	10.9
Eastern Asia/Oceania	17.4	25.8	8.5	12.5	18.1	11.2
of which: China	15.5	23.5	9.0	11.5	16.0	12.2
Southern Asia	26.1	36.9	7.2	17.1	26.3	8.5
of which: India	23.8	34.0	7.6	14.6	23.7	9.4
Least developed countries	36.8	46.1	5.8	29.2	38.1	5.8

1. Percentage ratio of the population in each age-group to the population aged 15–64.

Source: United Nations Population Division database (1996 revision).

regions, are generally declining. In consequence, the educational 'burden' represented by the proportion of the adult population who must become teachers in order to provide education for any given percentage of young people is gradually diminishing, although more rapidly in the less developed than the more developed regions where it has almost levelled off. For example, with reference to Table 2.1: in Latin America and the Caribbean the percentage ratio of young persons in the age-group 6–14 to older persons in the age-group 15–64 is projected to decline from 32.5 in 1995 to 23.4 in the year 2015, whereas in North America over the same period the ratio is projected to decline from 19.8 to 17.0.

Two further aspects of the current demographic context may be noted. First, the percentage of the adult population aged 15–64 who are teachers in the formal education system is smaller in the less developed regions (13 teachers per 1,000 adults) than in the more developed regions (23 teachers per 1,000 adults) (see Appendix II, Table 10). In the least developed countries there are only 8 teachers per 1,000 adults. On a comparative basis, therefore, the less developed regions would seem to have a substantial 'margin' of adult labour potentially available for expansion of their teaching forces to meet increases in student enrolments.

Table 2.2
Number of teachers in the non-agricultural
labour force, by region, 1985 and 1995

	Number of teachers[1] (thousands)		Teachers per 1,000 persons in the non-agricultural labour force	
	1985	*1995*	*1985*	*1995*
WORLD TOTAL	45 499	56 645	41	40
More developed regions of which:	11 453	12 918	33	33
North America	4 030	4 469	31	30
Asia/Oceania	1 816	2 209	28	30
Europe	5 607	6 240	36	37
Countries in transition	6 232	7 361	40	44
Less developed regions of which:	27 829	36 354	46	42
Sub-Saharan Africa	2 128	2 962	36	34
Arab States	1 726	2 763	49	50
Latin America/Caribbean	4 749	6 400	45	42
Eastern Asia/Oceania	13 716	16 577	54	49
of which: China	9 398	11 117	57	53
Southern Asia	5 440	7 097	35	32
of which: India	3 914	4 852	36	32
Least developed countries	1 581	2 178	34	31

1. Only countries for which data on the non-agricultural labour force are available are included. The figures shown here, therefore, differ slightly from those shown in Appendix II, Table 9.

However, the adult population in the less developed regions is less well educated and has a higher percentage of illiterates than the adult population in the more developed regions. Correspondingly, a higher percentage of the adult population is employed in traditional agriculture than is the case in the more developed regions. Thus the real 'pool' of adults in the less developed regions who potentially could be teachers in the formal education system is smaller than is suggested above. As is shown in Table 2.2, the percentage of the non-agricultural labour force who are teachers is generally higher in the less developed regions than in the more developed regions, which suggests that the less developed regions might already be doing as much as they can to employ their eligible adult population in teaching.

In the more developed regions, now that a majority of young people in many countries can participate in formal education up until their early twenties, the adult population is running out of people to educate, so to speak, unless it starts educating itself. It could be partly for this reason that the idea of 'lifelong education' is gaining ground so rapidly in the industrial countries.

The changing educational policy environment

Educational policies worldwide are currently in a state of flux and common strands are difficult to identify except possibly at the regional and subregional levels. Student enrolments in the various regions of the world have been increasing at different speeds; at some levels of education in the more developed regions and countries in transition, for example, they have even been decreasing (Figure 2.3). In consequence, teacher recruitment priorities have been constantly shifting, with 'knock-on' effects on other educational priorities and plans. However, educational policies have also evolved in response to broader political and economic trends and developments.

Figure 2.3
Average annual growth rates in enrolment,
by level of education, in the more developed
regions and in countries in transition,
1980–85, 1985–90, 1990–95

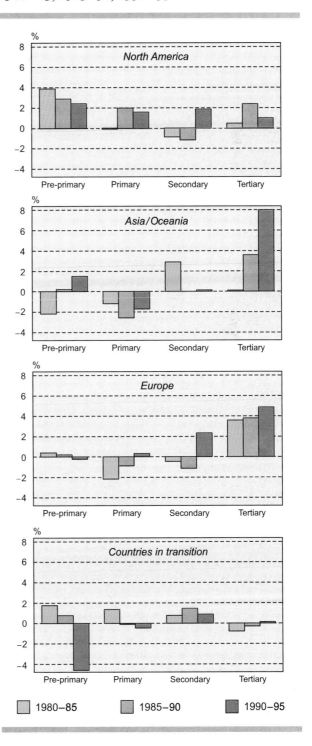

Box 2.3
'Four major trends in Canadian education'

The last several years have ushered in much change for Canadian education. The following is a summary of four major trends in Canadian education, which are captured in various sections of this report:
1. emergence of information technology at all levels of education;
2. retrenchment and restructuring;
3. redefining accountability structures; and
4. respect for diversity and gender equity.

Emergence of information technology at all levels of education
Information technology is emerging to pervade all aspects of education as a key learning and administrative tool. Technological developments of particular interest in this context are computers in education and distance education.

Computers and computer linkages have exploded onto the education scene. Access has been enhanced in the 1990s through technologically based lifelong learning and distance education. Education walls are becoming more permeable.

...

Retrenchment and restructuring
In the 1990s, all levels of government have struggled with increased debt loads, budget deficits, and stagnant revenues in what some have described as the emergence of a 'cuts culture'. In its efforts to put its fiscal house in order, the federal government has not been able to exempt transfer payments [to the provinces] from its deficit reduction exercise, given the magnitude of this support. The most frequent reaction of the provinces has been to reduce or at least cap expenditures, particularly in the social services envelope in which education is included.

...

Redefining accountability structures
Several provinces/territories have re-centralized functions that were previously shared with, or done solely by, district school boards, including defining standards, developing curriculum, and crafting assessment instruments. They also moved to reduce costs through tightened, centralized control of school board budgets.

The trend towards public accountability is pervasive. Accountability means clarifying the roles of all the players in the system, with mechanisms to assess whether these roles are fulfilled. It also means letting parents and community members have a greater say through school or parent councils, a development seen across Canada. Assessment also serves accountability. It implies a more open approach to sharing information with parents and the general public, about the good news and the bad. ...

Respect for diversity and gender equity
Respect for diversity in Canada has been safeguarded and extended through the 1990s, particularly in the teaching of languages, in the design of curriculum, and in programmes that fight racism and promote multiculturalism. ...

Access has been bolstered for a whole new generation of adult learners through an astonishing variety of formal and non-formal programmes: vocational, training, literacy, and general interest, at schools, colleges, and universities, and in the private sector.

Gender equity remains an important topic in Canadian educational discourse in the 1990s. Inroads in this area have been significant, with more females than males graduating from secondary schools, colleges, and undergraduate university programmes (though graduate school is still dominated by males). Significantly more females have enrolled in professional programmes leading to high-income careers.

Source: The Development of Education/Le développement de l'éducation, pp. 1–3, Toronto, Council of Ministers of Education/Conseil des Ministres de l'Éducation, 1996. (National report presented at the 45th session of the International Conference on Education, Geneva, 1996.)

In a global perspective, the two main strands of educational policies are the deepening commitment of most countries to the democratization of education (Education for All and Education throughout Life) and the tendency towards a more productivist view of educational quality and purposes. 'Assessment', 'adjustment', 'effectiveness', 'performance', 'outcomes', 'fiscal constraints' and of course 'human capital' are just some of the signs of how widely the productivistic view has permeated educational policies, compared, say, with thirty years ago. A third strand, 'accountability', is linked to the other two; sometimes it is mainly associated with policies designed to decentralize/democratize educational decision-making and at other times it is more closely associated with demands for improved educational 'effectiveness' and 'performance'.

There are, of course, many substrands and variations according to particular national circumstances, but it is becoming increasingly apparent that the two main orientations of educational policy do not sit quietly together. Teachers are aware of this. They are caught in the middle, regarded on the one hand as carriers of light into dark places, be it tolerance, international understanding or respect for human rights (e.g. Box 1.1), and, on the other hand, as costly 'factors of production' in an enterprise which absorbs a significant proportion of public budgets. If the latter is rarely stated as bluntly outside of professional economic journals, the consequences for teachers of current worldwide efforts to hold down public expenditures are nonetheless real enough.

During the 1990s, the double orientation of educational policies noted above has been evident in every region of the world, although there is of course great variation among countries and regions in the specific contents of policies. In the *more developed regions,* most countries have been engaged – like Canada (Box 2.3) – in a process of retrenchment and restructuring of public expenditure, including expenditure on education, while at the same time seeking to redefine accountability structures and continuing to democratize access to and participation in education, especially at the tertiary level, which is becoming increasingly diversified with respect to institutional forms and programmes, student populations and funding arrangements.

Retrenchment and restructuring of public expenditure have, of course, been key features of the economic and social transformation now under way in the *transition countries* of East and Central Europe and the Russian Federation, but the objective conditions have been much more

---

Box 2.4
'Poland is still a country in a transition period'

The prospects of the Polish educational system as the XXI Century approaches are further transformations and reforms that began in 1990. The last six years showed that reform of the education system is an arduous and long-term process, and the effects of the activities undertaken will only be seen many years later. The political, social and economic context of the state has an essential importance for the harmonious course of this process.

Poland is still a country in a transition period. The period of general transformation does not by its nature favour quiet and long-term activities. Political instability manifests itself by the three alterations in the composition of Parliament since 1990 as well as still more frequent changes of the Cabinets (since 1993, there has already been in operation the third government under the rules of the same parliamentary coalition), and – as consequence – also changes of ministers of national education and their closest collaborators, which does not favour steady reformatory activities. Added to all this are the constantly insufficient financial resources which the state budget allocates to education.

At the same time it must be emphasized that despite such a complicated situation, transformations and modernization of the Polish education system have been continued.

Source: Development of Education in Poland, pp. 137–8, Warsaw, Ministry of National Education, 1996. (National report presented at the 45th session of the International Conference on Education, Geneva, 1996.)

---

difficult, and education budgets have suffered (e.g. Box 2.4), impeding the educational reform process and causing considerable hardships for teachers, notwithstanding the role they are called upon to play in helping to forge new political identities and cultures. A notable casualty of the economic dislocation in the transition countries has been pre-primary education, where enrolments have fallen sharply (Figure 2.3). This level of education was traditionally provided mainly by

Figure 2.4
Average annual growth rates in enrolment, by level of education, in the less developed regions,
1980–85, 1985–90, 1990–95

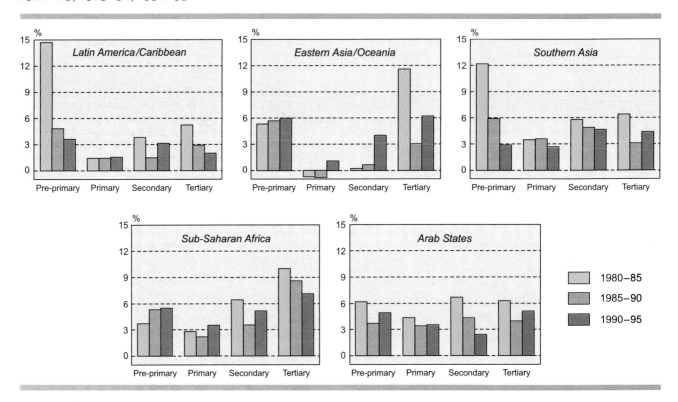

enterprises for the children of their employees, but the difficulties of adjustment to the market economy have forced most enterprises to cut back on their social services, including kindergartens and pre-school programmes, and many teachers in these programmes have lost their jobs.

In both the more developed regions and the transition countries, the ageing of the population has been an important (though little noticed) indirect contributory source of pressure on state education budgets, because of the competing demand it makes for funds to pay for social security and retirement benefits within the overall social sector budget envelope.

In the *less developed regions,* where population pressures are still strong and student enrolment growth rates generally have been positive (Figure 2.4), Education for All goals, including improvement in the quality of basic education,

have been the main focus of educational policies, at least to the extent that political and economic conditions have allowed, since many of the same impulses towards public expenditure retrenchment and restructuring which have constrained educational policies in the more developed regions have also been at work. There have been differences of emphasis among the less developed regions in how these constraints have been handled, because of the differences between regions in the stages of development of their educational infrastructures and differences too in their systems of governance.

In the *Latin American/Caribbean region,* where broadly speaking the educational infrastructure is more highly developed than in the other regions, the 1990s have witnessed several major initiatives towards the decentralization of once-monolithic state education systems, e.g.

Argentina (Box 2.5), Brazil, Colombia and Mexico. In each case, this has entailed, among other things, complex and protracted discussions with teachers' unions, which traditionally had negotiated teachers' salaries and conditions of service at the national level and were still wary of further erosion of their incomes coming after the experiences of inflation and structural adjustment policies in the 1980s.

In the *Eastern Asia/Oceania region,* where economic growth has been strong, there has not been the same degree of emphasis on retrenchment and restructuring of public expenditure as in Latin America. The overall pattern of educational development has also been different: that of the Republic of Korea, for example (Box 2.6), has perhaps been paradigmatic. The region's figures for enrolment growth rates are heavily weighted by China, where there has been a marked decline in the birth rate. Nevertheless, it is generally the case in this region that universal access to primary education has virtually been achieved, that rapid progress is being made towards the universalization of access to secondary education and that pressures are building up for expansion of tertiary level education. Given the region's favourable economic situation, there has been more scope for teachers' incomes to rise, although in many countries there is evidence of widespread moonlighting by teachers in second jobs. In fact, moonlighting by public school teachers to supplement their low official salaries has been an important source of supply of teachers for private schools throughout the region. The same phenomenon has also been evident in other regions, especially in Latin America.

In the *sub-Saharan Africa, Arab States and Southern Asia regions,* which include most of the least developed countries, educational policies have been very much hostage to economic and political circumstances although, as already noted, there has been a certain measure of success over the last decade and a half in responding to the great population pressures for increasing edu-

---

Box 2.5
Structural reform of education in Argentina

A structural transformation of education has been under way in Argentina since 1993. The basic legal framework for these changes consists of three laws:
Law No. 24.049, Transfer of Educational Services to the Provinces, 1992; transfers the educational services that still depended on the National Government to the Provinces.
Law No. 24.195, known as the Federal Law of Education, passed in 1993; states the basic outlines for the transformation of education at primary and secondary levels. This law establishes new objectives, a new academic structure and the need for new contents at all levels. It also sets the rules for the decentralized government of education; assigning the State the role of policy-maker, assessment in education and compensating balance, whereas the actual educational services are directly supplied by the provincial governments.
Law No. 24.521, Law of Higher Education, passed in 1995; deals with the tertiary level, both university as well as non-university tertiary studies, teacher development being one of them.
This legal framework is completed by a clear political determination which guarantees the economic resources required for the transformation, stated in the Federal Educational Pact signed by the President, the Governors of the Provinces and the Mayor of the City of Buenos Aires, on September 11th, 1994, according to Article 63 of the Federal Law of Education.

Source: Fortalecimiento de la función del personal docente en un mundo cambiante. Propuesta argentina/Strengthening the Work of the Teaching Staff in a Changing World. Argentine Proposal, pp. 20–2, Buenos Aires, Ministerio de Cultura y Educación de la Nación/Ministry of Culture and Education of the Nation, 1996. (National report presented at the 45th session of the International Conference on Education, Geneva, 1996.)

---

cational enrolments. That enrolments in tertiary level education in these regions have grown as fast as, or faster than, in primary and secondary level education (Figure 2.4) is probably more a reflection of the low starting base of tertiary level enrolments (especially in sub-Saharan Africa) than of policy preferences in favour of tertiary level education as such. Nevertheless, it has been a bone

Box 2.6
The evolution of educational development
policies in the Republic of Korea
from the 1950s to the 1980s

With scarce natural resources, Korea has relied heavily on human resources to develop its economy. Education being a major source for trained manpower, educational policies have changed in accordance with the types of human resources demanded by a changing economy. In the 1950s, when low-level skilled workers were needed in manual industries, efforts were geared to undertake a massive scale literacy campaign to produce a manual workforce. In the 1960s, skilled workers were in great demand for light industries, and the focus was shifted to expand vocational education at the secondary school level. As the importance of heavy industries grew in the 1970s, technicians who could deal with complex modern manufacturing processes were in demand. The government responded by expanding junior technical colleges. The number of junior colleges nearly doubled in this period. In the 1980s, economic competitiveness based on high-level technology and information industries became fierce and this challenge urged the Korean government to strengthen research and education in basic science and technology.

... In other words, Korea expanded and universalized elementary education followed by secondary education, and only after achieving this, shifted its emphasis to the expansion of higher education. This sequence of policies fits well into the economic development plan.

Source: The Development of Education, National Report of the Republic of Korea, p. 1, Seoul, Ministry of Education, 1996. (National report presented at the 45th session of the International Conference on Education, Geneva, 1996.)

regions which have been free of war and violent political conflict, economic conditions have improved since the beginning of the 1990s compared with the previous decade and many countries are beginning to make progress towards Education for All goals (e.g. Box 2.7). Where violent internal political conflict has ocurred, the effects on education have been disastrous (e.g. Box 2.8).

Box 2.7
Progress towards 'Education for All'
in Mauritania

The overall objective of the Mauritanian education system is to give Mauritanian children the basic education necessary for the development of their personality, in accordance with the precepts and principles of the Muslim religion, national culture and the requirements of life in a modern society, and to offer a training enabling them to find a job thanks to general secondary and higher education or to the network of technical and vocational education.

At the level of basic education, priority is given to enhancing admission capacity with a view to achieving by the year 2000 the enrolment of all children from 6 to 11 years and providing them with basic instruction. Efforts are thus continually being directed towards building classrooms, the initial and ongoing training of teachers and improving the curricula and material conditions in schools. Emphasis is placed on reducing regional disparities and those between boys and girls.

It should be noted that the gross enrolment ratio [in primary level education] rose from 44 per cent in 1987/88 to 64 per cent in 1992/93, 82.78 per cent in 1995/96 and 88.87 per cent at the start of the 1996/97 school year (estimate), when 80 per cent was the objective set for 1998. This rapid growth, which was more marked in regions where the enrolment ratio was below the national average, makes full enrolment by the year 2000 a certainty.

Source: Développement de l'éducation. Rapport national de la République islamique de Mauritanie, p. 5, Nouackchott, Ministère de l'Éducation Nationale, 1996. (National report presented at the 45th session of the International Conference on Education, Geneva, 1996.)

of contention with external financing agencies strongly influenced by interpretations of the educational foundations of the East Asian development 'miracle', in particular the idea that the universalization of primary and secondary education should precede (as in Box 2.6) any shift of emphasis to the expansion of higher education.

In the large majority of countries in the sub-Saharan Africa, Arab States and Southern Asia

Box 2.8
The effects of a worsening economic, social and political situation on education in Burundi

Since the last country report on the development of the Burundi education system submitted at the forty-third session of the ICE in 1992, the country's economic, social and political situation has continually worsened, as can be seen from the failure to publish a country report for the forty-fourth session of the International Conference on Education (ICE), held in October 1994.

...

The assassination on 21 October 1993 of the first President elected by universal suffrage plunged Burundi into an unprecedented socio-political crisis, jeopardizing chances of improving the socio-economic conditions of the people of Burundi. The widespread massacres left countless victims, orphans, widows and widowers, displaced persons and refugees. The number of orphans is estimated at 17,600 and the displaced at more than 200,000, while the number of refugees resulting from the October 1993 crisis exceeded 140,000 in 1994.

All the social indicators show a sharp deterioration in social services. Over 80 per cent of the population live below the poverty line and more than half have an annual per capita income of less than US $90. Life expectancy at birth has dropped. The national health care system functions at 70 per cent of its pre-crisis capacity.

The education system has also suffered from the crisis. Intake capacity, which had expanded across the country, has been significantly reduced in terms of staffing, and quality has declined.

In 1992–1993, public and private schools in Burundi had 649,999 pupils enrolled in primary education, 48,851 in secondary and teacher education and 5,505 in technical secondary education.

In 1994–1995, there were 167,009 fewer pupils enrolled in primary education, i.e. a drop of some 25 per cent, while the teaching staff was reduced by 34 per cent. At the secondary and higher levels, a significant number of pupils and students have left their boarding schools and campuses. Some primary and secondary schools are still closed on account of the prevailing situation of insecurity in the country.

In terms of quality, the Burundi education system had its flaws and failings even before the crisis, for example from the point of view of the purpose of primary education, the professionalization of secondary education, access and equity, upgrading of the teaching profession, improvement of infrastructures, teaching aids and equipment for the education system as a whole, the introduction of new curricula incorporating education in values and citizenship and the diversification of higher education courses in response to the employment situation.

These difficulties, which in normal circumstances are a natural result of the expansion of an education system, were aggravated by the events, which led to the destruction of infrastructures, teaching materials and equipment, balkanization in schools and the exodus of foreign (Rwandan and Zairian) teachers and Burundian teachers (refugees). The quality of education has suffered terribly and it is still very difficult to evaluate the incalculable effects of the crisis on the system. In any event, it is a system that urgently needs to be rebuilt.

Source: Développement de l'éducation: rapport national du Burundi, pp. 1–2, Bujumbura, Ministère de l'Éducation, de l'Enseignement de Base et de l'Alphabétisation des Adultes, Ministère de l'Enseignement Secondaire, Supérieur et de la Recherche Scientifique, 1996. (National report presented at the 45th session of the International Conference on Education, Geneva, 1996.)

In the less developed regions of the world generally, economic and social changes in recent years have reinforced the impulse towards the democratization of education (e.g. Box 2.9), establishing a momentum of rapid growth in most education systems that tends continously to push up against existing limits placed on the public budgetary resources available for education. In consequence, the teaching force is constantly growing and mutating in a situation of severe resource constraints. These conditions are not favourable to improvements in the status of teachers. Even in countries which in recent years have experienced rapid economic growth and increasing prosperity, the status of teachers has hardly improved and may even have declined

Box 2.9
Economic and social changes and their effects on education in Bahrain

Bahrain society has been submitted – as all other Arab States – to profound changes in its structure and function. The transformation from a society dependent on pearl-diving, fishing, dhow-building and agriculture to one based on oil industry and then non-oil industrial and services activities has led to the emergence of various kinds of position and expertise which have brought about changes in Bahrain's social structure. ...

The changes in the social structure ... have created an increasing social demand for education which has affected the education system as follows:

1. The population growth in Bahrain is one of the most important factors that has contributed to the increase of school population. This has required more school buildings and equipment, and more qualified teaching and administrative staff to be employed.

2. The construction and expansion of new cities in Bahrain has resulted in a movement of population to these new cities. This has increased the number of students in those areas and obliged the Ministry to make efforts to provide the necessary educational services, side by side with the other services in those areas.

3. The growth of the industrial and business sectors in Bahrain and the development of the economic situation have generated an obvious demand for education. They have also led to an attempt to develop technical and vocational education adequate for the growing industrial needs.

4. The development of people's acceptance of girls education has certainly increased the number of female students steadily at all levels of education. The factors behind this are: the development of religious perspective towards the role of girls' education in the economy, and the needs for knowledge felt by girls in order to participate in the society. These factors have required changes in the quality of programmes offered for girls, just as that offered for boys.

5. As a result of the education development itself and the contact with the modern scientific and technological civilization, the people's attitudes towards technical and vocational education have been developed greatly and obviously, which has assisted the development of this type of education and the emergence of new areas of studies in Bahrain.

6. The society's perception and attitude towards education as a basic ladder for social promotion and social status improvement have assisted the development of education in Bahrain.

7. The political, economic and civilization factors have generated new values in Bahrain that have helped the educational development quantitatively. Among these values are new cultural-humanistic values that necessitate the linking of the national heritage with modern world civilization. Other values are the feeling of national pride and the will to follow scientific advancement.

Source: Development of Education in Bahrain, 1994/95–1995/96, pp. 13–4, Manama, Ministry of Education, 1996. (National report presented at the 45th session of the International Conference on Education, Geneva, 1996.)

(e.g. Box 2.10). In other developing countries, the pursuit of Education for All goals is often still constrained by structural adjustment programmes. Although such programmes today are conceived with more consideration for the needs of the social sectors than was the case in the 1980s, some of the effects of the earlier programmes on the employment and conditions of service of teachers are still being felt, the most notorious probably being the encouragement given by these programmes to the hiring of 'contract' teachers at lower rates of remuneration than the rates

accorded to already employed teachers with similar qualifications (e.g. Box 2.11).

This practice – highlighted in ILO's 1996 report, *Impact of Structural Adjustment on the Employment and Training of Teachers* – is flatly contrary to the provisions (Section X) of the *Recommendation.* In fact, no other aspect of structural adjustment programmes has demonstrated so clearly the increasing tendency of national development policies to subject education to the same cost-cutting logic of market forces that is applied to the overall system of production: if qualified people are willing to teach for less pay than the standard rates, then why not hire them?

The emerging status and profile of teachers

The status and profile of the world's teachers that emerges from the development of education over the last decade is highly differentiated with respect to countries and regions, in particular their overall development experience and the stages of development of their education systems. In a relatively small minority of countries, teachers have

---

Box 2.10
Declining status of teachers in Thailand

Major problems facing teachers are as follows:
- The status of the teaching profession is deteriorating, discouraging competent and 'good' people to enter the profession. Some teacher students enroll in the programme without serious commitment as it is their low priority when taking the entrance examination. Their attitude and faith in the profession are not favourably contributive to their teaching career. Some are concerned over the limited teaching positions available and their lower remuneration in comparison with other careers.
- Teachers' incomes are low while their workload is heavy. Since promotion does not correspond with their professional development, teachers suffer low morale. Some spend their time moonlighting for more income. Their pride in being good teachers has decreased. Consequently, society respects the teachers less as some of them do not behave properly.
- Teacher development programmes are not seriously and consistently carried out. Consequently, in-service teachers have the tendency to have a lower level of academic competence, knowledge transmission skills and sense of professionalism.

Source: Development of Education, pp. 23–4, Bangkok, Ministry of Education, 1996. (National report presented at the 45th session of the International Conference on Education, Geneva, 1996.).

Box 2.11
Recruitment of teachers under 'structural adjustment' constraints in Togo

Since the introduction of the Structural Adjustment Programmes, the Ministry of Education, faced with staff shortages, has recruited teachers to a variety of posts whose common denominators are precariousness and especially lower remuneration for the same qualifications and the same duties as other teachers. Although this category of teacher is smaller in primary education (24 per cent), it represents the majority in the last two years of secondary education. In some establishments, teachers on short-term contracts represent 90 per cent of the teaching staff. It is highly unlikely that a majority group which is marginalized in any organization will not be tempted to demand its rights. There is therefore a risk that the whole system might be deadlocked if two categories of teachers continue to coexist.

Source: Développement de l'éducation: rapport national du Togo, p. 42, Lomé, Ministère de l'Éducation Nationale et de la Recherche Scientifique, Commission Nationale pour l'UNESCO, 1996. (National report presented at the 45th session of the International Conference on Education, Geneva, 1996.).

---

reasonably comfortable incomes and conditions of employment; most of them are higher education graduates and, in addition, they generally have been trained as teachers. In a minority of other countries, teachers can barely survive on their official salaries (when they are paid at all), have other jobs too and in many cases have not themselves received an education at a level much higher than the students they are required to teach. The majority of the world's teachers fall somewhere in between these two extremes.

There are few signs that this situation is likely to change significantly in the near future. Although teaching is a 'growth' occupation in a majority of countries – demographic pressures virtually guarantee continuing increases in student enrolments and hence the need for more teachers – the economics of the education sector have not markedly favoured improvements in

Figure 2.5
Public expenditure on education as a percentage
of GNP, by region, 1980–1995

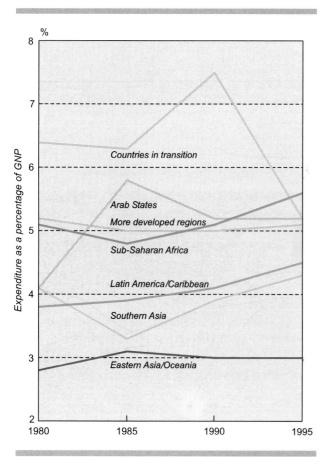

teachers' incomes in the past when teachers have been in short supply; too often the educational authorities have simply lowered the standards of recruitment for new teachers.

Thus, in none of the several regional meetings of experts and observers convened by UNESCO in preparation for the 45th Session of the International Conference on Education (1966), devoted to the theme 'Strengthening the Role of Teachers in a Changing World', was it felt that the status of teachers had improved in recent years. In fact, the general feeling in most regions was that there had probably been a decline; likewise in the majority of the replies by national authorities to the questionnaire administered by the Inter-

national Bureau of Education (IBE) in preparation of the Conference. Only in a handful of wealthy industrial countries with relatively stable teaching forces (e.g. Austria, Canada, Finland, Germany and Switzerland) and a few others was it claimed that the general standing and remuneration of teachers was not a cause for anxiety.

The prospects of reversing the apparent decline in the status of teachers mainly depend on the readiness of countries to finance educational expenditure more generously than they have done in the past, on the ability of teachers to make their claims for improved incomes and status heard, and on the changing profile (age, sex, and education and training background) of teachers themselves. These factors are considered in turn in the remainder of this chapter.

First, as regards *educational expenditure:* since teachers' salaries and allowances in most countries typically account for the two-thirds or more of such expenditure, the scope for improvement in teachers' incomes depends in part on the priority accorded to education in the overall allocation of national resources. Even so, an increasing priority for education will not necessarily benefit teachers, particularly if the additional resources are mainly used for expansion of the education system on the basis of existing conditions. This appears to have been the experience in many countries over the past decade. In the more developed regions, and in sub-Saharan Africa, Latin America and the Caribbean, and Southern Asia, the estimated share of education in GNP is larger than it was a decade or fifteen years ago (Figure 2.5). Only in the Arab States and Eastern Asia/Oceania regions, and in the countries in transition – especially the latter – is the share estimated to be stationary or lower. Yet in every region, as noted above, informed observers believe that the status of teachers has declined.

The expectation at the end of the 1980s in many countries that education could benefit significantly from the relaxation of international political tensions, in the form of a 'peace dividend'

Figure 2.6
Changes in the average percentage shares of defence and education in central government expenditure, in selected countries,[1] 1985–89 and 1990–94

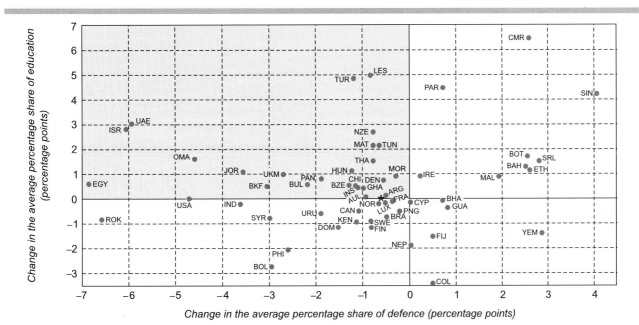

Country names abbreviations: ARG: Argentina; AUL: Australia; BHA: Bahamas; BAH: Bahrain; BZE: Belize; BOL: Bolivia; BOT: Botswana; BRA: Brazil; BUL: Bulgaria; BKF: Burkina Faso; CMR: Cameroon; CAN: Canada; CHI: Chile; COL: Colombia; CYP: Cyprus; DEN: Denmark; DOM: Dominican Republic; EGY: Egypt; ETH: Ethiopia; FIJ: Fiji; FIN: Finland; FRA: France; GHA: Ghana; GUA: Guatemala; HUN: Hungary; IND: India; INS: Indonesia; IRE: Ireland; ISR: Israel; JOR: Jordan; KEN: Kenya; LES: Lesotho; LUX: Luxembourg; MAL: Malaysia; MAT: Malta; MOR: Morocco; NEP: Nepal; NZE: New Zealand; NOR: Norway; OMA: Oman; PAN: Panama; PNG: Papua New Guinea; PAR: Paraguay; PHI: Philippines; ROK: Republic of Korea; SIN: Singapore; SRL: Sri Lanka; SWE: Sweden; SYR: Syrian Arab Republic; THA: Thailand; TUN: Tunisia; TUR: Turkey; UAE: United Arab Emirates; UKM: United Kingdom; USA: United States; URU: Uruguay; YEM: Yemen.

★ This symbol is used for Austria (−0.58, −0.08) and Netherlands (−0.57, −0.02).

1. Countries for which data are available for the two periods, excluding the following three countries where the changes in the percentage shares fall outside the ranges presented in this diagramme: El Salvador (−10, −3), Kuwait (21, −4) and Mexico (1, 12).

Source: Government Finance Statistics Yearbook, Washington, D.C., International Monetary Fund, various issues.

from reduced defence expenditure, seems not to have been realized, or at best only moderately so. This emerges from UNESCO's examination of changes in the average percentage shares of central government expenditure devoted to defence and education respectively in sixty-two countries for which data are available for the late 1980s and early 1990s. While defence is mainly a central government responsibility in every country, this is not always the case for education, although every central government incurs at least some direct expenditure on education. In countries where the financing of education is not mainly a central government responsibility, a reduced share for defence in central government expenditure could benefit education either directly, or indirectly through an increased general transfer of funds to lower levels of government which are responsible for education. Any such indirect benefit is very difficult to identify. As regards direct expenditure, and with reference to the periods 1985–89 and 1990–94, the average percentage share of central government expenditure devoted to defence fell in forty-four countries, and in twenty-five of these (shown in the top left quadrant of Figure 2.6) the average percentage share devoted to education increased. In Jordan, for example, the average percentage share of central government expenditure devoted to defence fell by 3.57 percentage points between 1985–89 and 1990–94, while at the same time the average percentage share devoted to education increased by 1.10 percentage points. However, in nineteen countries where the share of defence fell, the share of education also fell: these countries are shown in the bottom left quadrant of Figure 2.6.

Thus, it seems that in so far as the share of education in GNP has been increasing in recent years, this has probably been due mainly to the continuing expansion of education systems rather than to a fundamental shift in public expenditure priorities, let alone significant improvements in teachers' incomes. In no region of the world at present has the average share of educational expenditure in GNP yet reached the 6 per cent level recommended by the International Commission on Education for the Twenty-first Century, although a number of individual countries have reached this level (see Appendix III, Table 10).

Moreover, external aid to education, after a jump at the end of the 1980s, appears to have levelled off (see Appendix II, Table 14).

Global trends in *teachers' incomes* are very difficult to identify. The available evidence is mostly circumstantial and ad hoc. In their replies to IBE's questionnaire, mentioned above, a number of countries reported measures recently taken to increase teachers' salaries, but it is unclear whether these increases were designed to improve teachers' incomes relative to those of other groups, or were simply part of all-round public sector salary increases.

A certain amount of systematic information was assembled in the late 1980s/early 1990s in studies carried out by various international organizations (including UNESCO and ILO), as well as by independent researchers, into the effects of the structural adjustment programmes. In general, most of these programmes froze (or even reduced) public sector salaries, especially in sub-Saharan Africa

and Latin America. Still, in the more stable economic conditions of most regions in the 1990s, it is possible that the real incomes of teachers in many countries are rising again. Whether they are keeping up with average incomes generally is difficult to say; reliable evidence on movements in teachers' salaries relative to those of other major occupational groups in different countries is very scarce. The numerous studies of the effects of the structural adjustment programmes of the 1980s, for example, never clearly established whether teachers' incomes generally suffered more than those of other public sector employees.

More recently, OECD has assembled systematic data on primary- and secondary-teachers' salaries scales in its member countries (published in *Education at a Glance,* Paris, OECD, 1996), but these data refer only to a recent year (1994) and comparable data for other occupational groups are still lacking. However, even if such data were available, international comparisons of teachers' economic status are especially difficult to make because of differences between countries in the educational backgrounds and working conditions of teachers, as well as of other professional groups.

Consider, for example, India and the United States. Data for the various Indian states on the starting level salaries of public primary-school teachers and other government employees with comparable educational backgrounds, reported by India in its national report to the 1996 International Conference on Education, show that the salaries of primary-school teachers tend to lie in the middle of the range, somewhat less than those of trained nurses but more than those of policemen. In the United States, where primary-school teachers in general have a college (university) degree, unlike in India, quite different occupations are usually chosen for comparison. Thus, the National Commission on Teaching and America's Future compared the average annual earnings of teachers with those of physicians, lawyers and judges, engineers, accountants and auditors, social

Figure 2.7
Distribution of countries[1] by percentage of private-school teachers in primary and secondary general education, by region, 1995[2]

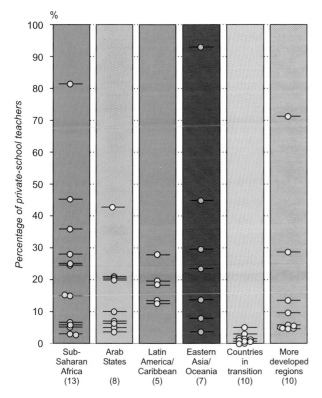

1. Each dot represents one country. For each region, the total number of countries for which data are available is shown in parentheses.
2. Or latest year available.

workers and other occupations which normally require a college (university) degree and found that teachers lie at the bottom of the range (*What Matters Most: Teaching for America's Future,* New York, National Commission on Teaching and America's Future, 1996).

The fact that the majority of teachers in most countries are not employed in the private (Figure 2.7) but in the public sector, where the salary scales of the different categories of employees are typically linked together, offers a certain amount of protection against loss of economic status relative to other occupations, but this also depends in part on the viability and coherence of the public sector itself. Where the latter has collapsed, as in the countries of the former Soviet Union, teachers along with other public servants have suffered dramatic erosions of their incomes.

Teacher attrition, i.e. the percentage of teachers who leave the profession each year, excluding retirees, could be a useful indicator of the relative status of teachers compared to other occupational groups, but reliable, internationally comparable data on teacher attrition rates do not exist and even national data are very scarce. In most countries, a certain amount of teacher attrition is accounted for by transfer and/or promotion to administrative and managerial positions within the education system itself; because of this, teacher attrition rates may tend to be higher in the less developed regions of the world, where education systems are rapidly expanding, than in the more developed regions with low birth rates and slowly growing student enrolments. In the 1960s and 1970s, ex-teachers could be found throughout the state administrations of most of the newly independent countries. However, in recent years, teacher attrition rates have probably been highest in East and Central Europe, and the countries of the former Soviet Union, partly because of the difficulties facing all categories of public sector employees in most of these countries, but also in part because many teachers found that they had skills (e.g. foreign languages, information technology) which have been in demand in the burgeoning private industrial and service sectors.

In sum, it is hard to find, for any region of the world, clear evidence of an overall trend towards improvement in teachers' economic status. Probably there is no country even where it can be confidently asserted that such a trend has ocurred.

Finally, it may be noted that part of the difficulty for teachers in getting their claims for improved economic status heard is that there still are many countries in which teachers do not have well-established *collective bargaining rights.* This is itself partly due to education's position in the

Box 2.12
**Freedom of association
and collective bargaining rights of teachers
in the Indian context**

In the domain of the rights and responsibilities of teachers, the Indian context enjoins a fair degree of freedom and flexibility based on a framework outlined by the respective state governments on the issue of freedom of association. In every state, teaching and non-teaching personnel have their unions/associations. These organizations have powers of collective bargaining to secure better service conditions for their members. State level organizations have joined together to form federations of educational organizations for primary, secondary and college stage education. These federations negotiate with the central government to secure better pay scales and other service conditions. The central question under Indian laws is whether a 'teacher' can be equated to a 'workman', the latter being defined in the Industrial Disputes Act 1947. Various suggestions in this respect are being considered by the Ministry of Labour to amend the Industrial Disputes Act and initiate reforms to grant teachers the same protection as other workers. On the question of the rights of teachers (in particular, salaries), these are structured as per norms as laid down by the government from time to time.

Source: Development of Education in India, 1995–96, with Special Reference to Teacher Education, pp. 44–5, New Delhi, Department of Education, Ministry of Human Resource Development, 1996. (National report presented at the 45th session of the International Conference on Education, Geneva, 1996.)

public sector. Where teachers are considered to be public servants, their collective bargaining rights are often restricted.

Governments traditionally have been cautious in their readiness to recognize formally the collective bargaining rights of their own employees. Thus, whereas 120 states (as of 1 October 1997) have ratified ILO's *Freedom of Association and Protection of the Right to Organize Convention* (1948) and 134 states have ratified ILO's *Right to Organize and Collective Bargaining Convention* (1949), the latter specifically 'does not deal with

the position of public servants engaged in the administration of the State' (Article 6), and only 30 states have ratified the *Labour Relations (Public Service) Convention* (1978), which specifically 'applies to all persons employed by public authorities' (Article 1). The *Recommendation concerning the Status of Teachers* provides for 'both salaries and working conditions' of teachers to be 'determined through the process of negotiation between teachers' organizations and the employers of teachers' (Section VIII), but actual practice, as in respect to other provisions of the *Recommendation,* is another matter. An independent review of the situation, based on a selected sample of ten developed and developing countries, carried out for ILO in 1994, concluded that although political changes were moving towards more effective recognition of teachers' rights to freedom of association, free collective bargaining was still the exception, and that prevailing economic trends were undermining the role of collective bargaining in many countries, even those with long traditions of respecting the rights of teachers and other workers to bargain. Probably it is still only a minority of countries that can match India's claim to provide a 'fair degree of freedom and flexibility' in respect to the 'rights and responsibilities of teachers' (Box 2.12).

Despite their numbers, therefore, teachers in a majority of countries have not been in a strong position to resist the apparent erosion in their economic status in recent years.

It remains now to consider whether the *profile* of the world's teachers has changed. As regards *sex:* the percentage of teachers who are female varies considerably among the different regions of the world, but is rising in all regions (Figure 2.8). In the less developed regions, as was noted in the *World Education Report 1995,* this has probably facilitated the increasing educational enrolment of girls. In countries where female teachers are a majority, it has sometimes been argued that the fact that teaching is more of a 'woman's profession' than most other professions has negative

Figure 2.8
Number (millions) of teachers in pre-primary,
primary and secondary education, by sex
and region, 1980 and 1995

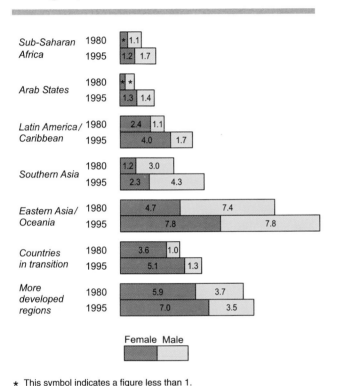

* This symbol indicates a figure less than 1.

resistance from employers. In any case, in some of the countries (chiefly in sub-Saharan Africa and Southern Asia) where teaching is still mainly a male profession, survival on a teacher's salary is pretty difficult for both men and women.

Secondly, the composition of the world's teaching force is also changing with respect to the *age-profile* of teachers (Figure 2.9). Teachers in the less developed regions of the world gener-

Figure 2.9
Age-profile of teachers in primary and
secondary education, selected countries, 1994[1]

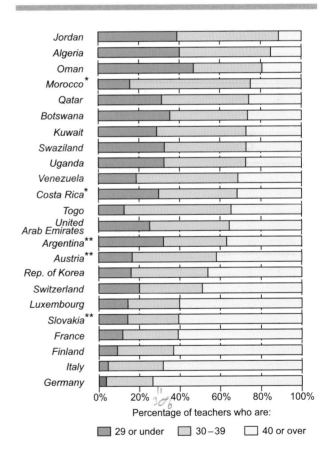

* Teachers in primary education only.
** Age-groups: 30 or under; 31–40; 41 or over.

1. Or latest year available.

Source: National replies to the questionnaire administered by the International Bureau of Education in preparation of the 45th session of the International Conference on Education (Geneva, 1996).

implications for the status of teachers. This could of course be true in so far as society accepts discrimination against women. While there probably are very few (if any) countries today where women teachers are paid on different salary scales from their male counterparts, at least in the public sector, it could be argued that the overall levels of teachers' salaries are kept below the levels which would prevail if teaching were a 'male profession', but this is speculation and very difficult to prove empirically. In probably a majority of countries, though, women still are underrepresented in educational leadership and management positions. Conceivably, if progress continues to be made worldwide in eliminating discrimination against women generally, improvements in teachers' incomes could encounter less

Box 2.13
Raising of the level at which primary-school teachers are recruited in France

Since 1992, all teachers recruited and trained to work in nursery and primary schools are known by the new term of *'professeurs des écoles'* which therefore replaces the traditional term of *'instituteurs'*.

The decision taken in 1990–91 to improve the status of teaching staff in the primary sector led to the creation of a new body of teachers. These *professeurs des écoles* (who are classed as Category A civil servants whereas *instituteurs* come under Category B) are totally comparable in terms of level of recruitment, pay and career structure to qualified teachers in middle schools *(collèges)* and secondary schools *(lycées)*. All new recruits belong to this new teaching body ... The raising of the level at which primary school teachers are recruited comes at the end of a relatively rapid process: only fifteen years separate the last intake of trainee teachers *('élèves maîtres')* recruited after their fourth year of secondary education (1976) from the first competitive examinations to recruit primary school teachers *(professeurs des écoles)* in possession of a degree (1992). This development admittedly came at a time when the teacher training schools in the primary sector were also undergoing very rapid and far-reaching change. It was not until 1973 that these *'écoles normales'* devoted themselves solely to the initial and continuous vocational training of primary school teachers. Previously, they had also prepared the trainees for their *baccalauréat*. From 1979 onwards they began to cooperate on a regular basis with universities, first of all in order to set up courses leading to a special DEUG (general university qualification) tailor-made for primary school teacher trainees as an integral part of their training course (at the time they were recruited at *baccalauréat* level), and then also in order to arrange for research teachers to participate in the training of trainees recruited at the level of the DEUG. Lastly, in 1990, some, and in 1991, all, the *écoles normales* were closed and their training capacity and resources transferred to the University Training Institutes for School Teachers (IUFM).

Source: Jean-Claude Ermin, 'Recruitment of Primary School Teachers under the New System', *Éducation et Formations*, Vol. 37, March 1994, p. 106. (Special number: Connaissance des enseignants.)

ally are younger than their counterparts in the more developed regions. Among other things, this implies a need for well-designed systems of professional guidance and supervision, but this need has not always been given the attention which it merits. It also implies a built-in pressure on education budgets as teachers grow older and move up their salary scales – a process which probably has largely stabilized in the more developed regions.

Thirdly, the composition of the world's teaching force is changing with respect to the *educational backgrounds* of teachers. As noted earlier in this chapter, the *Recommendation* considered that completion of secondary education should be the minimum educational background for prospective primary teachers and that they should have teacher preparation in addition. Since then, most of the industrial countries have moved towards requiring all teachers in primary and sec-

ondary schools to have a university degree or its equivalent. A recent example is France (Box 2.13). While this undoubtedly represents the long-term trend for the world's education systems, the distance still to be travelled by countries in the less developed regions is considerable (Table 2.3).

The percentage of the world's teachers who have received at least a secondary education is almost certainly higher than thirty years ago, but there still are many countries where significant numbers of teachers have received less. In Togo, for example, according to the national report presented at the 1996 International Conference on Education, over one-third of primary-school teachers themselves possess only a primary-school-leavers' certificate, which is probably representative of the situation in a number of other sub-Saharan African countries, although systematic data for the region are not available. In Uruguay, to take another example, notwithstand-

Table 2.3
Education and training backgrounds
of primary- and secondary-school teachers,
in selected countries, 1994[1]

	Percentage of teachers with university or equivalent educational qualification		Percentage of teachers who have received pedagogical training	
	Primary	Secondary	Primary	Secondary
Argentina	17	39	90	59
Ecuador	1	1	86	58
Egypt	55	100	36	49
Ghana	...	...	69	72
Indonesia	5	62	91	84
Japan	79	93	...	...
Jordan	42	75	...	...
Kuwait	41	90	...	...
Lesotho	14	44	77	79
Nigeria	9	...	...	...
Panama	6	9	...	...
Poland	61	91	...	...
Qatar	74	98	55	44
Slovakia	78	69	...	...
Swaziland	1	47	90	87
Uganda	1	25	61	80
United Arab Emirates	32	96	...	...
Venezuela	...	...	78	84

1. Or latest year available.

Source: National replies to the questionnaire administered by the International Bureau of Education in preparation of the 45th session of the International Conference on Education (Geneva, 1996).

ing that it has a much more highly developed education system than Togo, the 1995 Secondary Education Teachers' Census found that one-third of secondary teachers had never completed their university studies and another 11 per cent had themselves never gone beyond the secondary level. Although systematic data for the region again are not available, the situation in Uruguay is probably not a lot different from that in a number of other Latin American countries.

The situation as regards *teacher preparation or training,* as distinct from teachers' general education backgrounds, is hardly any better, because most countries, whatever their level of development, have at one time or another temporarily waived pre-service training requirements in order to fill urgent gaps in the teaching force. To take Uruguay as an example again: fully 70 per cent of secondary-school teachers have never completed their teacher-training studies. In the first (lower) cycle of secondary education in Togo, the corresponding figure is 84 per cent, and in primary education it is 36 per cent. Other examples could be given. Untrained teachers can also be found in

---

Box 2.14
Shortages of qualified teachers in
the United States of America

Although parents might assume that teachers, like other professionals, are educated in similar ways so that they meet the same standards before they are admitted to practice, this is not the case. Unlike doctors, lawyers, accountants, or architects, teachers do not have the same training. Some teachers have very high levels of skills – particularly in states that require a bachelor's degree in the discipline to be taught; coursework in teaching, learning, curriculum, and child development; extensive practice teaching, and a master's degree in education. Others learn little about their subject matter or about teaching, particularly in states that have low requirements.

And while states have recently begun to require some form of testing for a teaching license, most are little more than multiple-choice tests of basic skills and general knowledge, widely criticized by educators and experts as woefully inadequate to measure teaching skill. Furthermore, in many states the cutoff scores are so low, there is no effective standard for entry.

These difficulties are barely known to the public. But the schools' most closely held secret amounts to a national shame: Roughly / of newly hired American teachers lack the qualifications for their jobs. More than 12 per cent of new hires enter the classroom without any formal training at all, and another 14 per cent arrive without fully meeting state standards.

Source: National Commission on Teaching and America's Future, *What Matters Most: Teaching for America's Future. Summary Report,* p. 7, New York, National Commission on Teaching and America's Future, 1996.

countries in the more developed regions of the world (e.g. Box 2.14). The problem is often associated with shortages of teachers in specific subject-areas, most frequently in science.

The general picture which emerges from all this is one where the ideal laid out in the *Recommendation* – 'completion of an approved course in an appropriate teacher-preparation institution should be required of all persons entering the profession' (Section V) – is quite far from being realized. Lack of such preparation is not always regarded as an obstacle to being employed as a teacher, especially when increases in student enrolments have outrun the supply of trained teachers. In that respect, the situation in many countries today is not essentially different from that of thirty years ago.

In sum, the emerging profile of the world's teachers, aside from those employed in a relatively small number of industrial countries, and possibly a few others, has doubtfully strengthened their claims for improved status. Although they are better educated than thirty years ago, so is the general population who are not teachers. The fact that society still is willing to accept at all that people can be employed as teachers without having received any specific preparation for the job

points to the difficulty for teachers in getting their claims heard. Probably no other aspect of teacher employment policies has done as much to retard progress towards recognition of teaching as a profession.

In the period since the *Recommendation* was adopted, teachers and teaching have not really been central concerns of educational policies. As was seen earlier in the chapter, most governments have been pre-occupied by other aspects of education: while wanting continued progress towards the democratization of education and the expansion of educational opportunities, they have at the same time been concerned to hold down educational expenditure and to make education systems more 'accountable' for such expenditure. This policy environment has not been favourable to improvements in the status of teachers.

Yet in the 1990s at least, there also have been signs of increasing concern over the quality of education. If this trend continues, teachers and teaching are likely to come more into focus than has been the case up to now. In the next chapter, therefore, consideration is given to what teachers are expected to do. Does their uncertain status in much of the world today accord with what society demands of them?

3
Teaching contexts and pressures

WHAT SOCIETY expects of teachers depends in large part on what it wants from education. Since the beginning of the 1990s, national educational policies have been marked by an increasing concern for quality and relevance, especially in basic education. Education systems, it is widely felt, are not performing effectively, not doing what they should be doing to ensure that the young people passing through them learn well what they are supposed to learn, and are well prepared to assume their future adult roles and responsibilities in the family, the workplace, and the wider community and society. In many countries there is a growing sense that education is the key to the future, and that the challenges and jobs of tomorrow will require an education of better quality than that which most students receive today.

Increasingly, educational quality and relevance are defined by reference to students' learning outcomes. 'The focus of basic education', the World Conference on Education for All declared, 'must ... be on actual learning acquisition and outcome, rather than exclusively upon enrolment, continued participation in organized programmes and completion of certification requirements' (World Declaration on Education for All, Article 4).

Yet if learning is to improve, teaching will need to contribute to that improvement. For the International Commission on Education for the Twenty-first Century, 'the importance of the quality of teaching, and therefore of teachers, cannot be overemphasized' (Box 3.1). This will require additional resources, as the Commission itself recognized. Yet the assumption underlying many educational policies in recent years, as seen in the previous chapter, is that 'more can be achieved with less', in effect, that the quality and relevance of education in general, and learning outcomes in particular, can be improved in the context of existing resource constraints.

This chapter considers the changing contexts and pressures facing teachers in the light of both the increasing focus of national educational poli-

cies on students' learning outcomes and the continuing resource constraints facing a majority of the world's education systems. There are six sections. In the first two, the origins of the current concern for educational quality and relevance are recalled, and the impulse which this concern has given to the monitoring and evaluation of education is noted. In subsequent sections, the growing pressures on teachers and policy issues relat-

---

Box 3.1
'The importance of the quality of teaching, and therefore of teachers'

The importance of the quality of teaching, and therefore of teachers, cannot be overemphasized. It is at an early stage of basic education that the principal attitudes toward learning as well as the self-image of the learner are formed. The role of the teacher at this stage is crucial. The greater the handicaps the children coming to school have to overcome – in terms of poverty, difficult social environment or physical impairments – the greater the demands on the teacher. He or she, to be effective, must draw upon a broad range of teaching skills, as well as on the human qualities of empathy, patience and humility, as a complement to authority. When a child's or adult's first teacher is poorly trained and poorly motivated, the very foundations on which all subsequent learning will be built will be unsound. The Commission feels that reasserting the importance of teachers in basic education and improving teachers' qualifications are tasks to which all governments must address themselves. The measures needed to recruit future teachers from among the most motivated students, improve their training and encourage the best among them to take on the most difficult posts need to be determined in relation to the specific circumstances of each country; but such measures must be taken, since, without them, it is unlikely that there will be significant improvements in quality where they are most needed.

Thus, improving the quality and motivation of teachers must be a priority in all countries.

Source: J. Delors et al., *Learning: The Treasure Within. Report to UNESCO of the International Commission on Education for the Twenty-first Century,* p. 146, Paris, UNESCO, 1996.

ing to teaching and learning conditions, teacher education and the assessment of teacher effectiveness are considered.

The concern for quality and relevance

Trends and developments in earlier decades, both within and outside education, contributed to the upsurge of concern for educational quality at the beginning of the present decade. In the less developed regions of the world, the dramatic expansion of educational enrolments in the 1960s and 1970s severely strained the qualitative foundations of many, if not most, education systems. Pressures on teacher demand-supply balances were noted in the previous chapter, but there also were pressures on educational management and administration, on the physical infrastructure of education and on the availability of instructional materials. The difficulties faced by many countries in tackling these problems were compounded by the economic circumstances and budgetary constraints of the 1980s. Growing numbers of school leavers and higher education graduates entered adulthood ill-prepared for the difficult futures that awaited them.

In the more developed regions of the world, where the expansion of educational enrolments had been less dramatic, there too was a widespread feeling that standards of educational quality had declined. Anxiety increased in the 1980s with the rapidity of changes in the world economy and the resulting pressures on countries to adjust to a more competitive global economic environment in which the 'educated intelligence' of a country's population – 'human capital' – was coming increasingly to be recognized as a strategic resource.

If there has consequently been a tendency in some countries to consider the quality and relevance of education mainly in terms of education's contribution to the successful pursuit of economic goals and purposes, in other countries sweeping

---

Box 3.2
Towards 'an education of one's choice'
in the Russian Federation

Today the strategy in the field of education is to facilitate the solution of global social problems through educational means, in particular:
- To strengthen and develop democracy;
- To consolidate national identify, harmonize ethnic relations, to ease social tensions;
- To develop the Russian economy's potential under new conditions.

The way to accomplishing these aims is through:
- Ensuring guarantees of citizens rights to get an education;
- Transition to an education of one's choice and ensuring an opportunity to get education in accordance with one's talents, abilities, interests and health;
- Maintaining a common educational space;
- Modification of the education content, its humanization;
- Ensuring a high-quality education.

The main direction of the reform is to create certain conditions for a transition from a unified, standardized, uniform education *to an education of one's choice*. The educational system should change to meet educational needs of children, families and different communities.

Source: Russia's Educational System: National Report of the Russian Federation, p. 5, Moscow, Ministry of Education, 1996. (National report presented at the 45th session of the International Conference on Education, Geneva, 1996.)

---

political and economic changes and developments have brought a broader range of objectives to the fore. In the countries of east and central Europe and the former Soviet Union, for example, the depoliticization of educational contents, and the establishment of a new pattern of relations between the education system and children, families and communities (e.g. Box 3.2), have redefined the reference points or criteria from which to judge quality and relevance: how successful is education in preparing young people to help 'strengthen and develop democracy, . . . consolidate national identity, harmonize ethnic relations,

Box 3.3
**Focus on the evaluation and measurement
of the quality of education
in Latin America and the Caribbean**

*Evaluation and measurement of the quality of edu-
cation: taking responsibility for educational results*

• Using appropriate criteria and procedures so
that an evaluation can be made not only of the
results but also of the processes undergone by the
students while developing the various types of
skills. Now that in many countries education systems are in a process of transition from quantitative to qualitative expansion, it is necessary to
develop both qualitative and quantitative evaluation indicators.
• Carrying out national assessments to determine
the level of skills attained, establishing assessment
systems and improving the methods and instruments used.
• Developing comparative assessments at different levels. Establishing machinery for regional
analysis of school results in order to carry out
studies of attainments and performance factors at
various stages in the educational processes, in different types of schools and in a range of contexts.
• Developing systems of indicators for the performance evaluation of schools that include not only
factors such as the attainments of pupils but also
others that have to do with the performance of the
institution.
• Devising ways of making better use of information. Adopting methods of communicating the
results of assessments of educational quality that
will enable ministries, schools, parents and educational communities to adopt and implement
measures to improve results, together with better
arrangements whereby society can monitor the
performance of schools.

*Source: Seventh Conference of Ministers of Education of Latin
America and the Caribbean, Kingston, Jamaica, 13–17 May
1996. Final Report.* Recommendation, Article VI. Santiago,
UNESCO, 1996. (Document ED/MD/201.)

... develop [the] national economy under new
conditions'?

The current widespread concern for educational quality and relevance, therefore, has
complex origins and many nuances depending on

the particular experiences of individual countries
over the past quarter of a century. It has taken the
form of a growing interest among national policy-
makers in the monitoring, measurement and
evaluation of educational processes and outcomes. The Recommendation adopted by the
Ministers of Education of Latin America and the
Caribbean at their conference in Jamaica in 1996
is a recent example (Box 3.3). This movement has
significant implications for the world's teachers.
Questions concerning educational quality and relevance, national policy-makers have realized,
cannot be answered properly, or be opened up to
democratic debate, in the absence of systematic
information on what is happening in the schools
and why.

The trend towards
monitoring and evaluation

Monitoring and evaluation of education are not in
themselves new; educational research has largely
been defined around them. What is new is both
the interest of national policy-makers and the
scope of their concerns, which extend to the
entire education system or to entire sub-sectors of
it such as basic education or higher education.
Until very recently, most educational research had
focused on small groups of pupils or students,
often located in a single educational institution or
handful of institutions; few studies aimed to consider the education system as a whole. This has
begun to change.

Although more than a decade has passed since
UNESCO last surveyed the situation worldwide,
there are signs that more educational research is
being carried out. At least, educational research
has now taken root in many countries where ten
or twenty years ago it was virtually unknown.
Government financial support is still very modest;
even in wealthy industrial countries the sums
involved hardly compare to those allocated for
research in other areas such as agriculture or

health, let alone defence. Nevertheless, it is significant that even in countries where education budgets are very tight, some official support is given for educational research.

The World Conference on Education for All helped to bring to the fore the need for more research in the field of basic education in the world's less developed regions and the need too for increased support for co-operation among educational researchers in these regions. In response to the World Conference's call for countries to 'define acceptable levels of learning acquisition for educational programmes and to improve and apply systems of assessing learning achievement', UNESCO, in collaboration with UNICEF, has sought to strengthen national capacities in this field; a joint UNESCO-UNICEF Monitoring Learning Achievement Project involving five countries (China, Jordan, Mali, Mauritius and Morocco) was launched in 1992. In addition, established networks of co-operation, such as the Information Network on Education for Latin American and the Caribbean (REDUC) and UNESCO's Asia and the Pacific Programme of Educational Innovation for Development (APEID) were given a fresh impetus, and new networks such as the recently formed Southern Africa Consortium for Monitoring Educational Quality (SACMEQ), involving Botswana, Kenya, Malawi, Mauritius, Namibia, Swaziland, the United Republic of Tanzania, Zambia and Zimbabwe, have emerged.

Given the scarcity of funds available for educational research in the world's less developed regions, much of the research carried out in these regions necessarily is highly pragmatic and down-to-earth, focused on concrete obstacles or handicaps in the way of improving educational quality. In Africa, for example, many studies concern different aspects of textbooks: their cost (e.g. a study of parents' purchasing power with respect to buying school textbooks in Mozambique), their distribution (e.g. a study of the distribution and modes of utilization of school textbooks in

Guinea) and their contents (e.g. an evaluation of textbooks for Arabic, French, mathematics and 'awakening to science' for fourth grade pupils in Tunisia).

The growth of educational research activity in the less developed regions has begun to lay the foundations of systemwide mechanisms for the monitoring, measurement and evaluation of edu-

Box 3.4
Development of a National System
of Evaluation of Basic Education in Brazil

The Ministry [of Education and Sports] has attached priority to the production of information in the area of evaluation and statistical data, through the restructuring, in 1995, of the National System of Evaluation of Basic Education, and through the implementation of the Integrated System of Educational Information. ...

The National System of Evaluation of Basic Education ... provides data on the level of performance and the acquisition of skills in reading and interpretation of texts, problem-solving and the use of mathematical concepts.

In 1995 tests were given to a selected sample of 95 thousand pupils of public and private schools in the 4th and 8th grades of primary education and the 2nd and 3rd grades of secondary education. The research had different focal points, such as structural and sociopolitical aspects of the school and the school organization, psychological, pedagogical and technical aspects, including the instruments for the evaluation of pupils, teacher-student relations, class dynamics and the resources used in the learning process.

In addition to the pupils, 3,400 directors, 7,000 teachers and 3,600 schools were also studied. The results can be utilized by educational administrators, researchers and teachers, and should soon be available on the Internet. The analysis of the results will assist actions which aim to correct the distortions identified and to improve school teaching.

Source: Development of Education in Brazil, p. 59, Brasilia, Ministry of Education and Sports, 1996. (National report presented at the 45th session of the International Conference on Education, Geneva, 1996.)

cational quality. A small but growing number of countries – up to now chiefly in Asia and Latin America – are beginning to set in place national systems of evaluation (e.g. Box 3.4). In many countries, the poor state of national educational statistics has been a handicap.

It has been mainly among the OECD countries that the development of systemwide mechanisms has gone furthest. These countries have given a high priority to improving the coverage, reliability and policy relevance of their national educational statistics, as well as their international comparability, and have co-operated with UNESCO for that purpose; this has been an area of concern to the Organization since its earliest days (see Appendix I).

Much of the co-operation among the OECD

countries has focused on the development of internationally comparable indicators of the various aspects of the quality and performance of their education systems: educational participation and attainment, education finance, students' learning outcomes, adult literacy, education and the labour market, the functioning of schools and school systems, and public attitudes towards education.

The indicators of learning outcomes have been drawn mainly from the studies carried out by the International Association for the Evaluation of Educational Achievement (IEA). As noted in previous editions of the *World Education Report*, these studies have mainly focused on cognitive outcomes; the most recent study – the largest conducted to date (forty-three systems) – focused on students' learning achievement in mathematics and science. The IEA studies have also collected a great deal of background information on students and teachers; specific findings from the most recent study are quoted later in this report.

The pressure on teachers

The movement towards monitoring and evaluation of the quality and performance of national education systems has undoubtedly begun to have an impact on the way in which education is regarded both by society at large and by the people directly involved, not least teachers. While education is opened up to democratic debate, it also becomes another 'industry', like mining or construction, with indicators too of inputs, process and output, as well as of 'market conditions' for the product. Not all educational policy-makers are comfortable with this trend (e.g. Box 3.5).

It is still unclear how far the concern for productive efficiency in education can be pursued. Much depends on the way learning outcomes are interpreted. (Are slow learners to be regarded as 'costly'?) Much also depends on teachers, more

---

Box 3.5
Reservations concerning a 'product-oriented' view of education (Malaysia)

A high quality teaching force – one that is always learning – is a *sine qua non* of coping with the dynamic complexity of a changing world. There are simply no substitutes to having better teachers.

However, the status and image of teachers accorded by society do not seem to be commensurate with these expectations. Teachers' pay remains comparatively low and opportunities for career advancement are limited. All these are issues related to the assessment of the worth of the teaching profession. However, we should not assess education solely from the socio-economic perspective for otherwise we run into the danger of using performance indicators to appeal to economics and business sense and thus subjugate the influence of teaching professionals under the control of managerial authority. This in the end may only further limit the development of the profession and promote the development of a product-oriented rather than process-oriented view of education.

Source: Strengthening the Role of Teachers in a Changing World. Country Paper, pp. 2–3, Kuala Lumpur, Ministry of Education, 1996. (National report presented at the 45th session of the International Conference on Education, Geneva, 1996.)

Box 3.6
Towards 'a new culture of evaluation' of education in France

Assessment of pupils' proficiency and knowledge has been enhanced both by:

- ongoing monitoring activities (evaluation on completion of the lower secondary level ('*collège*') in 1995 in all subjects, except the arts and physical education and sport); and
- innovative comparative time studies (trends in academic achievement among the elite over the past forty years; pupils' proficiency in French and mathematics today as against the 1920s on the basis of primary school-leaving certificate examinations) and international comparisons (participation in the third international evaluation of achievement in mathematics and science).

Further work has been done on the evaluation of educational personnel, through two approaches:

- gaining a better understanding of the various categories of educational personnel (teachers, inspectors, documentalists, chief administrative officials, guidance counsellors-psychologists, head teachers) by conducting studies on how they and the other actors in the system perceive their role and activities;
- further research on teacher impact at the primary and lower secondary level (French and mathematics). These research studies are intended to highlight professional practices which, in a given context, are instrumental in improving pupils' performance.

Evaluation of state educational policies designed to improve pupils' performance has focused on the steps taken at the *collège* level to remedy the shortcomings observed at the beginning of the first year of secondary school and prevent subsequent learning difficulties – more flexible hours, tutorials, remedial classes or groups – and to give the pupils a greater sense of responsibility through education for citizenship.

The evaluation of educational establishments has progressed with the continued annual publication of performance indicators for the *lycées* (upper secondary schools) and research on the functioning of the *collèges*. This has provided an increasingly accurate and scientifically based picture of the added value of school establishments.

The evaluation of the education system is now the subject of analysis both at the national level with *'L'état de l'école'* and in academic terms with *'Géographie de l'école'*, two publications which use some thirty indicators to provide a yearly survey of the activities, cost and performance of the education system. They are particularly useful tools for assessing the system's effectiveness overall and as pointers for future action.

The publication of all evaluation studies has created a greater awareness among all actors involved nationally and locally in teaching and decision-making of the effects of individual or collective action taken within the system.

This new awareness is the first stage in the development of a new *culture of evaluation*. It would, however, be insufficient if it were not followed up by the use of evaluation tools conducive to self-evaluation by all parties concerned.

Source: Rapport de la France, pp. 41–2, Paris, Ministère de l'Éducation Nationale, de l'Enseignement Supérieur et de la Recherche, 1996. (National report presented at the 45th session of the International Conference on Education, Geneva, 1996.)

---

closely involved with these outcomes than anybody else except the learners themselves.

Teachers have always had their own individual methods of evaluation in the classroom and most countries have systemwide school-leaving examinations of one kind or another. What has been called the 'new culture of evaluation', though, is something quite different and more all-embracing (Box 3.6). It does not necessarily make for comfortable relations with teachers. There have been instances (e.g. in the United Kingdom) where teachers have not been convinced of the validity or fairness of a given evaluation or monitoring activity and, with the support of skeptical parents, have successfully blocked its implementation and/or caused the procedure in question to be revised.

The *Recommendation concerning the Status of Teachers* provides no direct guidance on the relationship of teachers to mechanisms of evaluation and monitoring imposed on schools from outside, whether these are public examinations of the traditional kind or the 'learning achievement' tests generally favoured by educational researchers. It says only that 'Teachers should be free to make use of such evaluation techniques as they may deem useful for the appraisal of pupils' progress, but should ensure that no unfairness to individual pupils results' (Section VIII). The 'new culture of evaluation' has emerged in the years since the *Recommendation* was adopted.

Teachers' discomfort with the intrusion of outside evaluation mechanisms into their relationship with pupils and students is probably increased where these mechanisms have extended to the evaluation of teachers themselves, notwithstanding that they have always been subject to some form of supervision and assessment. While such extension is to some extent inevitable if the educational authorities are ever to identify ways in which teaching can be improved, the co-operation of teachers depends critically on their confidence in the validity and fairness of the evaluation/assessment mechanism. This question is taken up later in the present chapter.

Moreover, teachers are aware that the concern for educational quality and relevance has not generally been matched up to now – as seen in the previous chapter – by a greater willingness in national development policies to provide more resources for education. This has probably increased teachers' sense of being under pressure, for it seems to suggest that the education system is expected to improve its performance with the means already to hand.

Teaching and learning conditions

Improved learning outcomes can hardly be expected of schools, or of educational institutions generally, if the conditions under which teaching and learning take place are not conducive. In many countries, the conditions are difficult, whether they relate to the physical state of schools and the availability of teaching and learning materials, class sizes, or the changing characteristics of the student population.

First, concerning *the physical state of schools and the availability of teaching and learning materials,* the desperate situation in some parts of the world's less developed regions needs to be emphasized. The situation is masked by existing international educational indicators, which mainly concern student enrolments without regard to the educational conditions in which the students are enrolled, thus giving the false impression that the students reportedly enrolled at any given level of education in the different countries are all enrolled in something which is basically quite similar.

With a view to correcting this impression and testing the feasibility of developing international indicators of teaching and learning conditions that could be useful and informative for educational policy-makers in the world's less developed regions, UNESCO, in co-operation with UNICEF and the countries concerned, commissioned in 1995 a pilot sample survey of primary schools in selected least developed countries. Specific findings are shown in Tables 3.1 and 3.2.

In a majority of the countries surveyed, the average classroom is not much more than a designated meeting place for a teacher and a group of pupils: in ten out of the fourteen countries, one-third or more of the pupils are gathered into classrooms without a usable chalkboard. In virtually all countries there are no teaching aids such as wall charts and almost no pupil will ever see a world map. In ten out of the fourteen countries, one-third or more of the pupils are in classrooms without a teacher's table and the situation is only marginally better with respect to a chair for the teacher. In eight out of the fourteen countries, more than 90 per cent of the pupils attend schools which do not have electricity; almost as many attend schools without piped water and one-third

Table 3.1
Teaching conditions in sampled primary schools,[1] in selected least developed countries, 1995

	Number of schools in sample	Percentage of pupils in classrooms not having:						Percentage of pupils in schools not having:				Percentage of pupils in schools needing major repairs or rebuilding
		Usable chalk board	Wall chart	World map	Cup-board	Teacher table	Teacher chair	Piped water	Any water	Elec-tricity	First aid kit	
Bangladesh	141	47	80	92	98	44	31	90	23	95	93	42*
Benin	30	2	25*	99	97	35*	29*	77*	46	88*	87*	90*
Bhutan	54	3*	52*	76*	76	12*	17*	40*	5	69*	73*	10*
Burkina Faso	103	79	6	94	89	14	15	88	39	92	81	37*
Cape Verde	20	42	92	97	77*	49	45	21*	0	42*	62*	0
Equatorial Guinea	25	48*	96	99	95	76*	85	93*	42	98	100	...
Ethiopia	99	36	97	99	100	92	90	94	72	93	96	72*
Madagascar	108	51	48	89	88	48	47	58*	36	55*	79*	39*
Maldives	20	51	78*	98	82*	54*	50	90*	10	35*	68*	...
Nepal	158	...	...	...	...	...	...	65*	28	91	85	38*
Togo	24	8*	75*	97	83*	31*	32*	77*	67	83*	72*	36*
Uganda	30	35	70	93	91	70*	56*	98	35	92*	71*	55*
U. Rep. of Tanzania	25	54*	90	91	94	91	97	91*	36	100	100	39*
Zambia	20	44	88*	100	86*	64*	68*	80*	30	95*	80*	45*

1. The figures in this table need to be interpreted with caution, bearing in mind that they are drawn from a sample of schools in each country and hence are subject in each case to sampling error. For example, for the column 'Usable chalk board' in the case of Bangladesh, where the standard error is 1.7, it can be said that there is a 95 per cent probability that the true figure for the country's whole population of primary-school pupils lies in the range 47 ± (2 x 1.7), that is to say, between 43.6 and 50.4. The standard errors of sampling are not shown in this table. Instead, an asterisk (*) is shown next to figures where the standard error is equal to or greater than 5.0.

Source: Andreas Schleicher, Maria Teresa Siniscalco and Neville Postlethwaite, *The Conditions of Primary Schools: A Pilot Study in the Least Developed Countries. A Report to UNESCO and UNICEF,* pp. 97 and 125–6. Paris, UNESCO, 1995. (Mimeo.)

or more of the pupils attend schools which do not have any water at all. Moreover, in half the countries (mainly in Africa) over 90 per cent of the pupils in the final grade of primary education do not have any textbook in their mother tongue, over a third of them do not have a maths textbook in any tongue and over a third (not shown in Table 3.2) do not have a desk or writing place, as distinct from just a place to sit.

The main finding, though, is a general one: if education is to be expected to help the poor to lift themselves out of poverty, then in the poorest countries education itself needs first to be lifted out of poverty. In this perspective, structural adjustment programmes designed to eliminate waste in public services could usefully be complemented by investment in the physical infrastructure of education: providing schools with water and electricity, and reasonably solid walls and roofs, plus furniture and of course textbooks and other teaching materials.

The tremendous expansion of education and the pauperization of teaching and learning conditions associated with this expansion in many parts of the less developed regions of the world over the past thirty years were not foreseen when the *Recommendation concerning the Status of Teachers* was adopted: 'School buildings should be safe and attractive in overall design and functional in layout; they should lend themselves to effective teaching, and to use for extra-curricular activities and, especially in rural areas, as a community centre; they should be constructed in accordance with established sanitary standards and with a view to durability, adaptability and easy economic maintenance'. All over Africa, Asia and Latin America, there are thousands of schools which do not meet these standards. Learning out-

Table 3.2
Availability of textbooks in sampled primary schools,[1] in selected least developed countries, 1995

	Percentage of pupils whose home language is different from the medium of instruction	Percentage of pupils in the highest grade who do not have:	
		Mother tongue textbooks	A maths textbook
Bangladesh	_[2]	...[3]	...
Benin	99	...	78
Bhutan	86	...	4*
Burkina Faso	94	100	95
Cape Verde	100	100	7
Equatorial Guinea	98	99	72*
Ethiopia	16	35*	20*
Madagascar	84	70	81
Maldives	8*	...[3]	52*
Nepal	34	84	58
Togo	99	94	68*
Uganda	60	99	55
U. Rep. of Tanzania	91*	98	48*
Zambia	100	95	59*

1. The same caution indicated in footnote 1 of Table 3.1 applies in this table.
2. Less than 1 per cent.
3. No data were collected, since textbooks are normally available in the mother tongue.

Source: Same as for Table 3.1, pp. 87 and 103.

comes will not be significantly improved until they do meet them.

The difficulties relating to the physical state of schools and the availability of instructional materials are compounded by *class sizes*. The issue of class size, though, cuts across all regions of the world. It is a matter of continuing controversy, because in most countries it has always been felt by teachers – and by parents too – to be a critical aspect of teaching and learning conditions, yet for the educational authorities it has major budgetary implications. Class sizes translate into the number of teachers needed for any given school population, while teachers' salaries in most countries typically account for two-thirds or more of total educational expenditure.

Although international indicators of class sizes

at the various levels of education in different countries are not available, it is reasonable to assume that pupil-teacher ratios (for which data are available) broadly speaking correlate with them and thus can point to trends in class sizes over time and across major regions of the world. In most regions over the last decade or so there was little change, with the possible exception of some upward pressures in primary and secondary education in Southern Asia, where pupil-teacher ratios are markedly higher than in other regions (Table 3.3).

The very high pupil-teacher ratios observed in a number of individual countries in the less developed regions (see Appendix III, Table 7) are probably in many cases associated with the operation of double (or even triple) shifts of pupils morning and afternoon in the same school premises. This has been one solution countries have adopted for coping with the under-capitalization of the physical infrastructure of education, although it invariably means reducing the average hours of instruc-

Table 3.3
Pupil-teacher ratios in primary and secondary education, by region, 1985 and 1995

	Primary		Secondary	
	1985	1995	1985	1995
WORLD TOTAL	27	27	17	17
More developed regions	17	16	14	14
of which:				
North America	14	16	16	16
Asia/Oceania	22	18	17	14
Europe	17	16	13	12
Countries in transition	22	19	15	12
Less developed regions	30	30	20	20
of which:				
Sub-Saharan Africa	38	39	24	25
Arab States	26	23	19	16
Latin America/Caribbean	27	24	15	15
Eastern Asia/Oceania	26	24	18	17
of which: China	25	23	17	16
Southern Asia	43	45	24	30
of which: India	47	47	26	32

Figure 3.1
GNP per capita and pupil-teacher ratio in primary and secondary education, by region,[1] 1995

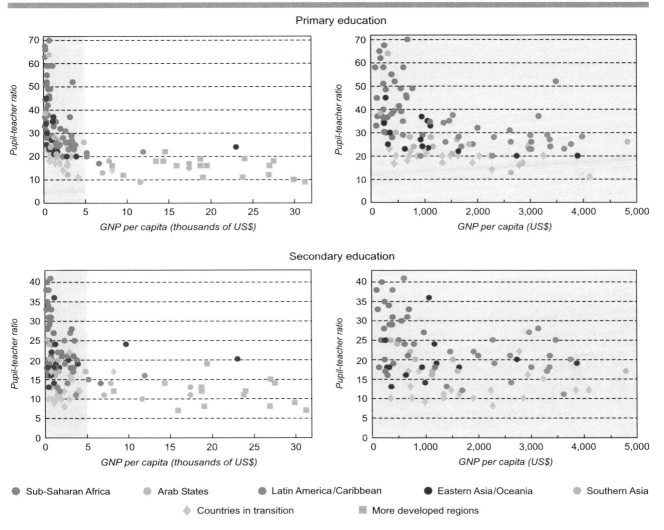

Primary education

Secondary education

● Sub-Saharan Africa   ● Arab States   ● Latin America/Caribbean   ● Eastern Asia/Oceania   ● Southern Asia

◆ Countries in transition   ▦ More developed regions

1. Individual countries within each region are represented by dots, diamonds and squares.

Note: The graphs on the right show separately countries for which the GNP per capita is lower than US$5,000.

tion per pupil per year while at the same time probably increasing the hours of instruction required of teachers (in so far as the latter are required to teach in two or more shifts).

Since pupil-teacher ratios, in a global perspective, are broadly correlated with levels of GNP per capita (Figure 3.1) the logic underlying them probably has a lot to do with whether countries can afford to reduce them. For many countries, especially in the less developed regions of the world, this has been a long-standing dilemma.

The horns of the dilemma are partly economic and partly educational and social. Some economists, believing that students' learning can be understood essentially as a production process which requires a number of 'inputs', including a teacher, have argued that the issue of class size should be decided on the basis of which input, if

Box 3.7
Class sizes and teachers' workloads in India

The workload of teachers is often judged in terms of amount and type of work done by them. A sample survey carried out in 1990 (J. C. Goyal and R. K. Chopra, *Elementary School Teachers: A Profile,* National Council of Educational Research and Training, 1990) found that 42 per cent of primary school teachers teach two classes or more at a time. About 50 per cent of upper primary/middle school teachers report that they teach four or more subjects. More than 60 per cent of teachers teach about 50 students on average, 34 per cent teach between 51–100 and about 5 per cent more than 100 students. This means that on average about 39 per cent of teachers teach more than 50 students in the primary school. At high/higher secondary levels, however, the teacher-pupil ratio was 1:16 in 1994–95. It is evident that primary school teachers are working under stress, especially those teachers who are handling multi-grade classes.

Education codes in different states specify the number of class periods teachers at different levels have to teach. The above-mentioned sample survey found that about one-fourth of primary school teachers teach 31–35 class periods and a similar number teach more than 36 class periods a week. In middle schools, nearly half of the teachers teach 31–40 class periods a week, whereas, 12 per cent teach more than 40 class periods.

Besides teaching, elementary and secondary school teachers have to spend a fair amount of time on co-curricular activities, especially in private schools. In addition, teachers have to do clerical work and other miscellaneous work like organizing relief work, collecting census data, participating in family planning campaigns, and population control drives, helping in the smooth conduct of elections, etc.

Source: Development of Education in India, 1995–1996 with Special Reference to Teacher Education, pp. 37–38, New Delhi, Department of Education, Ministry of Human Resource Development, 1996. (National report presented at the 45th session of the International Conference on Education, Geneva, 1996.)

increased by a given amount of expenditure, would produce the largest gain in students' learning achievement. Usually the argument has been presented as a trade-off between additional expenditure on teachers – with a view to reducing the student-teacher ratio – on the one hand, and additional expenditure on instructional materials on the other hand.

For countries such as those that participated in the UNESCO-UNICEF pilot survey, where the pupils have teachers but few textbooks or other learning aids, it can be plausibly argued on common-sense grounds that the trade-off favours expenditure on additional instructional materials rather than additional teachers. However, for the majority of countries, where teaching and learning conditions are better, the trade-off is more difficult to decide and in any case is rarely posed for educational policy-makers in such simple terms. In many countries, the overall pupil-teacher or pupil-class ratio usually masks a wide variation in teachers' workloads; in some cases even, teachers could be teaching very large classes composed of multiple grades (e.g. Box 3.7).

Moreover, in most of the world's less developed regions, the whole question of class size is complicated by the fact that pupil drop-out rates are so high (Figure 3.2). Very large classes – sometimes 75 to 100 pupils – are common in the first grade in some countries, but a third or more of the pupils drop out of school before reaching the fifth grade. In these countries, overall policies on class size cannot be meaningfully formulated without reference to the educational and social conditions which determine whether pupils will remain in school at all.

Up to now, very few of the studies of the effect of class size on students' learning achievement have been rigorous enough to warrant giving much confidence to the possibility of generalizing their findings to the level of a national school system. Indeed, few have fully recognized that the notion of 'class size' itself is problematic: the size of the class today or last month? Or five years ago when the child started to read? How long do children have to be in a class of a given size before reliable measures of the 'effect' can be made? And how can these children be meaningfully compared with another group of different children in a larger (or smaller) class with a different teacher?

In light of these difficulties, it is not surprising that the majority of studies have found only a modest effect of class size on learning achievement and not really noticeable unless quite small classes – say below twenty students – are taken into account. However, this finding could be culture-specific and doubtfully relevant to regions such as sub-Saharan Africa and Southern Asia where average class sizes are large, since most of the studies have been carried out in North America where there is little variation in class size and average class sizes are small.

More research is still needed into how the effect is produced: what aspects of teachers' and pupils' behaviour are different in small compared with large classes? There is evidence, for example, that both teachers' and learners' stress is less in small classes. Such findings could help to shift the focus of the class size debate which up to now has mainly been on cognitive outcomes. Children with special educational needs, for example, are very relevant to this debate; the advantages of small classes which more easily allow for such children to be educated alongside other children are universally recognized.

Much more needs to be known about the effects of class size on students' attitudes and social behaviour, which have been of growing concern in a number of countries, especially where various forms of student violence – bullying, assaults on teachers, property damage – have been on the increase. Japan's National Institute for Educational Research, for example, currently has underway a major study of school bullying. In Canada, a recent study carried out by the Ontario Teachers' Federation reported 441 episodes of major physical assaults by students on teachers in Ontario during a three-year period and 6,300 cases of minor abuse. Other industrial countries have experienced similar phenomena.

Having regard to such problems, not to speak

Figure 3.2
Estimated survival rates[1] to Grade 5 in primary education, in the less developed regions

1. Percentages of the 1994 cohort reaching Grades 2, 3, 4 and 5.

of the currently overworked state of so many of the world's teachers, the whole question of class size clearly needs to be situated in a broader context than cognitive outcomes. On the evidence available to date, educational policy- and deci-

---

Box 3.8
'When half the class has problems ...'

'If there are five or six problem children in a class of 30, the teacher can take care of the problem. But when half the class has problems the teacher cannot really cope. But in addition, most of our teachers do not come from our neighbourhoods, and that poses a problem ...'

'Teaching today is not what it was ten years ago: a teacher must now be priest, cop, and so on. Are teachers capable of that? They would say no. What they say is, 'We can play that role up to a point, but after that the State must assume its responsibilities'. But something more than teaching is called for, and that is the human capacity to understand all the problems. What we need today is teachers who are involved. And that goes far beyond mere time-tables. It is a fact that children and adolescents succeed when they come upon a teacher who shows interest and confidence in them. It is what we define as human warmth. Are we capable of providing human warmth in a class in which more than half the pupils have problems of one kind or another? ...'

'All we teachers do is sow the seeds. We have no way of knowing what our efforts will produce. Some students will take nothing in. But others, years later, will say: 'I remember you once told me such and such; it made an impression on me and it taught me something' ...'
(Rachid Benzine, a secondary school teacher in Trappes, France.)

'Most teachers [in this school] work individually with each student and we've worked it out as a system, with a sense of family. Young people are reasonable. They are looking for someone who treats them with respect. The message that I try to transmit is that whatever they do now will have an impact in their future, in their life, in their society ...'

'For me teachers are more than instructors. I wish I would become a lifelong teacher, which is teaching how to learn, the ability to analyze, share possibilities in unique and innovative ways to solve problems. Teachers are renaissance people. We are not licensed to counsel, we are not licensed to preach, but we preach ...'
(Mimsie Robinson, biology teacher at Unity High School and New York's '1997 Teacher of the Year', United States.)

Source: Learning to Live Together. Interviews from around the World on the Role of Education, pp. 34, 50–1, Paris, UNESCO, 1997. (Mimeo.)

---

sion-makers would be wise to favour smaller classes when budgets permit. Even in those countries – many of them Asian – that traditionally have favoured (and still have) large classes while being able, in a comparative international perspective, to afford smaller ones, the long-term trend in class sizes is downwards.

More than most issues in education, the class size issue brings out vividly the implications of applying the cost-effectiveness line of thinking to education generally. Whether this line of thinking can be pursued very far on the basis of the teacher as a disembodied 'input' into the learning process – on the same level as textbooks or wall charts – rather than as a creative partner in this process is quite doubtful. The danger is of slipping into the view – strongly criticized, for example, in the recent report of the National Commission on Teaching and America's Future – that schools can 'be run like factories and managed by top-down controls rather than by investing in teachers' capacities to make good decisions'.

The class size issue cannot easily be divorced from the third aspect of teaching-learning conditions that needs to be mentioned: the *changing characteristics of the student population.*

In the industrial countries, the expansion of educational opportunities at post-compulsory levels in recent years has brought to these levels a more diverse student population in terms of social backgrounds, interests and abilities. In some countries, immigration has brought more ethnic diversity. In other respects too the student population has changed. As a result of the breakdown of the family especially, most observers agree, the student population today has a frequency of social problems that few teachers who have been teaching for more than fifteen to twenty years anticipated when they began their careers. In the poorer neighbourhoods of large cities particularly, where these problems are common, teachers are called upon to perform roles – parent, policeman, priest – far removed from the one for which in most cases they were formally prepared (e.g. Box 3.8)

Still, the tendency of educators in many of the industrial countries to attribute the current problems of the schools to social changes could be overdone. Educational policy-makers would be wise to scrutinize the continuing relevance of existing curricula. A remarkable (and hitherto unpublished) finding of IEA's recent Third International Mathematics and Science Study (TIMSS), based on national samples of 7th and 8th grade students (14-year-olds) in twenty-five countries and territories (Table 3.4), suggests that students' academic abilities and/or lack of interest in their educational programme could be bigger problems for teachers than either students' behaviour or backgrounds. In virtually every country, the percentages of students whose teachers report that their teaching is limited 'quite a lot' or 'a great deal' by students' academic abilities and/or lack of interest are higher than the percentages of students whose teachers report that their teaching is limited 'quite a lot' or 'a great deal' by students' backgrounds or disruptive behaviour.

The characteristics of student populations in the world's less developed regions are changing too as educational opportunities at the different levels improve, marked in varying degrees in different countries by the increasing educational participation of girls and of rural populations generally, including diverse social and ethnic groups which up to now have had only limited or no access to education. The complex and difficult role of the rural teacher in this movement towards Education for All has not always been fully recognized in educational policies. The need particularly for more female teachers in rural areas, in order to

Table 3.4
Secondary-school mathematics teachers' views concerning their students,[1] in countries and territories that participated in IEA's Third International Mathematics and Science Study (TIMSS), 1994–95

	Percentage of students whose teachers report that their teaching is limited 'quite a lot' or 'a great deal' by:[2]			
	Students' academic abilities	Students' wide range of backgrounds	Students' lack of interest	Disruptive students
Belgium (Fl)[3]	30	20	38	26
Canada	54	21	46	45
Cyprus	83	47	74	64
Czech Republic	70	8	54	30
England	35	13	30	27
France	66	21	59	36
Hong Kong	67	33	55	44
Hungary	91	38	68	57
Iceland	86	21	54	52
Iran, Islamic Rep. of	88	62	68	49
Ireland	62	19	43	38
Japan	62	...	35	...
Latvia[4]	81	15	64	27
Lithuania	88	11	57	33
New Zealand	50	26	40	39
Norway	67	16	39	29
Portugal	72	37	69	58
Rep. of Korea	77	24	67	65
Russian Federation	77	13	49	18
Singapore	56	34	48	45
Slovakia	68	21	71	44
Spain	82	17	88	64
Sweden	51	18	35	30
Switzerland	61	33	30	25
United States	48	17	47	36

1. Teachers of 7th and 8th grade students were asked whether a particular characteristic of their students, e.g. students' academic abilities, limited their teaching either 'not at all', 'a little', 'quite a lot' or 'a great deal'.
2. The TIMSS sampling targeted the 7th and 8th grade student population in each system. Thus, this table shows the views of teachers of nationally representative samples of 7th and 8th grade students. For example, with reference to Belgium (Fl): an estimated 30 per cent of 7th and 8th grade students had teachers who report that their teaching is limited 'quite a lot' or 'a great deal' by their students' academic abilities.
3. Flemish-speaking schools.
4. Latvian-speaking schools.

Source: TIMSS International Study Center, Boston College.

Box 3.9
The language question in Niger

In Niger most schools use French, as they were established in a non-French-speaking environment by the colonizer. Since then, they have been unable to put this 'original sin' behind them. In order to understand the kind of anathema that schools in Niger labour under one needs to be aware of Niger's situation as regards language and culture.

Niger is at the heart of the African continent, almost equidistant from all the seas, and appears in the middle of the Sahara like a kind of buffer against which, from time immemorial, waves of populations bringing Arab-Berber, Guinean, even Bantu influences, not to mention those of great medieval empires of Africa (Mali, Songhay, Kanem), were brought to a halt. This meeting-point function is seen clearly on a linguistic map of the country. It does not have exclusive possession of any language but shares them all with other countries.

- Hausa, with Nigeria;
- Gurmanche, with Burkina Faso;
- Sonaï Zarma, with Mali, Benin and Burkina Faso;
- Tamajak, with the Libyan Arab Jamahiriya, Algeria and Mali;
- Fulfulde, the language of the Peuls, spoken in some 15 African countries;
- Tabu, with Chad;
- Arabic, the language of the liturgy of 95–98 per cent of the country's Muslims and mother tongue for some isolated population groups; and lastly
- French, the official language, the language of the administration and above all the main language of education, has been pinned on top of this patchwork, and the people of Niger who speak it have an ambivalent attitude towards it. It is hardly ever used in everyday exchanges in cultural and social life, where French merely emerges, it seems, as a bulwark against the real or imagined threats posed by the mass of illiterates, non-French speakers, or 'barely-French-speakers', which various efforts to democratize power structures over the last few years have made more aggressive. French, which has for a long time been and still is the language of social advancement, has played a part, here as in other African countries, in creating a dichotomous society that pits the political and administrative elite against the bulk of the population.

Source: Rapport national sur le développement de l'éducation au Niger, 1994–1996, pp. 7–8, Niamey, Commission Nationale Nigérienne pour l'Éducation, la Science et la Culture, Ministère de l'Éducation Nationale, 1996. (National report presented at the 45th session of the International Conference on Education, Geneva, 1996.)

---

provide more encouragement for families to send their girls to school, was stressed in the 1995 edition of this report.

For the rural teacher in the least developed countries, school conditions, as already noted, are often such as to permit only minimal forms of educational activity to be carried out, and structures and mechanisms for providing professional support to the teacher are often lacking. In these countries, the question of educational quality and relevance, and the role of the teacher is of an altogether different order from that facing countries in the more developed regions of the world.

For many rural teachers in Africa, Asia and Latin America, the material difficulties in carrying out their teaching duties are compounded by the nature of the teaching challenge itself, in particular having to deal with multigrade classes because of the scattered nature of the rural population. Although international data on this phenomenon have not been collected since 1959, when IBE obtained information from around forty-five countries on the numbers of, and enrolment in, one-teacher primary schools, in the years since then the specific challenges of multigrade teaching have been the focus of international discussion at experts' workshops and seminars organized from time to time (most recently in 1995) by APEID. Multigrade classes and/or small schools that have more grades than teachers are unofficially estimated to number in the hundreds of thousands in China and India, and are common elsewhere in the Asia-Pacific region as well as in Latin America (e.g. Brazil, Mexico and Peru).

The material and pedagogical challenges facing the rural teacher are complicated in many countries by difficulties relating to the medium of instruction for minority language groups. Even where the merits of providing initial education in the mother tongue are officially recognized, shortages of appropriate learning materials and trained teachers have handicapped the efforts of many countries to provide such instruction. The problems are acute in Africa, where such shortages and the great multiplicity of languages have made it virtually impossible in some countries to conduct classes in the mother tongues of most learners, while attitudes towards the use of a former colonial language (English, French, Portuguese or Spanish) as the medium of instruction are often ambivalent, for the reasons highlighted in Box 3.9.

In sum, whichever way teaching-learning conditions are considered, whether from the standpoint of the physical state of schools, the availability of teaching and learning materials, class sizes or the characteristics of the student population, the education sector cannot easily be regarded as conspicuously prone to the waste of resources. Nor can the teacher's job be regarded as a particularly comfortable one. In many countries, both teachers and students need more support if learning outcomes are to be improved.

Teacher education

While teaching and learning conditions are important, teachers are central to the question of education's quality and relevance. How they are educated and prepared for their work is a critical indicator of what kind of educational quality and relevance is being sought. Although it is still common, as was noted in Chapter 2, for persons who have never participated in a teacher-education programme to be appointed as teachers, the educational authorities in most countries today are probably more reluctant to resort to this expedient than they were ten or twenty years ago. The World Conference on Education for All pointed educational policies away from measures designed merely to permit increases in student enrolments without doing anything to improve students' learning outcomes.

Approaches to teacher education, however, are as varied as the tasks and roles for which teachers are intended to be prepared, whether in the classroom, school or other educational setting, or in the wider community. In so far as there can be said to be any international consensus at all on such a complex matter, given the differences in national and cultural contexts, it is that 'teaching should be regarded as a profession'. This is what was agreed when the *Recommendation* was adopted.

'Teaching', the *Recommendation* affirms, 'is a form of public service which requires of teachers expert knowledge and specialized skills, acquired and maintained through rigorous and continued study; it calls also for a sense of personal and corporate responsibility for the education and welfare of the pupils in their charge' (see Box 2.1).

Approaches to the pre-service and in-service education of teachers have essentially been based on conceptions of the teacher's teaching and other roles, choices concerning the form and contents of teacher-education programmes, and the priority given to enabling teachers to continue learning while keeping up to date and abreast of developments in their fields.

Conceptions of the teaching role have strongly influenced *pre-service teacher-education programmes,* but the emphasis typically placed on this role has often led to the neglect of preparation for other aspects of the teacher's life in the school and the community (e.g. Box 3.10).

Given the emphasis on the teaching role, global trends in teacher education can be broadly interpreted as a shifting balance between a concern mainly to prepare teachers who can implement effectively their school systems' mandated cur-

---

Box 3.10
'Little or no time is spent preparing the trainee teachers for their real life in these difficult contexts'

The [Conference's] Roundtable on Teaching in Difficult Contexts commenced with presentations outlining either recent practice or identifying possible issues in different regions, including Viet Nam, Pakistan, Thailand and Myanmar. ...

One of the major issues identified was the recruitment of local teachers, that is teachers who come from the same difficult context and who therefore understand the nature of the situation. This is often not possible and therefore offers a new set of challenges for teachers who come to the area from outside. This then has implications for how these teachers are trained.

Locally recruited teachers have the advantage of understanding the local conditions but are often disadvantaged through the same factors that make the situation difficult. In many cases of minority people, they are further disadvantaged by having to be trained in what is for them their second language. For women, it is particularly difficult for them to leave their local area to attend training. Thus, training of an intensive nature which is provided in the local environment is a useful innovation. ...

For teachers who come from outside the disadvantaged region, there are additional complexities to their work. Often, they are expected to be more than teachers. In many cases, they will be the most educated person in the village and demands will be placed upon their specialist skills and knowledge. Thus, additional responsibilities will be given to them. At the same time, survival skills for these teachers are neces-

sary so that they can cope with their new environment and can 'get on' with the local community. In some cases, this can expand into a new role of community resource person. This role may be formalized in some cases where a stronger link between the school and the community is an explicit aim of an educational intervention, or it may simply evolve.

In any case, there is a need for a symbiotic relationship between teacher and community since local support is essential for teacher survival. In some cases, for example in communities which are very poor and almost all parents are illiterate, this relationship will seem unbalanced and teachers will have difficulty in knowing how to involve the community in the activities of the school. ...

The implication for teacher development is clear. Teacher educators spend significant periods of time teaching pedagogy, curriculum and the disciplines of student development. Little or no time is spent preparing the trainee teachers for their real life in these difficult contexts. In order to cope with their life in such contexts, they need additional skills. The basic skill which is needed is self-security, a strong sense of who they are and what they are doing in their life. In their work, they need to see themselves as at the centre of the community rather than being only in the classroom. As such, they need to be self-reliant and skilled in promoting community participation. This of course requires high level skill in communication and negotiation.

Source: Partnerships in Teacher Development for a New Asia, pp. 391–2, Bangkok, UNESCO (Asia-Pacific Centre of Educational Innovation for Development), 1996. (Report of an International Conference organized by UNESCO and UNICEF in association with the Office of the National Education Commission, Thailand, held in Bangkok, 6–8 December 1995.)

---

ricula and a concern mainly to prepare teachers who can respond effectively to the diversity of students' learning needs and interests generally. In practice, this distinction is not a hard and fast one, but is mainly a question of orientation; it echoes to some extent other distinctions which are often made in education, for example, between socially utilitarian and humanistic educational purposes, or between subject-centred and learner-centred approaches to teaching. The balance which is struck at any time reflects many

of society's basic expectations of schools and schooling.

In a global perspective, a historic shift towards more humanistic educational purposes occurred at the beginning of the present decade in the Russian Federation and the countries of east and central Europe. This shift, which was considered in the 1993 edition of this report and is acknowledged in Box 3.2, set in train a radical rethinking of teacher education. At the same time, a shift in the other direction occurred elsewhere, notably in the English-speaking countries, marked by the introduction of national curricula for primary and secondary education in the United Kingdom, and the movement towards voluntary national curriculum standards for primary and secondary education in the United States. This shift has also set in train a rethinking of teacher education.

The overall global trend towards either a loosening of the bounds of mandated curricula and teaching protocols on the one hand, or a tightening on the other, is difficult to assess. There possibly is a convergence from different directions, as indicated above, towards a middle ground. Countries have different starting points and national circumstances vary. In some countries, highly competitive examinations have distorted the best intentions of the curriculum designers (e.g. Box 3.11). India (with one out of every twelve teachers in the world) has recently moved towards more rigorous standards, marked by the establishment in 1993 of a National Council for Teacher Education with a wide range of functions including the laying down of national norms and guidelines for teachers' qualifications and the forms and contents of courses of teacher education. There also have been signs of a trend in the same direction in Latin America, with reforms of school curricula and teacher education in Argentina, Brazil, Mexico and Venezuela.

In general, the growing sensitivity of educational policies worldwide to the international dimension of educational quality and relevance, provides less room for open-ended school curricula with uncertain standards. Teacher-education programmes could face increasing pressures to adjust accordingly, particularly with respect to the types of competencies that are emphasized. Aware of this, some observers have expressed fears of a trend towards the 'deprofessionalization' of teachers and teaching, with the teacher's role reduced to that of a technician primarily responsible for implementing prescribed procedures, rather than for making a professional judgement about the instructional approach that would be

---

Box 3.11
**The danger of schools becoming
'mere training camps to pass examinations'
(Republic of Korea)**

The university-entrance-focused secondary school education has been the most stigmatizing problem in Korean education. It has been the cause of almost all aberrant educational practices occurring in the schools. For example, as the main concern of all educational agencies is to prepare their students to obtain high scores to enter a prestigious university, no matter how sound a curriculum is developed, it has not been and cannot be implemented as intended. Private tutoring became a 'virtual school curriculum', a means for every student to use to win a competitive edge for entering universities and colleges. This, in turn, causes a soaring of private educational spending far above the level of public educational spending.

The heated competition to enter universities stems, in part, from an educational system which focuses on academic education only and which provides few learning opportunities outside of formal school settings. Those who fail to advance to the next level of schooling upon graduation find little chance to pick up the opportunity at a later. Especially since learning at a higher education institution can only be available to those who manage to win the fierce competition. Students rightly fear their futures depend upon passing the university entrance examination.

In so far as the schools have become mere training camps to pass examinations, they have not been the most ideal places for learning.

Source: The Development of Education. National Report of the Republic of Korea, p. 86, Seoul, Ministry of Education, 1996. (National report presented at the 45th session of the International Conference on Education, Geneva, 1996.)

---

most appropriate and effective in the particular situation. However, these fears could be overstated since the higher standards of effective teaching that are being sought are unlikely to be achieved unless there is a corresponding rise in levels of professional competence. School systems can hardly avoid tendencies to favour some teaching methods and procedures over others, nor can

Box 3.12
Learning better to understand (John Dewey, 1859–1952)

By science is meant that knowledge which is the outcome of methods of observation, reflection, and testing which are deliberately adopted to secure a settled, assured subject matter. It involves an intelligent and persistent endeavour to revise current beliefs so as to weed out what is erroneous, to add to their accuracy, and, above all, to give them such shape that the dependencies of the various facts upon one another may be as obvious as possible. ... Both logically and educationally, science is the perfecting of knowing, its last stage.

Science, in short, signifies a realization of the *logical* implications of any knowledge. Logical order is not a form imposed upon what is known; it is the proper form of knowledge as perfected. ...

To the non-expert, however, this perfected form is a stumbling block. Just because the material is stated with reference to the furtherance of knowledge as an end in itself, its connections with the material of everyday life are hidden. ... The necessary consequence is an isolation of science from significant experience. The pupil learns symbols without the key to their meaning. He acquires a technical body of information without ability to trace its connections with the objects and operations with which he is familiar – often he acquires simply a peculiar vocabulary.

There is a strong temptation to assume that presenting subject matter in its perfected form provides a royal road to learning. What more natural than to suppose that the immature can be saved time and energy and be protected from needless error by commencing where competent inquirers have left off? The outcome is written large in the history of education. Pupils begin their study of science with texts in which the subject is organized into topics according to the order of the specialist. Technical concepts, with their definitions, are introduced at the outset. Laws are introduced at a very early stage, with at best a few indications of the way in which they were arrived at. The pupils learn a 'science' instead of learning the scientific way of treating the familiar material of ordinary experience. The method of the advanced student dominates college teaching; the approach of the college is transferred into the high school, and so down the line, with such omissions as may make the subject easier.

The chronological method which begins with the experience of the learner and develops from that the proper modes of scientific treatment is often called the 'psychological' method in distinction from the logical method of the expert or specialist. The apparent loss of time involved is more than made up for by the superior understanding and vital interest secured. What the pupil learns he at least understands. Moreover by following, in connection with problems selected from the material of ordinary acquaintance, the methods by which scientific men have reached their perfected knowledge, he gains independent power to deal with material within his range, and avoids the mental confusion and intellectual distaste attendant upon studying matter whose meaning is only symbolic. Since the mass of pupils are never going to become scientific specialists, it is much more important that they should get some insight into what scientific method means than that they should copy at long range and second hand the results which scientific men have reached. Students will not go so far, perhaps, in the 'ground covered', but they will be sure and intelligent as far as they do go.

Source: John Dewey, *Democracy and Education*, pp. 256–8, New York, Macmillan, 1916.

teacher-education programmes. Such tendencies often reflect the experience of the best teachers.

This debate doubtless will continue. Its resonance with other educational debates to which allusion was made earlier suggests that it ultimately cannot be resolved without a better understanding of how different teaching methods and approaches assist students' learning. Teaching methods matter; while other thinkers could equally well be cited, the classic statement in favour of this by the great American educational philosopher John Dewey is recalled in Box 3.12. Thus, teaching about teaching methods to prospective teachers matters also. However, little systematic information is currently available at the international level on the effectiveness of different teaching methods or approaches in different subject areas in different countries, or on the qualities which teachers need to possess in order to implement them effectively. Methods which help pupils better to understand scientific principles (Dewey's example) could well apply everywhere. For other things that 'a sense of personal and corporate responsibility for the education and welfare of their pupils' beckons teachers to help pupils understand, for example, the nature of the obstacles to living better together (e.g. Box 3.13), different methods might be equally effective.

So long as the nature of good teaching remains elusive, the design of teacher-education programmes will continue to be uncertain. Although educators have long been aware that subject matter knowledge, knowledge of general pedagogical principles and knowledge of learners are essential components of the knowledge base that teachers must possess if they are to be effective, the challenge still rests for teacher-education programmes to integrate these components into the 'content-specific pedagogical knowledge' (how best to teach maths or history or human rights) which some researchers claim to be the key to effective teaching.

While the central concern of pre-service teacher education in most countries in coming years will continue to be preparation for teaching as such, other aspects of teachers' work could also come more into focus. They have not often been given the attention which they merit, in so far as teaching is only one of the challenges facing teachers when they graduate and take up their duties in the schools. For many teachers in the world's less developed regions, but not only there, skills in non-formal education and in relations with parents and the local community generally – as can be seen for example in Box 3.10 – are sometimes critical for survival even as a teacher, yet few teacher-education programmes currently provide serious preparation for handling them. The situation of teachers in some of the urban schools of the industrial countries, which was featured in Box 3.8, poses a parallel challenge for teacher education. But quite aside from the specific

---

Box 3.13
Learning to stop bullying

The attitude of society to bullying [in schools] needs to be urgently examined. As long as there is a heritage of opinion which considers that it can be sorted out among the children themselves, that it is a valuable learning experience, that we cannot and need not, as adults, do anything constructive to help, then bullying in schools is being covertly supported. Within the school a sense of community can be developed where all, pupils and staff, take responsibility for each other. If pupils witnessing bullying feel confident to alert staff in the context of taking responsible action, rather than telling tales, this could be a most powerful preventative strategy. If pupils are alerted to the subtleties of bullying so that they recognise it and can see that it is the dominance of the powerful over the powerless, and as such warrants no kudos, a change in attitude could be brought about.

Source: Valerie Besag, 'Management Strategies with Vulnerable Children', in: Erling Roland and Elaine Munthe (eds.), *Bullying: An International Perspective*, pp. 84–5, London, David Fulton Publishers Ltd., 1989.

---

natures of these challenges, relations with parents and communities could become more important for teachers generally, as a result of trends in national educational policies (noted in Chapter 2) towards the decentralization of the management and accountability of school systems to school and local community levels.

The institutional arrangements of teacher education are changing. The long-term secular trend worldwide is towards the consolidation of pre-service teacher-education programmes at the tertiary level of education, but there still are differences among countries in where they are positioned in respect to this trend, depending on the stages of development of their education systems. Some countries are educating virtually all their teachers in universities or equivalent level institutions while others still have primary-school teacher-training colleges which accept partici-

Box 3.14
**Components of the initial training
programmes for teachers in Portugal**

In accordance with the legislation governing the initial and in-service training of pre-school, basic education and secondary school teachers, the initial teacher-training must include a content training component in the subject area(s) to be taught, which should not exceed 60 per cent of the total hours of training for pre-school and basic education first cycle (primary) teachers and 70 per cent for basic education second- and third-cycle teachers. As regards secondary school teachers, the training is given in one subject area only and must not exceed 80 per cent of the total hours of training. Subject areas are the responsibility of the respective departments.

The sciences of education components are organized with the aim of providing psychological and pedagogical training appropriate for the exercise of the responsibilities of a teacher, particularly through a knowledge of the principal theories of development and their educational implications, through the development of awareness of interpersonal relations, and through training in the various methods and techniques of education, in models of curriculum organization and in evaluation processes, to quote the most significant themes of the syllabuses.

These components, particularly that concerned with the methods and techniques of education, take into account, directly and systematically, questions such as the new technologies (computer-assisted and computer-managed teaching, and multimedia systems) and also, less-systematically, civics education, values education and multicultural education.

Source: Développement de l'éducation. Rapport national du Portugal, pp. 282–3, Lisbon, Ministère de l'Éducation, Bureau des Affaires Européennes et des Relations Internationales, 1996. (National report presented at the 45th session of the International Conference on Education, Geneva, 1996.)

pants after completion of the first cycle of secondary education. However, in the majority of countries in every region, preparation for secondary-school teaching is now generally conducted at the tertiary level.

This trend is being reinforced by the changing orientation of teacher-education systems towards primary- and secondary-school teachers. In the more developed regions, the numbers of secondary-school teachers are half as many again as the numbers of primary-school teachers, whereas in the less developed regions the situation is the reverse, but the numbers of secondary-school teachers in the latter regions are growing rapidly (see Appendix II, Table 9). In consequence, the global balance of teacher education is shifting towards the preparation of secondary-school teachers.

The content-orientation of the world's teacher education programmes is therefore changing, since the goals of primary- and secondary-school teacher education are somewhat different, the latter usually being more subject-centred (e.g. Box 3.14). Indeed, primary-school teachers have been known to say that secondary-school teachers are more concerned about teaching subjects than children. There is an element of truth in this; primary-school teachers in most countries generally teach several subjects to a particular class or group of children with whom they are normally in contact most of the day, whereas secondary-school teachers generally teach only one or two subjects to several classes, in each case for only part of the day. Thus, in virtually every country for which UNESCO has data (assumed to be basically comparable within countries but not necessarily between them), the primary-school teacher has longer teaching hours per week (Figure 3.3). Taking into account the different orientations in the preparation of primary- and secondary-school teachers, and the trend towards consolidation of primary- and secondary-teacher education at the tertiary level, the more child-centred concerns of primary-school teaching could in many countries receive less of a hearing in teacher-education policies in the future. This may well have occurred in the industrial countries over the past thirty to forty years.

The speed at which countries have been able to

move towards raising the educational level required of entrants to pre-service teacher-education programmes has been determined by several factors. While the status of the teaching profession has often made it difficult to attract the most able secondary-school graduates, the sheer size of the teacher recruitment needs of the education sector in many countries where student enrolments have been growing rapidly has also been a factor. In regions such as Western Europe, where enrolment growth has slowed, most countries have had little difficulty in recent years in selecting persons whom they consider to be suitable candidates for teacher-education programmes. In the world's less developed regions, raising the educational levels of teacher recruitment has often been constrained by budgetary considerations, in particular fears of increased expenditure on teachers' salaries; such considerations have been an issue in many of the structural adjustment programmes, especially in Africa, that were noted in Chapter 2. Recruitment for technical-vocational teacher-education programmes has presented special difficulties in many countries, because the abilities needed in candidates are frequently those which provide ready access to engineering qualifications and employment at higher salaries in industry.

Although the main focus of teacher-education policies in most countries continues to be the pre-service preparation of teachers, the *in-service or further education of teachers* has grown in importance over the last thirty years. In some countries, the term 'continuing education' is used. Increasingly it is appreciated that teaching, like other professions, is a 'learning' occupation in which the practitioners need to have opportunities throughout their careers for periodically updating and renewing their knowledge, skills and capabilities. The classroom and the school, it is realized, are relatively small worlds which do not in themselves provide opportunities for teachers to share in the broader educational community's growing and constantly changing body of knowledge and experience of teaching.

Figure 3.3
Average teaching hours per week of primary- and secondary-school teachers, in selected countries, 1994[1]

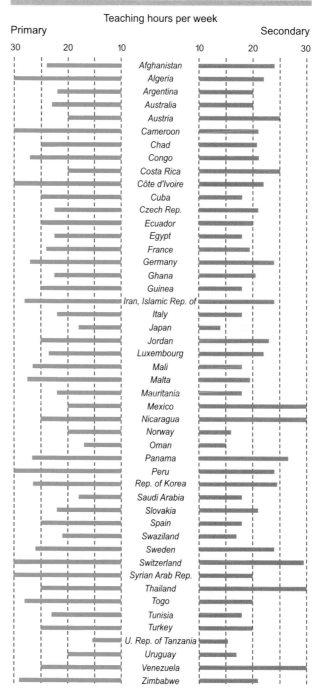

1. Or latest year available.

Source: Same as for Figure 2.9.

Box 3.15
The evolution of in-service education
for primary school teachers in China

Teacher training schools in China, strengthened and rebuilt in the early 1980s, have been a major base for the in-service training of primary school teachers. There are at present 2,153 such institutions, with almost one for each county and city district.

From 1980 to 1995, more than two million teachers were trained in these schools. In the first four years, training focused on enabling teachers to master subject matter and develop basic teaching competence. From 1984 to 1990, the training objective was to help unqualified teachers obtain a diploma of secondary normal education.

As a result of the 15-year endeavour, the percentage of unqualified primary school teachers decreased from 53 per cent to 12 per cent of the 5,664 million teaching force in 1995. Given this condition, the training priority for most parts of China has changed from training for qualification (diploma of secondary normal education) to continuing education.

Continuing education is offered through various programmes to serve the professional needs of all qualified teachers. The programmes include training for the following: new teachers, key teachers, teachers in new teaching posts, and potential key teachers, with emphasis on the first two.

Source: Teachers as Lifelong Learners: Case Studies of Innovative In-Service Teacher Training Programmes in the E-9 Countries, p. 15, Paris, UNESCO, 1997. (Mimeo.)

The potential for in-service teacher education to contribute to the improvement of the quality and relevance of education has been recognized since the 1960s at least if not earlier. The *Recommendation concerning the Status of Teachers* affirms that both 'The [educational] authorities and teachers should recognize the importance of in-service education designed to secure a systematic improvement in the quality and content of education and of teaching techniques'. It affirms too that the educational authorities, 'in consultation with teachers' organizations, should promote a wide system of in-service education, available free to all teachers', and that 'teachers should be given both the opportunities and incentives to participate in courses and facilities [of in-service education] and should take full advantage of them'.

At the time when the *Recommendation* was adopted, organized and systematic in-service teacher education was a comparatively recent development; before the Second World War, most programmes were informal and voluntary, often centred on the activities of teachers' own professional associations. Formal officially-organized programmes became common from the 1960s and 1970s onwards. In some countries it was necessary to train the large numbers of unqualified teachers who had been recruited at that time to meet the expansion of student enrolments; in other countries, major changes in school curricula (e.g. the introduction of the 'new' mathematics) provided the main impulse.

In various forms, in-service teacher-education programmes now serve many different purposes ranging from the renewal and updating of teachers' subject area knowledge and teaching techniques to training in the application of new student assessment procedures. The large-scale national level in-service programmes that were initiated in the 1970s and 1980s in a number of countries in Africa, Asia and Latin America, and designed to facilitate the upgrading of the qualifications of entire cohorts of teachers, have mostly given way to a more diverse array of smaller scale, often innovative programmes designed to serve recurrent needs at the provincial, district and local levels. The evolution of primary-school teacher in-service education in China (one out of every five teachers in the world) is representative of this trend (Box 3.15). In Europe and North America, the early emphasis of many in-service programmes on subject area knowledge and teaching skills has been supplemented by additional concerns ranging from student guidance and assessment to the inclusion of children with special educational needs, school management and administration, and educational technologies. The 1996 International Conference on Education recommended that 'special priority should be given to the in-service training and education of those involved in the management, supervision and evaluation of teachers'.

With the growth of in-service teacher education over the last thirty to forty years, experience of its strengths and limitations as a means to improve the quality of education has grown too. While there exist some remarkably sophisticated programmes, notably those found in east Asia that are conceived for the induction of beginning teachers (e.g. Box 3.16), most in-service programmes typically are modest in scope and of short duration. In a number of countries they are often school-based, which some observers believe to be a growing trend, although fears have been expressed that this could signal a tendency to substitute in-service training for the practicum component of pre-service teacher education. In probably the majority of cases they consist of a short course, workshop or seminar lasting a few days and focused on selected aspects of subject area knowledge, teaching technique, or classroom and school management. Teachers' normal workloads constitute a basic constraint on their participation in anything more elaborate except during school vacations, and even then most teachers often have preferred alternatives for the use of their time unless specific incentives to participate in a course are offered.

Still, in countries where there exist extensive networks of teacher-education institutions and school advisory and support services able to mount short in-service courses, either on their own initiative or at the request of schools, it is possible to involve quite high percentages of the total teaching force in any year. The percentages are probably higher in Western Europe than in any other region of the world, although the figures for a few east Asian countries may be comparable. Thus, in France, where primary-school

---

Box 3.16
Induction for beginning teachers in New Zealand and Japan

In *New Zealand*, though registration is not a compulsory requirement, new teachers are not eligible to become fully registered until they have completed at least two years' classroom experience. An 'advice and guidance' programme is available to all beginning teachers during their initial two years. The programme includes resources and personal support from colleagues; a programme of visiting and observing experienced teachers; meetings with other staff; appraisals of the beginning teacher's progress, and a written record of the induction programme. In addition, primary schools that employ beginning teachers receive 0.2 teaching entitlement per week for each new teacher's first year, to facilitate released time for the beginning teachers or senior staff working with them.

In *Japan*, beginning teachers maintain a lighter work load of teaching duties; attend in-school training two times per week, with assistance from designated guidance teachers; and receive out-of-school training once per week. Out-of-school training covers a wide range of activities including volunteer work, lectures, seminars and visits to other schools, child welfare facilities, and private corporations. To support induction activities, schools employing one beginning teacher are assigned a part-time lecturer; those employing two beginning teachers are assigned a full-time teacher.

Source: Linda Darling-Hammond and Velma L. Cobb (eds.), *Teacher Preparation and Professional Development in APEC Members: a Comparative Study,* p. viii, Washington, D.C., U.S. Department of Education, 1995.

---

teachers are offered a variety of short courses and training workshops of one to four weeks duration, it is estimated that around 40 per cent of teachers participate each year. A similar figure is estimated for the Republic of Korea. A study of in-service teacher education in Western Europe carried out by EURYDICE (the educational information network of the European Union) in 1994 found

Table 3.5
Percentage of employees who participated in courses in 1993 in enterprises employing 10 or more people in Western Europe[1]

By industry:	
Mining and quarrying	32
Manufacturing	24
Electricity, gas, water	49
Construction	14
Wholesale, retail, repair	25
Hotels and restaurants	24
Transport, communication	37
Financial intermediation	55
Services for enterprises, renting, real estate	34
TOTAL	28
By size of enterprise:	
10 to 49 employees	13
50 to 99 employees	19
100 to 249 employees	24
250 to 499 employees	30
500 to 999 employees	35
1 000 and more employees	44
TOTAL	28

1. The twelve member countries of the European Community before the coming into existence of the European Union.

Source: Statistical Office of the European Communities (EUROSTAT).

that an estimated 85 per cent of primary- and secondary-school teachers in Austria had participated in at least one training course in the previous three years, and that around a third of the teachers in Denmark and the Netherlands had participated in a training course in the previous year. In some European countries, the participation of teachers for a few days each year in in-service courses or workshops is a requirement of their conditions of employment.

However, to put all this activity into perspective: the corresponding participation rates for in-service education and training in many parts of private industry are just as high if not higher, especially in the larger enterprises (Table 3.5).

The critical issue for the future evolution and development of in-service teacher education could be the question of incentives and the related question of teachers' willingness to invest in their own professional development. Little information is available on these questions at the international level, although it has been observed in many countries that in-service education programmes which specifically enable teachers to obtain career development qualifications, and hence improvements in their individual salaries, have little difficulty in engaging teachers' interest and participation. Moreover, the strong participation of teachers that is frequently found in open university and other general-purpose distance-education programmes that enable participants to obtain such qualifications, e.g. a master's degree in education, is evidence that teachers are often willing to invest substantial amounts of their own time in professional development independently of any in-service programmes which are officially organized during normal working hours. In this perspective, the existence of an adequate structure of career development rewards could largely determine whether in-service teacher education will evolve mainly as a top-down supply-driven activity dependent on policy-makers' assessments of the professional development needs of the teaching force, or as a bottom-up demand-driven activity responsive to teachers' own judgements of where their professional capabilities can best be improved. In countries where teachers need to take on second jobs in order to make ends meet, the issue is more complex.

Assessing teachers' effectiveness

While teacher-education programmes are expected to do their best to prepare good teachers and to help serving teachers improve their skills, their success in achieving these objectives depends on how teachers' effectiveness is assessed and on whether the qualities required in

Box 3.17
The career structure for primary-school teachers in Lesotho

Classroom positions
On first appointment, the teacher will be allocated to salary grade and step within that grade according to his/her qualifications and experience. Allocation will be at the discretion of the Teachers' Service Commission (TSC). The teacher will then proceed by annual increment to the top step of the grade. At this point no further progress can be made without applying to TSC for advancement. Advancement will only be granted on a satisfactory assessment of the teacher's performance, experience and qualifications. This will be assessed by consideration of a report from the teacher's Principal on behalf of the Management Committee, together with assessment of any additional qualifications which the teacher has gained.

On satisfactory assessment, the teacher will be allocated to the next grade, normally at the first step of that grade. Allocation to a step above the first will be at the discretion of TSC, taking account of exceptional performance, experience, qualifications.

Advancement can continue to the top of the Senior Teacher Position grade. At that point advancement ceases. Further progression in the career struc-ture is by competition and interview for Leadership Positions.

Leadership positions
Leadership positions in the primary school include the posts of Head of Department, Deputy Principal and Principal. When these posts become vacant they will be advertised nationally by TSC and all teachers eligible ... may apply. The posts will be filled by TSC on the recommendation of the Management Committee responsible for the school.

Advisory positions
Advisory positions are so defined because they involve giving advice and support to schools across the districts and across the country. They are normally filled by appointing exceptionally well-qualified and experienced Principals who have been noted for their excellent performance in their schools. The positions include District Resource Teacher and Senior Resource Teacher. Advisory posts will be advertized nationally and will be filled by TSC in consultation with the Chief Education Officer (Primary).

Source: The Development of Education, 1996–1998, p. 36, Maseru, Ministry of Education, 1996. (National report presented at the 45th session of the International Conference on Education, Geneva, 1996.)

teachers for effective performance of their work are those which have been developed in their teacher-education programmes.

Teachers are assessed throughout their careers, at entry into the profession and at successive stages thereafter up to leadership and supervisory positions; the Lesotho example in Box 3.17 illustrates the general case. In most countries, however, the main concern of teacher assessment is not the advancement of knowledge about teacher effectiveness but the well functioning of an employment system which requires that judgements be made about whom to select or hire as a teacher and whom to promote, give tenure to, demote or dismiss. In consequence, the advancement of knowledge about teacher effectiveness has been slow. The main repositories of such knowledge are school systems' inspectorate and supervisory services, at least to the extent that their functions are largely professional rather than administrative, but links between these services and the educational research community are not always well-established.

The interest of educational policy-makers in improved methods of assessing teachers' effectiveness has grown with the concern for improved learning outcomes and better school system performance generally. There also is an accountability dimension. The trend in many countries towards the decentralization of the governance of school systems to the local level has brought local communities into direct contact with questions of school performance and teacher assessment. This point, among others, is made in a background paper prepared for this report on assessing teachers' effectiveness in India, where the

73rd Constitution Amendment Act (1992) vests
the education committees of panchayats (village
councils) with responsibilities for school governance including the recruitment and assessment
of teachers.

Without fair and valid systems for assessing
their work, teachers are in a vulnerable position.
The problem was foreseen in the *Recommendation concerning the Status of Teachers,* which
affirms that 'direct assessment of the teacher's
work … should be objective, and should be made
known to the teacher, … [who] should have the
right of appeal against assessments [deemed] to be
unjustified'. The *Recommendation* makes a distinction between this kind of assessment and 'systems of inspection or supervision … designed to
encourage and help teachers in the performance
of their professional tasks', a distinction which
corresponds broadly to that made by educational
researchers between 'summative' and 'formative'
evaluation.

As in the case of teaching methods, little information is available at the international level on the
methods utilized in different countries for assessing teachers' effectiveness. Where formal systems
of assessment exist, the school's head teacher
usually plays a key role along with the school district or regional supervisor(s). The Oman case
shown in Box 3.18 is probably representative. It
also points to the gap in international information
on teacher assessment: what kinds of things are
the head teacher and the supervisor supposed to
take into account when they fill in the forms? In
that regard, the extract of various items concerning teacher behaviour from a checklist recently
proposed by a Chinese research group to be utilized for the purposes of formative assessment in
the schools of Beijing is of interest (Box 3.19),
because the mix of objective and subjective indicators on the list illustrates the general problem:
even when there exists agreement on which
aspects of the teacher's behaviour should be
assessed, there still is a need for the observer
(head teacher or supervisor) undertaking the

Box 3.19
Proposed checklist of teacher behaviour items to be utilized in the appraisal of primary- and secondary-school teachers in Beijing

Item	*Objectives*
Preparation of classes	Fulfilment of teaching plan in accordance with requirements; proper basic ideological and educational goals, and measures aimed at developing pupils' abilities and intelligence.
Homework	Punctual correcting of pupils' homework; provision of specific guidance; proper amount and relevance of homework.
Tuition	Provision of guidance according to individual needs; emphasis both on helping pupils with difficulties, and on encouraging outstanding pupils.
Evaluation	Regular and fully recorded classroom observation and evaluation; proper evaluation criteria and objective evaluation results.
Attendance per semester	Percent days absent.
Amount of work	Number of teaching hours assigned; number of teaching hours actually taught.
Organization of teaching	Punctuality in starting and finishing classes, and maintenance of classroom discipline; encouragement of alertness among pupils, and fostering of a lively and orderly classroom atmosphere.
Classes	Fulfilment of teaching plans of the class; scientific and precise teaching content, laying proper emphasis on the most important points, and spreading difficult points out evenly.
Teaching methods	Proper use of teaching methods such as lecture, demonstration and student experiment, use of standard character forms on the blackboard, proper use of teaching aids tools, multi-directional classroom communication.
Teaching manner	Clear and simple vocabulary, dignified appearance, kindly attitude, persuasiveness.
Teaching effectiveness	Orderly teaching process; harmonious student-teacher relationship; students strongly motivated and eager to learn.

Source: National Commission of the People's Republic of China for UNESCO, *On the Methods of Appraising Middle and Primary School Teachers in China*, Beijing, 1996. (Mimeo. Report commisioned by UNESCO from the National Commission of the People's Republic of China for UNESCO.)

---

assessment to exercise sound judgement, both in respect to individual items and in arriving at an overall synthesis. For this reason, the Recommendation of the 1996 International Conference on Education stressing the priority to be given to the in-service education and training of persons 'responsible for the management, supervision and evaluation of teachers' is especially relevant.

However, without an adequate base of knowledge of what makes for effective teaching, valid and reliable assessment instruments cannot be devised and head teachers and supervisors can-not be properly trained in methods of assessment. In practice, it has proved very difficult to operationalize the notion of 'teacher effectiveness' in terms of student learning outcomes. At least, research in the United States going back sixty years or more has consistently found that head teachers' ratings of teachers' effectiveness have no appreciable correlation with students' learning outcomes no matter how much effort the head teachers put into getting their ratings 'right'.

Operationalization of the notion of 'learning outcomes' itself has given rise to much controversy. All students? Yet some students perform better than others. Then the majority of students? The 'average' student? The slower learners? The gifted students? Moreover, for how long do the 'learning outcomes' have to be retained by the students before the effectiveness of the teaching can be confirmed? Until the weekend after the test, or longer? Proposals which sometimes have been made to pay teachers ('merit' pay) on the basis of students' learning outcomes have foundered on such questions, among others.

The real difficulty, anyway, veterans of the classroom sometimes say, is to get students to take responsibility for their own learning. While this assumes the value of what the schools require the students to learn, it does at least indicate that there are limits to the responsiblity of the teacher.

To return to the beginning of the chapter: what society currently expects of teachers in most countries could be out of proportion to the rewards it is prepared to accord to teachers for their efforts, the means typically put at their disposal, the difficult conditions under which many of them work and the present knowledge base of what makes for effective teaching and learning. In the next chapter, it is shown how this knowledge base is beginning to unravel in the face of new technologies.

4
Teachers, teaching and new technologies

IN A GROWING NUMBER of countries, questions concerning teachers and teaching have emerged at the centre of debate over how education can make best use of the new information and communication technologies. At the international level, as was noted in Chapter 1, there are expectations that these technologies could facilitate progress towards 'Education for All' goals, in particular by enabling society to reach out more effectively to individuals and social groups whose basic learning needs are not being met by conventional educational means.

For the purposes of this report, the new technologies are understood to refer mainly to the computer and related communication equipment and software that enable one computer to communicate ('network') with other computers. It has often been suggested that education has up to now been relatively slow in making use of these technologies, despite their ability to facilitate access to knowledge and information. The Swedish authorities, for example, are surely not alone in their assessment of the possible consequences: 'if the methods for seeking knowledge inside the school and outside the school become too different, the school will end up in a crisis of legitimacy' (Box 4.1).

Although the prospects of such a crisis occurring may seem to be remote, there is little doubt that in helping to reconfigure how learners can acquire knowledge and information, the new technologies are beginning to present a very complex set of challenges for the world's formal education systems. This chapter considers selected aspects of these challenges with particular reference to teachers and teaching. The broader question of how existing and emerging technologies can be used to overcome multiple barriers to

---

Box 4.1
'If the methods for seeking knowledge in the school and outside the school become too different, the school will end up in a crisis of legitimacy' (Sweden)

The school must prepare young people for a reality involving computers. All pupils must be able to use IT (information technology) when leaving school. Education – learning – takes place under different conditions, e.g. dialogue and collaboration with other pupils and using libraries. Concurrently with the development of IT, computers as a pedagogical means of assistance and a tool have come into focus. Through access to international data networks, e.g. Internet, the pedagogical arena has widened far outside the wall of the schools. More and more pupils are accustomed to using computers and getting hold of information and knowledge through IT. Very often pupils' knowledge of using computers is on a higher level than that of their teachers. As IT affects the work in school, school-libraries change and get a more important role. In every teaching situation, the pupil must be in focus. The role of the teacher must be seen as a mentor supporting the pupil when seeking knowledge. The mass-availability of data and information in databases raises demands on capacity to formulate problems and on critical thinking in order to choose the relevant information. The role of the teacher becomes even more important as transferer of knowledge, as discussion-partner, etc. If the schools fail to cope with the development of IT and its integration into the teaching process, and if the methods for seeking knowledge in the school and outside the school become too different, the school will end up in a crisis of legitimacy. In a society rich in information the school no longer has a monopoly on facts, information and knowledge which means a change in the task for the schools. The development of knowledge and competence for the individual person will in the future take place in several arenas – in school, in the home, in social life and working life. This affects the schools' and the teachers' work.

Source: Reply of Sweden to the questionnaire administered by the International Bureau of Education in preparation for the Forty-Fifth Session of the International Conference on Education on the theme 'Strengthening the Role of Teachers in a Changing World', Geneva, International Bureau of Education, 1996, p. 30. (Mimeo.)

learning, which is the concern of UNESCO's 'Learning Without Frontiers' initiative, is not directly addressed.

The chapter has four sections. The first sketches the background to the challenges which the new technologies now pose for education. The second reviews briefly the key technological trends and developments that have implications for conventional teaching-learning processes. The third considers some of the ways in which the quality of the learning experience could be enhanced by the new technologies. The fourth considers some of the ways in which the teaching function and the role of the teacher could change. The chapter draws in part on the discussions at UNESCO's Second International Congress on Education and Informatics (Moscow, 1996), as well as on those at the UNESCO-sponsored International Colloquium on Virtual Learning Environments and the Role of the Teacher, which was held at the Open University, United Kingdom, in April 1997.

Hesitation towards the new technologies

Overshadowing the utilization of the new information and communication technologies in education are worldwide disparities in access to these technologies. A majority of countries lack the basic infrastructure needed for gaining access. All of Africa, for example, has barely more telephones than the city of Tokyo. A majority of the world's schools still do not have electricity.

The dangers of a widening gulf in the world between 'information rich' and 'information poor' countries have been of particular concern to UNESCO. A comprehensive overview of the current disparities in information resources across the different regions of the world is presented in the Organization's recently published *World Information Report* (Paris, UNESCO, 1997). Selected media and communication indicators are shown in Figure 4.1.

The utilization of the new information and com-

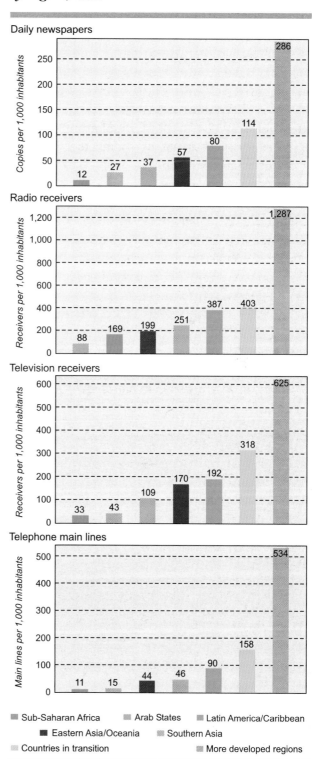

Figure 4.1
Media and communication indicators, by region, 1995

munication technologies is unevenly distributed among the various economic and social sectors. Skeptics have suggested that if the education sector has been hesitant up to now in making use of the computer and related communication equipment this could be due to the legacy of disappointing experience with older technologies – film strips, radio, television – which once were expected to transform education. Other commentators have suggested more thoughtfully that the nature of the sector's work could be partly responsible: an activity which traditionally has been so much dependent on the quality of human interaction for the fulfilment of its purposes would seem to be an unlikely candidate for technological improvement. Its 'output' is concerned with values and attitudes as much as with cognitive achievement, and the complex human processes involved are not fully understood.

Still other commentators have pointed to economic factors: in most countries, the education sector traditionally has provided few incentives and limited scope for acquiring new technologies, as the budgetary constraints highlighted in Chapters 2 and 3 would seem to bear witness. If essential and low-cost old technologies are underfunded – desperately so (from chalkboards to textbooks) in some countries – then the sector hardly represents a promising market for more costly innovations.

Whatever the reasons, while the form and character of educational processes have always been mediated by technology – the book, electric light, radio, television and the ball-point pen being obvious examples – it has rarely happened that major technological developments have been driven by the needs of education as such. Rather, the tendency has been for education to try to adapt for its own purposes the technology which has come into use elsewhere.

The current posture of the world's formal education systems with respect to the new information and communication technologies follows the historical pattern. The utilization of the computer for educational purposes is still at an experimental stage, whereas in other sectors – for example, financial services, many parts of manufacturing industry, commerce – its utilization has already altered core technical processes. In the education sector, the core process – face-to-face contact between the teacher and learners in a classroom – has as yet barely been touched.

Nevertheless, there are signs that the computer, in contrast to earlier technologies which never delivered on promises to transform education, could be different, for it has begun to intrude into the core process in a way that many of the older technologies never managed to do. This is a very recent development, not even a decade old. It has occurred in several steps.

Computers were originally introduced into a number of industrial countries' education systems in the 1980s for the purposes of school administration and as subjects of study, in the latter case to enable students to become acquainted with their basic modes of operation and some of their functions. In fact, this 'computer literacy' rationale is probably still the main driving force behind most countries' efforts to introduce computers into the school system. Students and their parents are increasingly aware of the need for computer-related skills: in the United States, for example, a presidential task force has estimated that up to 60 per cent of jobs in the year 2000 will require computer-literate employees.

Initially, little use was made of computers for the support of students' learning in other areas of the school curriculum. In the sole international survey (twenty countries) carried out to date on the uses of computers in schools, IEA in 1989 found that in almost all the countries surveyed computers were mainly located in special computer rooms. Besides the scarcity of funds for buying hardware, there was a dearth of appropriate educational software for the support of students' learning in standard curriculum subjects and most teachers did not have the skills needed for developing such software. In a special report on the

Figure 4.2
Trends in the number of Internet hosts
in the world, 1981–97

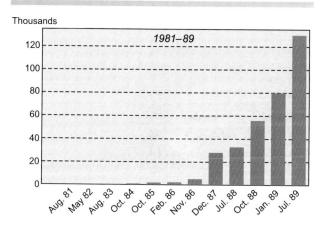

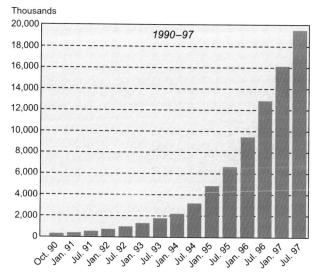

Source: Network Wizards (http://www.nw.com/), September 1997.

software problem at that time, OECD's Centre for Educational Research and Innovation (CERI) observed that there existed a chicken-and-egg situation: the limited availability of computers in schools provided a limited market for commercial software developers, while the limited availability of appropriate software provided little incentive for schools to devote their scarce resources to buying any more computers than were needed for computer literacy purposes.

Since then, the situation has eased. The power and capabilities of the personal computer have greatly increased, unit prices have fallen, schools have steadily increased their purchases of computers under the continuing pressure of students and their parents, and software developers have become more interested in the education market. In many of the industrial countries today, computers are now found in ordinary classrooms. Although systematic international data on school systems' stocks of computers are not available, a recent estimate for the United States places the ratio of computers to students in that country's K-12 (kindergarten, primary and secondary) school system as 1:6. In other industrial countries, the availability of computers in schools is probably more limited. Still, it is clear that computers are now beginning to be used by the schools for more things than just computer literacy.

Key technological trends and developments

Technological trends in both hardware and software have begun to change the educational status of the computer. On the hardware side, there has been a tremendous increase over the past few years in the data-processing power, capabilities and convenience of use of the computers that schools – indeed, ordinary families – in most of the industrial countries can afford to buy. The standard desktop or personal computer today has comparable processing power to some of the mainframe computers of 1985. In addition, as a result of digitalization – the storage of texts, images and sound in the same (digital) form on compact disks (CDs) – it has a multimedia capability (the ability to present text, images and sound to the user). Affordable equipment that enables one computer to communicate with another has also become available.

On the software side, too, there have been significant developments: first, in the ease of inter-

<hr />

Box 4.2
'Accessible Internet data: finding sites that suit your students' needs'

The Internet is fast becoming an important tool for Earth science teachers and students because it makes a vast wealth of data, both real-time and archival, easily accessible. Teachers no longer need to use small, contrived data sets [for] classroom discussions, and students can be given large sets of real data to create graphs, apply basic statistical techniques, construct models, and draw conclusion about how the Earth functions.

Montgomery Blair High School has had Internet access for a number of years, but use of the Internet has only recently extended to departments other than computer science. My initial excitement and plans for classroom applications were quickly squelched, however, when I realized that finding data that students can handle is quite difficult. Most online data are field specific and incomprehensible to those with limited experience in the field. Because data generally are presented with no explanations or labels, I had no idea what many numbers meant or what units they were in. Fortunately I was persistent. It took close to a year, but I finally found a student-friendly data set at the National Oceanic and Atmospheric Administration's (NOAA) Pacific Marine Environmental Laboratory

(PMEL). Since then I have found other online data sets appropriate for classroom use.

Realtime TAO Buoy Data Access
http://www.pmel.noaa.gov/toga-tao/realtime.html
This site stores daily real-time data, specifically sea surface temperature and wind vectors, from the TAO buoy array in the tropical Pacific Ocean. The user can choose the type of display: latitude-longitude maps, latitude-longitude time plots, or latitude-longitude depth profiles. All data are contoured and color coded for easy reading.

Daily Planet, University of Illinois, Urbana-Champaign
http://www.atmos.uiuc.edu/
Weather Pages, Penn State University
http://www.ems.psu.edu:80/wx/
Weather Processor, Purdue University
http://thunder.atms.purdue.edu/
These three locations provide up-to-date satellite imagery, both infrared and visible, and surface maps of the United States and other locations around the world. Students can track storm systems as they begin, develop, and dissipate.

Source: Sarah Clemmitt, 'Accessible Internet Data: Finding Sites That Suit Your Students' Needs', *The Science Teacher,* pp. 48–50, March 1996.

action between the user and the computer, in particular by means of 'graphical user interfaces' which make it possible to control many aspects of the computer's functions by pointing at pictures rather than by typing instructions; second, in the development of programs of interactive self-instruction for users; and third, in the ease of communication and interaction ('networking') with other computers.

Educationalists have begun to recognize that as a result of these developments modern computers with their convenient keyboards, small screen and pointing devices such as mice have evolved into personal media which for the user are similar to books and notepads while having additional properties such as multimedia and the ability to link up with the 'books' and 'notepads' of other

users, or indeed with whole libraries. In short, the computer is evolving into a tool to facilitate learning that appears to have most of the educational properties of older technologies (books, radio, film strips, phonograph records, television) with at least equal if not greater convenience of use plus communication capabilities in addition.

Up to now, a majority of commentators have focused on the trend towards the integration of computer and communication technologies as being likely to pose the most radical challenges to conventional formal education, because it could have implications for the modes of interaction between teachers and students. The emphasis of these commentators is mostly on educational methods. Other commentators have emphasized questions concerning educational contents. This divergence of emphasis is taken up later in the chapter. For the moment, key technological aspects are noted, in particular the development of the Internet and World Wide Web.

From its origins in 1969 as a technology for enabling the transmission of data between the computers of four universities in the United States, the Internet has grown exponentially into a worldwide network ('information superhighway') of host computers counted today in millions (Figure 4.2). However, it was not until the release in 1990 of the World Wide Web computer program – developed by a physicist at the Conseil Européen pour la Recherche Nucléaire (CERN) laboratory in Geneva – that it became relatively easy to establish links between different types of computers with different operating systems. Individual users can now easily gain access to multimedia documents or 'pages' stored on World Wide Web 'sites' in other computers located elsewhere, and schools can utilize such data and information for the purposes of enriching their curricula (e.g. Box 4.2). Searching among different World Wide Web sites has been facilitated by the availability (since 1993) of graphical user interface 'navigation' tools or 'browsers', which enable the user to scan ('surf the information highway') and download documents from other computers in content areas of interest.

There has come into existence, therefore, a geographically distributed, interconnected 'virtual' worldwide library of documents accessible in principle to anyone with a computer plus a communication device (modem) and a telephone. The possibility has been opened up too for different users to collaborate at a distance in creating documents (the original impetus for the development of the World Wide Web).

However, gaining access to the new virtual libraries of information and knowledge is still difficult for ordinary users because of technical constraints relating to both the speed of communication and the data storage and processing capacity of the average personal computer.

Box 4.3
'Information technology is not yet widely used in the Chadian education system'

Chad does not have the funds necessary to introduce information technology into teaching, and there is also a problem of human resources.

At the university, computer science is a timid newcomer, in two faculties only:

• the economics faculty, where computer science teaching is offered from the first to the third year to approximately 300 students by only two permanent teachers, has only four PCs, already very heavily used;

• the science faculty, where computer science is taught as from the second year. The training programme comes down to an introduction to the MS-DOS operating system and to the Turbo-Pascal programming language. Training is provided by two temporary teachers. The faculty has five computers at its disposal. A project to set up a computer network has been drawn up in collaboration with the *Institut universitaire technique* in Orléans on behalf of the science faculty.

As can be seen, information technology is not yet widely used in the Chadian education system.

Source: Rapport national sur le développement de l'éducation, p. 33, N'Djamena, Commission Nationale Tchadienne pour l'UNESCO, Ministère de l'Éducation Nationale, 1996. (National report presented at the 45th session of the International Conference on Education, Geneva, 1996.)

Although experts predict that the latter constraint will be overcome fairly quickly, there is agreement that the communication constraint will be more difficult to overcome because of the enormous investments which will be needed to upgrade the data-carrying capacities of existing telephone lines (currently the principal means of communication for ordinary users of the Internet/World Wide Web).

Towards virtual learning environments

The long-term implications of the technological trends and developments described above for the

---

Box 4.4
Creating Learning Networks for African Teachers

The emerging power of information technologies might contribute to resolving two of the central issues which are crippling African education systems today, namely: 1) the lack of access to necessary information and learning resources, which considerably lessens the chances of building up the existing formal system's capacity and 2) the lack of opportunities for communication among key players in the learning process (students and their parents, educators, researchers) and education officials (planners, policy makers and curriculum developers) which often results in a bureaucratic and top-down approach to the provision of learning with isolated or disconnected teacher training colleges.

With this in mind, a project, Creating Learning Networks for African Teachers, has been established by UNESCO to facilitate knowledge of and access to Internet in Africa. Considering the rapid expansion of affordable access to full Internet, even in some of the poorest regions of Africa, the World Wide Web and e-mail are increasingly becoming a possibility for challenging educators and formal systems of communication to overcome some of the existing barriers to learning.

The project, still in its pilot stage, will connect a number of teacher training colleges (four to six in twenty African countries) to the Internet in order to develop local, national and regional networks to initiate activities that focus on:

- enhancing dialogue between teacher training colleges, educational planners and policy-makers, researchers and practicing teachers on issues related to learning and teaching;
- accessing and assessing information on latest concepts, developments and experiments in the field of learning, teaching and education to enhance professional development, build local knowledge structures, and stimulate processes of change;
- stimulating the development of locally adapted and relevant curricula, appropriate teaching and print-based learning materials through groupwork and groupware, using locally relevant images and sounds (including otherwise inaccessible 'artifacts') in close collaboration with the relevant national education authorities;
- promoting the development and implementation of learning projects at teacher training colleges; targeting different learner groups of the communities around them;
- exploring the use of the Internet to stimulate more learner-centred and interactive approaches in the teaching-learning process at colleges and in the classroom.

Source: Technology and Learning, Cases, pp. 47–8. Paris, UNESCO, 1997. (Education for All: Making it Work: Change in Action.)

---

world's formal education systems are as yet unclear. However, in the foreseeable future it is likely that disparities in access to the new technologies will ensure that many countries will be little affected. In some of the world's poorest countries, even universities are only just beginning to utilize computers (e.g. Box 4.3); without substantial outside assistance, they could fall further behind. Assistance to teacher-training colleges in these countries could have significant multiplier effects (e.g. Box 4.4).

In the education systems of the advanced industrial countries, computers are currently utilized mainly in three roles: first, the traditional one as a means of ensuring that students acquire a minimum level of computer literacy; second, as a means of supporting and enriching the curriculum; and third, as a medium for interaction between teachers and learners, between learners and between teachers. The first role is becoming less important as more and more families purchase computers for use at home and children learn to operate them at an early age. The second and third roles are becoming more important. They are considered below.

Concerning the second role: as a result of digitalization and the convergence of media technologies that has enabled text, audio and video material to be stored on compact disks, the computer has emerged as a potentially powerful and convenient means of delivering support and enrichment for existing curricula. Early signs of its impact have been seen in distance education systems, which previously prepared separate sets of print, audio and video educational material for use by students. However, the preparation of effective multimedia educational material is very costly, requiring the services of teams of highly skilled designers and technicians. Thus, in most countries as yet there exists very little purpose-built multimedia educational material that can be fully integrated into existing curricula, although in certain areas of the curriculum where there is an overlap with training in industry relevant material is available; examples are accountancy and business studies, and engineering.

An insight into the current status of the use of computers for support of existing school curricula in science is provided by IEA's Third International Mathematics and Science Study, which was mentioned in earlier chapters. This study (carried out in 1994–95) found that in only four systems (Denmark, England, Scotland and the United States) did as many as one-third of the students (14-year-olds) report that computers were used in their science classes 'at least once in a while'.

As for the Internet and World Wide Web, while there is a growing number of sites with potentially interesting and relevant material about education (e.g. Box 4.5), there are practical difficulties in locating material which can be readily integrated into existing curricula, as is shown for example in the account given by the enterprising teacher in Box 4.2. In fact, the problem for the teacher (or student) of finding interesting and relevant teaching-learning material in the new virtual global library represented by the Internet/World Wide Web is daily becoming more complex; without effective navigation tools ('maps' and 'compasses', so to speak), teachers and students could find themselves endlessly 'surfing' the Internet/World Wide Web searching for such material (lost forever on the 'information superhighway'?). The development of improved navigational support

---

Box 4.5
Searching for information about education on the Internet/World Wide Web

It does not take long to discover that the World Wide Web features a wealth of entertaining sites that offer endless diversion. But what if you wanted to use resources on the Internet to help improve educational practice? What do the Internet and the World Wide Web offer today to K-12 educators, hype and hoopla aside?

The short answer to this question is plenty. An individual with 1) a starting point and 2) a strategy for negotiating the World Wide Web can find many high-quality Web sites specific to education in a relatively short period of time. These sites offer, among other things, dozens of on-line student and teacher publications, electronic news services that feature articles of particular interest to educators, subject-specific resources that provide in-depth and comprehensive information on nearly every topic imaginable, complete on-line texts of classics and more recent books, thousands of detailed lesson plans, information about how to apply for educational grants, 'home pages' of teachers eager to volunteer their own insights into classroom teaching and recommend other educational sites on the Web, maps to hundreds of networked K-12 schools, lists of students and classes looking for 'keypals', step-by-step instructions on how to construct your own Web site, and discussion groups that feature extensive conversation and idea-sharing with others around the United States and the world. Furthermore, provided that you have access to the Internet and the World Wide Web, practically all of this information is yours free of charge, twenty-four hours a day, to explore on-screen, print out as hard copy, or download onto your own computer.

Source: Edouard J. Miech, 'Editors Reviews', *Harvard Educational Review*, Vol. 66, No. 1, 1996, p. 128.

---

for learners is considered by some experts to be one of the key challenges of the coming five to ten years for effectively exploiting the information and knowledge resources of the Internet/World Wide Web for educational purposes.

Table 4.1
Selected characteristics of students' home backgrounds and use of time at home,
as reported by Grade 8 science students in countries and territories that participated
in IEA's Third International Mathematics and Science Study (TIMSS), 1994–95

Country/ territory[1]	Percentage of students reporting: More than 25 books at home	Percentage of students reporting: Have a computer at home	Average number of out-of-school hours per day spent: Studying or doing homework	Average number of out-of-school hours per day spent: Watching TV or videos	Country/ territory[1]	Percentage of students reporting: More than 25 books at home	Percentage of students reporting: Have a computer at home	Average number of out-of-school hours per day spent: Studying or doing homework	Average number of out-of-school hours per day spent: Watching TV or videos
Australia*	90	73	2.0	2.4	Kuwait*	51	53	5.3	1.9
Austria*	72	59	2.4	1.9	Latvia[4]	95	13	2.7	2.6
Belgium (Fl)[2]	71	67	3.4	2.0	Lithuania	80	42	2.7	2.8
Belgium (Fr)[3]*	83	60	3.0	1.9	Netherlands*	76	85	2.2	2.5
Canada	86	61	2.2	2.3	New Zealand	90	60	2.1	2.5
Colombia*	43	11	4.6	2.2	Norway	92	64	2.3	2.5
Cyprus	76	39	3.6	2.3	Portugal	64	39	3.0	2.0
Czech Republic	95	36	1.8	2.6	Republic of Korea	78	39	2.5	2.0
Denmark*	88	76	1.4	2.2	Romania*	54	19	5.0	1.9
England	81	89	...	2.7	Russian Federation	87	35	2.9	2.9
France	78	50	2.7	1.5	Scotland*	72	90	1.8	2.7
Germany*	78	71	2.0	1.9	Singapore	67	49	4.6	2.7
Greece*	73	29	4.4	2.1	Slovakia	87	31	2.4	2.7
Hong Kong	50	39	2.5	2.6	Slovenia*	83	47	2.9	2.0
Hungary	88	37	3.1	3.0	Spain	78	42	3.6	1.8
Iceland	94	77	2.4	2.2	Sweden	89	60	2.3	2.3
Iran, Islamic Rep. of	31	4	6.4	1.8	Switzerland	76	66	2.7	1.3
Ireland	77	78	2.7	2.1	Thailand*	51	4	3.5	2.1
Israel*	83	76	2.8	3.3	United States of America	79	59	2.3	2.6
Japan	...	...	2.3	2.6					

1. Countries marked by an asterisk * are not strictly comparable with other countries because they did not meet the study's agreed sampling standards.
2. Flemish-speaking schools.
3. French-speaking schools.
4. Latvian-speaking schools.

Source: Albert E. Beaton et al., *Science Achievement in the Middle School Years: IEA's Third International Mathematics and Science Study,* pp. 94–5, 106–7, Boston, Center for the Study of Testing, Evaluation, and Educational Policy, Boston College, 1996.

Although existing education systems do not at present have the capacity themselves to undertake on a large scale the preparation of multimedia materials for support and enrichment of school curricula, commercial software developers are showing an increasing interest in the education market. The original impulse seems to have come partly from computer games. In fact, it is common for commercial educational programs (e.g. *My First Amazing Dictionary, Dinosaur Adventure, Discover Astronomy,* etc.) to be marketed to the general public along with games under the generic heading of *Edutainment;* many such programs have entertaining interactive multimedia games-like features designed to engage the interest and enthusiasm of the learner.

Another impulse behind the increasing availability of commercially produced educational software has been the interest of book publishers, who have discovered a growing market for all kinds of interactive multimedia reference and self-instructional material: dictionaries, encyclopaedias, reference 'books' on health, birds, plants and so on, atlases and geographical exploration, musical instruments, teach yourself Arabic, Chinese, English, French, Russian, Spanish, etc. Many of these products are remarkably sophisticated and of very high quality.

The extent to which schools at present are buying such programs is not known, although there is plenty of circumstantial evidence (e.g. advertisements in educational magazines and journals) that schools are regarded as a serious market for these products. In the IEA study mentioned above, questions unfortunately were not asked about the nature of the computer software being utilized. Probably the main market for educational programs is still the home computer market, pointing to the discrepancy between in-school and out-of-school education alluded to at the beginning of this chapter. In a majority of the countries and territories surveyed by IEA, computers are almost as common in secondary students' homes as are books (Table 4.1), and if the time students devote to using their computers (unfortunately the survey did not elicit this information) were added to the time they spend watching television, the total time spent each day being informally (non-formally?) educated in front of a screen could be more than the time spent doing homework and almost as much as the time spent in school. As a result of all this, the school teacher who has been teaching for more than ten years – the majority of teachers in the industrial countries – is dealing with a different kind of student from the one he or she knew when first taking up teaching.

It is in respect to the third of the three roles mentioned at the beginning of this section – use of the computer as a medium for teacher-learner, learner-learner and teacher-teacher interaction – that the computer and associated communication technology could potentially have the most significant implications for conventional education. Up to now the main form of use of the computer as an educational medium has been computer

---

Box 4.6
'Virtual learning environments'

Virtual learning environments represent an entirely new form of educational technology. They offer the educational institutions of the world a complex set of opportunities and challenges. For the purposes of this report we will define a virtual learning environment to be an interactive educational computer program with an integrated communication capability. An example of a virtual learning environment is a program ... which supports learners as they work with mathematical formulae and makes it possible for them while using the program to send mathematical working, tables of values and mathematical sketches to other students and tutors, and to receive similar information back from them, either while they are working or later. It is the combination of individual adaptive interaction with communication on demand that provides the unique form of support for the learner. A classroom or a library is an example of a real learning environment, and a computer program which supports a non-trivial scientific simulation can be considered to be an interactive learning environment. A virtual learning environment may support similar forms of learning to a 'real' one but it is not a physical space like a classroom or lecture theatre, and learners may work closely together while not being active at the same time. In addition to having a different relation to space and time, a virtual learning environment is also different from a real one with respect to memory. Virtual learning environments are realized with computer technology, thus can be designed to have their own memory of what the learner or group of learners have been doing.

Virtual learning environments are a relatively recent development and they arise from the convergence of computer and communication technologies that has accelerated over the last ten years. ... The educational community has only recently begun to think through the possibilities for learning environments that are not restricted to particular places and times and that can remember past events.

Source: Tim O'Shea and Eileen Scanlon, *Virtual Learning Environments and the Role of the Teacher. Report of a UNESCO/Open University International Colloquium*, pp. 3–4, Paris/Milton Keynes, Unted Kingdom, UNESCO/Open University Institute of Educational Technology, 1997. (Mimeo.)

conferencing, in which materials for a course, say lecture notes, are placed by the teacher or course leader on a server computer which can be accessed from a distance by students taking the course. The server is programmed to receive and store messages from the students, as well as the teacher's responses to these messages, giving each participant in the course the possibility of consulting (and responding to) the interventions of other participants in the course as well as the teacher's responses and further instructions. The term 'virtual classroom' was coined by researchers in the mid-1980s to describe such a course, since it had most of the essential features of a course occurring in a real classroom but was not bound by place or time. The general term 'virtual learning environment' is more commonly used today (Box 4.6).

Computer conferencing is increasingly used in higher and distance education, but has not yet come into use on anything other than an experimental basis in regular school systems. Its advantages in higher and distance education are readily apparent, especially for part-time and off-campus students who are working in regular jobs and cannot easily participate in conventional full-time courses requiring attendance at lectures, seminars, etc. given on campus. In fact, it was reported by one participant at the UNESCO/Open University International Colloquium mentioned earlier that regular full-time students at his institution were registering for the 'virtual' courses in increasing numbers because of the greater convenience, lower fees and comparable (if not superior) effectiveness of the learning experience.

A number of commentators have suggested that there could be radical implications, including the possible future convergence of higher and distance education, especially if multimedia material could be readily incorporated into such courses. The asynchronous (not occurring in real time) nature of the courses could be one of their advantages, since it allows for the course participants to have different daily schedules and dispenses with

the need for restrictive timetabling. Synchronous audio- and video-conferencing including screen sharing and on-line chalkboards, which also have been utilized in higher and distance education, are correspondingly disadvantaged although they have more of the properties of regular face-to-face classroom contact. Some experts predict the eventual convergence of asynchronous and synchronous modes, permitting courses that could be run in both modes simultaneously, usage depending on the changing needs of individual learners. This development depends on designing computer programs that can be used on demand by groups of simultaneous users and which remain in the computer's memory while not in active use.

In assessing the support that computers can potentially provide for student learning, researchers have noted a number of unique properties of computers and their software that either are not provided by conventional educational means or are difficult to provide, for example the simulation capability (so that students can watch, for example, how plants grow or bridges collapse); the input and output devices which make it possible for disabled students with little movement to have the same degree of control over computers as other students; the ability to display authentic multimedia illustrations and demonstrations; the reprogrammability which makes it possible in principle to improve steadily and systematically existing learning materials; and the ability to interact adaptively with individual students.

The challenge for designers of the new virtual learning environments has been to exploit these properties in ways that can enhance student learning processes, but much more needs to be known about these processes. An example of the very rich agenda of areas where further research and development is needed is shown in Box 4.7. The need also for new evaluation and assessment paradigms that could better reflect the cognitive learning processes involved was stressed in the discussions at the Moscow Congress.

Box 4.7
The scope for computer enhancement of students' learning

The special properties of computers can be used to enhance student learning processes on a number of orthogonal dimensions.

1. *Visualization.* By augmenting simulation engines, symbolic calculators and other software with graphical output it becomes possible to support student visualization of highly abstract processes and procedures. ...

2. *Diagnosis.* By tracking student work on related tasks it becomes possible to distinguish 'accidental' errors from those which provide statistical evidence for failure to understand key concepts or to master critical skills.

3. *Remediation.* By systematically giving students greater access to relevant information or rehearsing them on weak skills it becomes possible to focus remediation on areas that the student, tutor or software has diagnosed as requiring attention. ...

4. *Reflection.* By giving the students access to records of their past working, the responses of the peers, tutors and systems they were working with, and by providing them with tools with which to annotate and file such work, it becomes possible to support systematic reflection on what they have learnt and on their own learning processes. ...

5. *Memory prostheses.* By giving students comprehensive access to their past computer mediated work and by providing them with appropriate search engines it becomes possible for students to have the self confidence to be very selective and focused about what they choose to attempt to memorise at any point in time, thus supporting much greater cognitive economy on the part of the learner. ...

6. *Scaffolding.* By tracking student learning gains and by human or system dialogue with the learner it becomes possible to dynamically vary the level of scaffolding provided for learners.

7. *Tackling the hypothetical.* By making it possible for students to set up counterfactual situations in simulations or to break laws in symbolic reasoning systems it becomes possible for students to investigate the fundamental principles which underpin formal scientific, mathematical and other models. ...

8. *Time travel.* By facilitating 'time travel' as a matter of routine in simulations and databases it becomes possible to help learners augment their understanding by focusing on the key issues of chronology and causality.

9. *Autonomy.* By taking the learner's viewpoint when designing instructional software it becomes possible to give the learner greater control over the degree to which there are external interventions in their learning processes. ...

10. *Pacing.* By providing a 'clock' based on the planned work of a cohort of learners or on an appropriate instructional design it becomes possible for learners to increase their motivation when engaged in sequences of learning activity over longer time periods such as terms and years.

11. *Redundancy.* By encoding the same learning material using different media elements it becomes possible for heterogeneous groups of learners with different learning style and media preferences to study the same curriculum content.

12. *Motivation.* By addressing issues of intrinsic and extrinsic learner motivation explicitly in the design of learning sequence supported by instructional software, and in the design of educational interfaces, it becomes possible to enhance motivation in ways that depend on the characteristics of the individual learner.

13. *Group working.* By supporting synchronous or asynchronous group working modes and by appropriate choice of design to support competitive, collaborative or complementary activity it becomes possible for learners to work in teams and to acquire higher order learning skills from each other.

14. *Knowledge integration.* By taking a chronological view when designing instructional software, by deliberately incorporating appropriate elements of media redundancy and by planning for student use of memory prosthetics it becomes possible for the learner to integrate diverse knowledge acquired at different times.

15. *Access.* By incorporating diverse prosthetics in learner interfaces and by designing for learner autonomy and pacing it becomes possible to extend access to learners who cannot take advantage of conventional modes of classroom delivery because of their special social or physical circumstances.

Source: Tim O'Shea and Eileen Scanlon, *Virtual Learning Environments and the Role of the Teacher: Report of a UNESCO/Open University International Colloquium,* pp. 14–16, Paris/Milton Keynes, United Kingdom, UNESCO/Open University Institute of Educational Technology, 1997. (Mimeo.)

Research and development in this area is costly and, as already noted, educational software has not up to now been an area of particular interest for major commercial software producers with the resources to undertake the big investment that would be needed. Thus, progress is likely to be slow, despite much speculation in popular discussion that education could soon experience radical changes similar to those which the new technologies have prompted in other sectors.

Implications for teachers and teaching

Although much more needs to be learned about the educational potential of the new technologies, it is clear that they are likely to have a bigger impact on the formal education system than most earlier technologies that have been applied to education. As suggested in the preceding section above, the impact is likely to be two-fold: on the nature and type of learning materials available to students, and on educational methods. Both are large topics which merit comprehensive review in a separate report. In this final section of the present report, only selected aspects directly related to teachers and teaching in the formal education system are considered.

First, concerning *teaching and learning materials*: current trends suggest that books could increasingly be complemented by multimedia computer software in the presentation of standard curriculum subjects. However, the quite modest use of the computer in the secondary schools of the industrial countries at present in a subject area such as science, noted earlier in this chapter, suggests that this development will be slow. There remain major constraints in regard to both the capabilities of the existing stock of computers in the schools and the availability of suitable software that can be integrated directly into existing curricula. The existing stock of computers includes large numbers of old models which cannot be used for much more than word processing and cannot handle multimedia software. The software problem relates to curriculum requirements. In fact, there may have been a tendency for advocates of greater use of the computer in schools to underestimate the extent to which most school systems have mandated curricula and learning goals that normally can be changed only after careful deliberation. Increased use of the computer in regular classwork is unlikely if it does not contribute to improved learning of mandated curriculum content.

The software question leads further, for it suggests that the computer, far from yet having solved the problem of enabling students to learn better, may actually have partly displaced the problem elsewhere. Are educational software designers anything other than 'virtual' teachers? This question was evoked at the UNESCO/Open University Colloquium. The preparation of good educational software, it was agreed, requires a range of skills that can only be provided by multi-disciplinary teams of technicians and educators; in this respect there is an important difference compared with the preparation of conventional textbooks. The need to involve teachers in the software development process, with a view to minimizing the difficulties that could later arise when utilizing the software in the classroom, was emphasized in the discussions at the Moscow Congress.

The continuing nature of the software problem, even in countries with highly developed software industries, points to larger policy issues. First, who will take responsibility for developing the software? The education system itself or commercial software producers? Several speakers at the Moscow Congress, for example, urged that the development of educational software should not be left to the commercial and industrial world alone. Yet if education systems themselves are going to get involved more than they are now in educational software research and development, resources for such activity will have to come from somewhere. At a time when most governments are trying to hold down public expenditure, how

---

Box 4.8
Issues relating to the introduction of the new technologies into education in developing countries

1. It was noted [in the discussions at the Round Table] that education has always made use of technology, with new waves of technology absorbing – not replacing – their predecessors. Thus, there has been a progression from oral transmission, to print, to computer assisted instruction and, now, to computer assisted learning.
2. It was noted that new technologies raised issues to do with (a) impact on culture, (b) impact on communities, (c) authority and control, (d) curriculum design and access, (e) the nature of the school, (f) teacher competence, and (g) equity and social justice.
3. In some countries, access to the Internet is being discouraged by the government because it has the potential to subvert the culture. However, it was noted that while it is possible to reduce access, it is not possible to eliminate it altogether.
4. Differences of opinions were expressed as to the role of computers – as aids to teaching or aids to learning. Some believed that the role of the teacher as a source of knowledge should be maintained, while others argued that students should be as independent as possible and should be encouraged to become interested thinkers.
5. Differential access to computers will further exacerbate differences within societies and will undermine democracy.
6. Investment in technology should be seen as just that

7. – investment which will have a significant return in the future.
8. Earth orbiting satellites have the potential to make information technology universally accessible.
9. Developing countries' access to computer technology varies according to their position on a spectrum of wealth.
10. Developing countries should tap in to companies' use of technology by developing school-business partnerships, with business being asked to assist with putting computers into schools in their communities and providing some training of teachers in computer technology.
11. Costs of technology are reducing and will continue to do so as demand increases and mass production takes place.
12. With network computers being introduced, the cost of access to information will dramatically decrease.
13. Under the principle of 'shared growth', developed countries could enter into partnerships with specific developing countries to provide technology.
14. Under the Florence Agreement, import taxes for educational equipment should be waived.
15. If expenditure on technology is consolidated, more computers could be introduced. The development of CD Roms could replace some other technologies.
16. The first step in introducing technology should be to provide one to act as a 'teachers' library.

Source: Re-engineering Education for Change: Educational Innovation for Development, Report of the Second UNESCO-ACEID (Asia-Pacific Centre of Educational Innovation for Development) International Conference organized by UNESCO-ACEID in co-operation with the Ministry of Education, Thailand, Bangkok, 9–12 December 1996, pp. 162–3, Bangkok, UNESCO Principal Regional Office for Asia and the Pacific, 1997. (Report of the Round Table on the theme: Re-Engineering Use of Educational Technology in Developing Countries.)

---

much priority are they ready to give to increasing investment in this area?

Second, there is the international dimension. At present, many of the concerns relating to the new technologies in the less developed regions of the world are focused on access to the hardware; the software challenge has not yet drawn the attention that it merits. This is evident, for example, in the discussion of issues relating to the introduction of the new technologies into education in developing countries at the recent Conference on 'Re-

Engineering Education for Change', organized by UNESCO for countries in the Asia-Pacific region in Bangkok in December 1996 (Box 4.8). Few countries in the less developed regions of the world have any real capacity to undertake software research and development. In consequence, even when they can afford to purchase the hardware they could be unable to exploit it fully for educational purposes.

Training in educational software development would seem to be a priority area for future inter-

Box 4.9
'Making educational and cultural buildings more intelligent' (Japan)

In recent years, along with the maturing of our society, the aspiration of people for learning has been growing, and their learning demands have become diversified and heightened. In this context, the National Council for Educational Reform proposed a concept of 'intelligent school building'. According to this concept, education, research, cultural and sports facilities in the community should become focal points for lifelong learning and information activities in the community through reorganizing and renovating these facilities as centres providing comfortable learning and living spaces equipped with high-level information and communications equipment.

In response to this proposal, the Ministry began to conduct studies on making educational and cultural buildings more intelligent, and in March 1990 published a report on 'Making educational and cultural buildings more intelligent'.

To follow up on this report, the Ministry started in 1990 to commission a number of local governments to conduct pilot studies on 'model intelligent schools'. On the basis of the results of these pilot studies, the Ministry is now studying how to carry out specific plans for making educational and cultural buildings more 'intelligent'.

Further, with a view to contributing to the diversification and upgrading of the functions of school buildings, the Ministry in 1992 launched a programme for making school buildings more intelligent for public elementary, lower secondary, upper secondary and special schools.

During the six years from 1990 to 1995 the Ministry commissioned 22 local governments and other organizations to conduct pilot studies on 'model intelligent schools'.

Source: Development of Education in Japan 1994–1996, pp. 101–2, Tokyo, Ministry of Education, Science, Sports and Culture, 1996. (National report presented at the 45th session of the International Conference on Education, Geneva, 1996.)

limited prospect of educators in one country being able to adapt easily for their own purposes the educational software which has been developed in another; differences between countries in language, culture and school curricula are formidable obstacles, as they are right now for the international exchange and adaptation of school textbooks. The prospect of computer-mediated distance education across national boundaries also would seem to be limited; as in the case of today's students studying outside their own countries there needs to be a commitment by the learner to encounter and successfully cope with the cultural and linguistic hurdles of the host country's educational programme.

The question of *teaching methods and approaches* is equally complex. Even where computer and communication equipment can be made readily available to schools, the scope for adopting alternative approaches based on different groups of learners than standard age-graded classes is constrained by both the inherited stock of school buildings and existing curricula. Most schools in the industrial countries, like the old office buildings and industrial plants which some of them resemble, were never designed to accommodate information and communication technologies, as some countries have begun to realize (e.g. Box 4.9). Experimentation with alternative teaching methods and approaches to formal education based on the systematic use of computers has therefore been largely confined up to now to pilot projects in conventional schools.

Observation of computer-rich classes in schools where standard curricula have been relaxed so as to permit learning activities specifically centred on the use of computers has found that there typically is a much higher level of collegiality or collaboration between students, and between students and the teacher, than in ordinary classes. Students enjoy using computers. Thus, it has been observed that students in the computer-rich class are more ready to assist each other, e.g. in exploring databases and Web sites, and in completing

national co-operation, as has already happened to some extent in respect to conventional distance education using older technologies such as radio and television. There would seem to be only a

group projects, while the teacher becomes more of a 'team facilitator' or 'learning coach' than chalkboard source of knowledge and information. A related finding has been the higher level of continuous individual learning activity in the computer-rich class compared with the ordinary class where at any time only a minority of learners are actively involved in proceedings with the teacher.

Such findings, though, have followed to some extent from the initial conditions, i.e. the availability of computers, and the activities which the students are requested to undertake with them. Whether the levels of collaboration are any greater than can be achieved with well-conceived group work in ordinary classes not having computers has not been decisively established, although the form of the collaboration clearly is different as well as the nature of the students' learning experiences. Depending on the kinds of learning materials that can be accessed with their equipment, e.g. simulations of physical events or biological processes, or sights and sounds from foreign countries, the learning experiences of the students in the computer-rich class are arguably more 'authentic' than those available to students in the ordinary class and possibly are more productive of deeper levels of understanding of given subject area content. In general, there still is a dearth of rigorous research findings demonstrative of clear learning gains over conventional classroom processes, other than the gain of learning how to utilize the new technologies themselves for different purposes, but it could be precisely the latter learning that is now becoming more and more useful in active life outside the school.

It is in regard to the role of the teacher that there has been the most potential for controversy. Some of the discussion in this area has tended to caricature the 'traditional' teacher mainly as a communicator of information – a role which increasingly can be performed, so it is claimed, by the new information and communication tech-

---

Box 4.10
Can anything be taught by words?
(Augustine of Hippo, A.D. 354–430)

What can be said in support of the view that words teach us something quite apart from their sound which strikes our ears? All that we perceive is perceived either with the senses or with the mind.

When we are asked about the former, we can give an answer only if the things we experience through the senses are actually before us; for example, when we are looking at the new moon and are asked what it is made of or where it is. In this case, if the questioner does not see it himself, he merely believes my words, and often, in fact, he does not believe them. It is quite wrong to say that he learns, unless he himself is seeing what is being spoken about. This is to say, he does not learn from the words which are uttered but from the things themselves and from his senses; for the same words sound in the ears of the person who sees a thing and of the person who does not see it. ...

When we consider the things we perceive with the mind,* that is, by means of the intelligence and reason, we are talking about what we are looking at *directly* in that interior light of truth by which what we call the inner man is enlightened and in which he delights. If at the same time the person who listens to me sees these realities for himself with his inner eye, he knows what I am talking about, not because he has listened to my words, but because he has contemplated the realities on his own account. ... If he is led along this path by the words of a questionner, he is not being taught by words; the words are merely raising questions which put him in a fit condition to learn inwardly. ...

[Therefore,] we go astray when we refer to 'teachers', since there are really no teachers at all. The reason that we speak in this way is that frequently there is no time lapse between the moment of speaking and the moment of learning. Because pupils are quick to learn within themselves in consequence of the teacher's instruction, they think that in fact they have learned externally, from the person who has instructed them.

* Editor's note: Elsewhere, Augustine gives '7 + 3 = 10' as an example of something perceived with the mind as distinct from something experienced by the senses.

Source: George Howie (ed.), *St. Augustine: On Education,* pp. 318–27, Chicago, Henry Regnery Company, 1969.

Box 4.11
Dear Mr Germain, … (letter from Albert Camus to his former teacher)

19 November 1957

Dear Mr Germain,

I let the flurry around me these last few days die down somewhat before writing to you from the depths of my heart. I have just been paid a great honour indeed,* which I neither sought nor solicited. But when I heard the news, my first thought, after my mother, was for you. Without you, without the affectionate hand that you held out to the poor child that I was, without your teaching and your example, none of this would have happened. I do not like making a big fuss over this kind of event, but this one is at least an opportunity to tell you what you meant and will always mean to me and to assure you that your efforts, your work and the generous heart that you put into it are still alive in one of your little pupils who, despite his age, has not ceased to be a grateful one. I hug you with all my might.

Albert Camus

* Camus had just heard that he had been awarded the Nobel Prize for Literature.

Source: Albert Camus, *Le premier homme*, p. 327, Paris, Gallimard, 1994.

this role, the favoured teaching methods or approaches have been variously described as 'experiential learning', 'inquiry learning', 'learning by discovery' and 'open classroom learning', which can be traced back to Dewey (Box 3.12) in this century and to other educational thinkers in other countries in earlier times. The influential idea of the computer and related communication equipment providing 'scaffolding' to support the learner – mentioned for example in Box 4.7 – has been drawn from the pedagogical theories of the Russian educational psychologist Lev Vygotsky (1896–1934).

History aside, the stimulation that has been given over the last decade or so in many countries to thinking and debate about teaching and learning has undoubtedly been one of the most important consequences of the introduction of the new technologies into the schools. More and more teachers are being drawn into such debate as they acquire computer literacy skills and begin to use the new technologies to 'network' with other teachers about what they are doing.

As their experience of the application of the new technologies grows, teachers are likely to exert a stronger influence than they have had up to now on the development of these technologies into effective teaching and learning tools. Like the development of good textbooks, the development of good educational software will be a long-term process of trial and error that will need continously to draw on the experience of the best teachers, those who are most observant of, sympathetic to and skilled in responding to the learning needs of individual pupils (e.g. Box 4.11).

nologies. However, the new role of 'learning coach' or 'facilitator' which the teacher is called upon to play is more traditional than is usually recognized (e.g. Box 4.10); successive waves of new technology rediscover it. Consistent with

Appendices

I. Statistical notes

THE FOLLOWING NOTES provide the historical back-ground to UNESCO's current concern to improve the international comparability of educational statistics.

Main steps in the movement towards the international standardization of educational statistics, 1853–1978

International Statistical Congress, Brussels, 1853. This Congress, the first of its kind, brought together some 150 people (from 26 countries) having an official or scholarly interest in statistics, the aim being to provide for an exchange of experience and views on both theoretical and practical aspects of statistics, including standard systems of classification. Education statistics was one of the eleven fields selected for discussion.

In its report concerning education statistics, the Congress adopted a classification system based on education and training institutions, which it recommended should be classified into four broad categories, the first three of which were also referred to as 'levels' of education:

1. Primary or first level education, including kindergartens, primary schools, primary teacher training institutions, schools for the blind or deaf, orphanages, schools annexed to industrial establishments, etc.;

2. Middle or second level education, including grammar schools, lycées, gymnasia, colleges, schools of agriculture, horticulture, navigation, etc.;

3. Higher or third level education, including universities, advanced schools of civil engineering, mining, agriculture and forestry, etc.;

4. Special education distinct from the preceding categories, including religious seminaries, apprentice workshops, schools of music, gymnastics, etc., military schools, etc.

Following the first International Statistical Congress, statistical societies in several European countries took it upon themselves to organize further congresses; these were held at two- to three-year intervals up until 1876 (e.g. Paris, 1855; Vienna, 1857; London, 1860), after which there was a hiatus until 1885. In the latter year, the participants from many countries who were in London for the golden jubilee celebrations of the Statistical Society of London agreed to found an inter-national society, the International Statistical Institute (ISI). The secretariat was initially based in Rome, but later moved to The Hague. ISI revived the international statistical congresses in the form of biennial general sessions of its members. Several papers relating to education statistics were presented at these sessions before the First World War; two papers in particular, prepared by Émile Levasseur, a professor at the Collège de France, contained unique compilations of statistics on the development of primary education in a number of countries in different regions of the world (see box below). In the inter-war years, and again after the Second World War, other papers were presented from time to time on diverse aspects of education statistics; facsimile copies of these papers have recently been brought together by ISI in a two-volume compendium,

---

'The terms "primary schools", "teachers" and consequently "pupils" do not have exactly the same meaning in all countries'

Statistical data are an instructive source of factual information and are very often the only precise source available to the social sciences. But the figures themselves and the variations they undergo from one period to another can only be understood if the nature of the facts they describe and the causes of change are known. This is why we have felt it necessary to give a brief history of primary education and an overview of the educational, administrative and financial organization of schools. The terms 'primary schools', 'teachers' and consequently 'pupils' do not have exactly the same meaning in all countries; hence the great difficulty in establishing international comparisons, and the need to look into legislation and administrative organization in order to ascertain what they mean. Defining them may not remove the difficulties, but will at least help in assessing them and in pinpointing the differences from one country to another.

Source: M. É. Levasseur, 'Rapport sur la statistique de l'enseignement primaire', *Education Statistics: an International Compendium (1853–1995)*, p. 112, Voorburg, ISI, 1995. (Initially published in Vol. II of the report of the third session of the International Statistical Institute, Vienna, 28 September–3 October 1891.)

Education Statistics: an International Compendium (1853–1995) (Vols. I, II, Voorburg, Netherlands, ISI, 1995).

Joint Committee on Intellectual Statistics, 1926. After the First World War, there emerged a demand for international education statistics on the part of a new international body, the International Institute for Intellectual Co-operation (IIIC), set up in Paris in 1924. The aim of IIIC was to foster international co-operation and exchanges in a wide range of fields of intellectual activity, and one of the new organization's earliest felt needs was for up-to-date international statistics relating to education, science and culture. In 1926 IIIC proposed to ISI that the two organizations set up a joint committee for the purpose of making recommendations on the compilation of such statistics. The committee's recommendations took the form of model national tabulations.[1] A minority of the tabulations (eighteen out of sixty-six) concerned scientific and cultural institutions and activities, e.g. museums, libraries, book production, cinema, radio broadcasting, etc. The majority concerned educational institutions, which the committee recommended should be classified into three levels (higher, secondary or middle, and primary or elementary) similar to the classification recommended by the first International Statistical Congress seventy-three years previously. In its detailed elaboration of the model national tabulations, the joint committee recommended that a distinction should be drawn, where appropriate, between institutions giving a general education and those giving a vocational or technical education, and called for detailed information to precede the tables concerning the organization, administration and inspection of the schools, as well as legislation regarding compulsory education, the qualifications of teachers, duration of courses, etc. The General Assembly of ISI, at its seventeenth session in January 1928, adopted a resolution calling on countries to compile and publish the tabulations

recommended in the joint committee's report, but there was no follow-up since neither ISI nor IIIC had any statutory capability of performing the role of collector/collator of international statistics in education or any other field.

International Bureau of Education (IBE). Originally established in 1925 as an offshoot of the Institute (School) of Educational Sciences of the University of Geneva, IBE was restructured in 1929 with new statutes which provided specifically for 'any government, public institution or international non-governmental organization' to become a member 'on payment of an annual contribution of not less than 10,000 Swiss francs'. IBE's goal was to serve as 'a centre of educational information', and in particular 'to collect documentation on educational research and its applications and to ensure a wide-ranging exchange of such documentation and information in order that each country will feel stimulated to benefit from the experience of others'. Besides the Canton of Geneva, several governments (Czechoslovakia, Ecuador, Egypt, Poland and Spain) became members straightaway and more joined later. IBE soon became very active in carrying out international surveys on selected educational topics by means of questionnaires addressed to the national educational authorities and leading institutions of educational research in different countries. In 1932 a number of countries were invited to submit reports (including statistics) on the recent development of their education systems; these reports provided the basis for publishing (from 1933 onwards) an *International Yearbook of Education*. From 1937 to 1939 the *Yearbook* included a section, 'Summary Statistical Tables', showing data for fifty-eight countries on the numbers of primary and secondary schools, pupil enrolments in primary and secondary schools, numbers of primary and secondary schools teachers, and public expenditure on education. These tables may be considered as the first-ever 'official' set of international education statistics.

Preparatory Commission of UNESCO, 1946. Article VIII of UNESCO's constitution, as adopted in London in November 1945, provided specifically for 'each Member State [to] report periodically to the Organization, in a manner to be determined by the General Conference,

1. The Committee's report entitled 'Rapport au nom de la Commission mixte de la statistique intellectuelle' was presented at the seventeenth session of ISI (Cairo, 1927–28) and published (in French only) in the *Bulletin de l'Institut International de Statistique*, Vol. XXIII, pp. 609–92, Cairo, Imprimerie Nationale, 1928. This report is not reproduced in the ISI compendium mentioned above.

on its laws, regulations and statistics relating to educational, scientific and cultural life and institutions ...'. In May 1946, the United States of America submitted to the Preparatory Commission of UNESCO two proposals, one of which concerned the setting up of an international service of educational statistics. This proposal was adopted by the General Conference of UNESCO at its first session in November 1946. As a result, the programme of the Organization for 1947, as approved by the Executive Board at its second session in May of that year, contained the following project under the section on education:

'*Educational statistics.* In collaboration with a committee on educational statistics the following activities will be carried on: (a) Assist in the co-ordination, standardization and improvement of national educational statistics. (b) Assist in the standardization of educational terminology. (c) Advise Member States and intergovernmental organizations on general questions relating to the collection, interpretation and dissemination of statistical data on education. (d) Explore the possibility of publishing an international education yearbook, which should contain information on educational policies and trends as well as statistics'.

Accordingly, over the next ten years, UNESCO's activity in educational statistics had two main thrusts: on the one hand, standard-setting and advisory services to Member States, culminating in the *Recommendation concerning the International Standardization of Educational Statistics,* adopted by the General Conference at its tenth session in 1958, and on the other hand development of data collection and analysis, culminating in the *World Survey of Education: Handbook of Educational Organization and Statistics* (Paris, UNESCO, 1955).

Recommendation concerning the International Standardization of Educational Statistics, 1958. The Committee on Educational Statistics which had been proposed by the Preparatory Commission of UNESCO met in March-April 1947 and drew up a plan for the collection of basic statistics on education. This eventually led to the establishment of a statistical service in UNESCO (April 1950), and to the setting up of a Committee of Experts on the Standardization of Educational Statistics (November 1951), which was charged with drawing up

a set of definitions, classifications and tabulations of statistics on illiteracy and education. As a result of the expert committee's work, the question of international regulation with a view to standardizing educational statistics was put to UNESCO's General Conference at its ninth session (1956), at which a resolution was adopted authorizing 'the Director-General to convene a Committee composed of technicians and experts nominated by Member States to prepare a draft recommendation for submission to the General Conference at its tenth session (1958)'. The *1958 Recommendation* as finally adopted had four sections: I. Statistics of Illiteracy; II. Statistics on the Educational Attainment of the Population; III. Statistics of Educational Institutions; and IV. Statistics of Educational Finance. Each section contained sub-sections giving definitions and classifications; in addition, the first two sections (on illiteracy and educational attainment respectively) also contained sub-sections suggesting methods of measurement, while the other two sections (on educational institutions and educational finance) contained sub-sections giving recommended tabulations. Among the more significant contents of the *Recommendation* were: the first-ever internationally agreed definitions of literacy/illiteracy ('... can/cannot with understanding both read and write a short simple statement on his(her) everyday life'), and the basic classification of education into three broad levels, first, second and third. Also significant was the definition of 'educational attainment' in terms of 'highest grade or level of education completed'.

World Survey of Education. Successive volumes served as UNESCO's main vehicle for publishing international educational statistics up until 1964 when the Organization brought out its first *Statistical Yearbook.* At the same time as the first *World Survey* (1955), the Organization also began publication of an annual series (discontinued in 1962) entitled *Basic Facts and Figures,* containing country tables of the main educational statistics then available. Five volumes of the *World Survey* were eventually published: at three-yearly intervals from 1955 up until 1961, then at five-yearly intervals in 1966 and 1971. The first volume was notable for offering, among other things, the first-ever statistical estimate of the extent of illiteracy in the world ('a reasonable estimate is that half of the world's [adult] population still cannot read and write'), as well as a unique appendix containing a comprehensive glossary of national terms for the different types of educational institutions and programmes in the various countries. The third volume (1961) was notable for its statistical analysis of the development of education by level of education and major world region; this analysis was further elaborated and updated in the fourth (1966) and fifth (1971) volumes.

UNESCO's Manual of Educational Statistics, 1961. Now out of print, the *Manual* was intended to serve as a means of disseminating and explaining the *1958 Recommendation* to producers and users of educational statistics. Besides the introduction and two general chapters at the beginning on the 'Nature and Sources of Educational Statistics' and 'International Comparability of Educational Statistics', the layout of the *Manual* followed that of the *1958 Recommendation* itself, covering first the sections on illiteracy and the educational attainment of the population, and then those on educational institutions and educational finance.

International Standard Classification of Education (ISCED), 1975. At the same time as the *1958 Recommendation*'s guidelines for classifying education were being developed, other statistical instruments were being developed elsewhere in the United Nations system, for example the International Standard Classification of Occupations (ISCO), the International Standard Industrial Classification (ISIC) and the System of National Accounts (SNA). When revisions of ISCO and ISIC were initiated in the early 1960s, it was felt in UNESCO that a comparable 'international standard classification' needed to be formulated for education, in particular one that could be linked to ISCO, the aim being to facilitate education-manpower planning, which at that time was being actively promoted in developing countries by UNESCO and other international organizations such as ILO and the World Bank, and in the industrial countries by OECD. For the purposes of education-manpower planning, the classification unit adopted by the *1958 Recommendation* – the educational institution – was considered to have the drawback that it could not be easily linked to the occupational categories defined in ISCO: most edu-

cational institutions normally provided a preparation of one sort or another for a variety of occupations. A more narrowly defined classification unit appeared to be needed. Thus, when UNESCO began work in 1966 on formulating an international standard classification of education, it was decided that the basic classification unit would be the educational programme rather than the educational institution, the aim being to enable countries to construct occupation-education matrices in which individual occupations or groups of occupations could be matched to educational programmes defined by level and field of study. Such matrices, it was argued, could be used by education planners to derive the required 'output' (graduates or leavers), and hence enrolments of the education system broken down by level of education and field of study, provided that national economic planners could deliver projections of future employment opportunities broken down by occupation. The first meeting of experts on ISCED was held in 1968. Two further expert meetings were held in 1972 and 1974 respectively, following which ISCED was presented to the 1975 session of the International Conference on Education. As finally adopted by the latter, ISCED contained several innovations compared to the system of classification built into the *1958 Recommendation,* notably: the replacement of the educational institution by the educational programme as the basic unit of classification; the formulation of so-called 'level categories' 0, 1, 2, 3, 5, 6 and 7,[2] with 0 corresponding to education preceding the first level, 1 to first level education, 2 and 3 to lower and upper second level education respectively, and 5, 6 and 7 to third level education not equivalent to a university degree, third level education leading to a university degree or equivalent qualification, and third level education leading to a higher or research degree, respectively. ISCED also elaborated (for the first time) a classification of fields of study. The intention of ISCED's architects was that any educational programme, whether in the regular education system that normally constitutes a 'ladder' from pre-primary education up to university, or in adult and/or out-of-school education, could be classified into one or other of the

---

2. A 'level category' 4 was not proposed.

new levels and one or other of the various fields of study.

Revised Recommendation concerning the International Standardization of Educational Statistics, 1978. Following the adoption of ISCED by the International Conference on Education, the Director-General was invited to submit a revised version of the *1958 Recommendation,* incorporating ISCED, to UNESCO's General Conference. Accordingly, ISCED was incorporated into the *Revised Recommendation concerning the International Standardization of Educational Statistics* adopted by the General Conference at its twentieth session in 1978. ISCED primarily affected the section of the *1958 Recommendation* concerning 'Statistics of Educational Institutions'. This section was substantially revised and renamed in the *Revised Recommendation (1978)* as 'Statistics of Enrolment, Teachers and Educational Institutions', beginning with a sub-section on 'Definitions' that included an explicit statement of what should be adopted as the 'basic statistical unit for which educational data are to be collected', namely, 'the programme', following which was presented the definition of a 'programme' as given in the ISCED manual. In the next two sub-sections, concerning 'classification' and 'tabulations' respectively, major changes were made to the *1958 Recommendation.* In the 'Classification' sub-section, the *Revised Recommendation* proposed that 'Education should be classified into the following major sectors:

(a) Regular education, (b) Adult Education'; the corresponding part of the *1958 Recommendation* had made a distinction between education that could be classified by level and 'Education which is not usually classified by level'. In the following sub-section, 'Tabulations', the text of the *1958 Recommendation* was replaced by a new text spelling out four sets of tabulations covering 'regular education', 'adult education', 'special education' and 'population data' respectively, in each case (except the last) with breakdowns drawn according to the ISCED levels and fields of study. Tabulations on 'adult education' had not been mentioned at all in the *1958 Recommendation,* nor had the distinction between 'regular' and 'adult' education. Within 'adult' education, the *Revised Recommendation* made a distinction between 'formal' and 'non-formal' education that also had not been made in the *1958 Recommendation.* As regards the other sections of the *Revised Recommendation* – i.e. those concerning 'Statistics of Illiteracy', 'Statistics on the Educational Attainment of the Population', and 'Statistics of Educational Finance' the original text of the *1958 Recommendation* was retained except for the inclusion of two new terms – 'functionally literate' and 'functionally illiterate' – accompanied by their definitions: 'can/cannot engage in all those activities in which literacy is required for effective functioning of his group and community and also for enabling him to use reading, writing and calculation for his own and the community's development'.

II. Regional tables

A NEW CLASSIFICATION approach to countries and regions is adopted in this report. The traditional 'developed' and 'developing' countries groups are replaced by 'more developed' and 'less developed regions' in order to acknowledge that there are differences in levels of development among countries within the same region. A third group of countries, 'countries in transition', is included so as to allow for a separate analysis of the particular situation(s) observed in the countries of East and Central Europe and the former Soviet Union. The classification adopted in this report is as follows:[1]

More developed regions

Northern America comprises Canada and the United States.

Asia and Oceania comprises Australia, Israel, Japan and New Zealand.

Europe comprises Austria, Belgium, Denmark, Finland, France, Germany, Greece, Iceland, Ireland, Italy, Luxembourg, Monaco, Netherlands, Norway, Portugal, San Marino, Spain, Sweden, Switzerland and the United Kingdom .

Countries in transition

Countries in transition comprises Albania, Armenia, Azerbaijan, Belarus, Bosnia and Herzegovina, Bulgaria, Croatia, Czech Republic, Estonia, Georgia, Hungary, Kazakhstan, Kyrgyzstan, Latvia, Lithuania, Poland, Republic of Moldova, Romania, Russian Federation, Slovakia, Slovenia, Tajikistan, The Former Yugoslav Republic of Macedonia, Turkmenistan, Ukraine, Uzbekistan and Yugoslavia.

Less developed regions

Sub-Saharan Africa comprises Angola, Benin, Botswana, Burkina Faso, Burundi, Cameroon, Cape Verde, Central African Republic, Chad, Comoros, Congo, Côte d'Ivoire, Democratic Republic of the Congo, Djibouti, Equatorial Guinea, Eritrea, Ethiopia, Gabon, Gambia, Ghana, Guinea, Guinea-Bissau, Kenya, Lesotho, Liberia, Madagascar, Malawi, Mali, Mauritania, Mauritius, Mozambique, Namibia, Niger, Nigeria, Rwanda, Sao Tome and Principe, Senegal, Seychelles, Sierra Leone, Somalia, South Africa, Sudan, Swaziland, Togo, Uganda, United Republic of Tanzania, Zambia and Zimbabwe.

Arab States comprises Algeria, Bahrain, Djibouti, Egypt, Iraq, Jordan, Kuwait, Lebanon, Libyan Arab Jamahiriya, Mauritania, Morocco, Oman, Palestinian Autonomous Territories, Qatar, Saudi Arabia, Somalia, Sudan, Syrian Arab Republic, Tunisia, United Arab Emirates and Yemen.

Latin America and the Caribbean comprises Antigua and Barbuda, Argentina, Bahamas, Barbados, Belize, Bolivia, Brazil, British Virgin Islands, Chile, Colombia, Costa Rica, Cuba, Dominica, Dominican Republic, Ecuador, El Salvador, Grenada, Guatemala, Guyana, Haiti, Honduras, Jamaica, Mexico, Netherlands Antilles, Nicaragua, Panama, Paraguay, Peru, Saint Kitts and Nevis, Saint Lucia, Saint Vincent and the Grenadines, Suriname, Trinidad and Tobago, Uruguay and Venezuela.

Eastern Asia and Oceania comprises Brunei Darussalam, Cambodia, China, Cook Islands, Democratic People's Republic of Korea, Fiji, Hong Kong, Indonesia, Kiribati, Lao People's Democratic Republic, Macau, Malaysia, Mongolia, Myanmar, Papua New Guinea, Philippines, Republic of Korea, Samoa, Singapore, Solomon Islands, Thailand, Tonga, Tuvalu, Vanuatu and Viet Nam.

Southern Asia comprises Afghanistan, Bangladesh, Bhutan, India, Islamic Republic of Iran, Maldives, Nepal, Pakistan and Sri Lanka.

Least developed countries comprises Afghanistan, Angola, Bangladesh, Benin, Bhutan, Burkina Faso, Burundi, Cambodia, Cape Verde, Central African Republic, Chad, Comoros, Democratic Republic of the Congo, Djibouti, Equatorial Guinea, Eritrea, Ethiopia, Gambia, Guinea, Guinea-Bissau, Haiti, Kiribati, Lao People's Democratic Republic, Lesotho, Liberia, Madagascar, Malawi, Maldives, Mali, Mauritania, Mozambique, Myanmar, Nepal, Niger, Rwanda, Samoa, Sao Tome and Principe, Sierra Leone, Solomon Islands, Somalia, Sudan, Togo, Tuvalu, Uganda, United Republic of Tanzania, Vanuatu, Yemen and Zambia.

---

1. The totals for each regional group include data and estimates for other small countries and territories not shown individually in Annex III's indicators tables. It should also be noted that the totals for 'Less developed regions' include data for Cyprus, Malta and Turkey, and do not double count data for the four countries (Djibouti, Mauritania, Somalia and Sudan) which belong to both the Sub-Saharan Africa and the Arab States groups.

Table 1
Dependency ratios[1] and population aged 15–64, 1985–2005

	1985				1995				2005			
	Dependency ratio (percentage)			Population (millions)	Dependency ratio (percentage)			Population (millions)	Dependency ratio (percentage)			Population (millions)
	0–5	6–14	65+	15–64	0–5	6–14	65+	15–64	0–5	6–14	65+	15–64
WORLD TOTAL	23.3	31.9	9.8	2 936	20.8	29.6	10.5	3 534	18.0	25.8	11.1	4 192
More developed regions of which:	11.9	19.1	18.4	523	11.2	17.3	20.9	557	10.0	16.0	22.9	581
North America	13.5	19.1	17.5	178	13.7	19.8	19.1	194	11.4	18.4	18.5	216
Asia/Oceania	11.6	21.1	15.1	97	9.5	15.8	19.8	105	10.0	14.7	25.9	105
Europe	10.9	18.2	20.4	247	10.0	15.9	22.8	258	8.9	14.6	25.3	261
Countries in transition	16.1	22.2	14.1	261	12.7	23.0	16.9	272	10.8	16.7	18.6	285
Less developed regions of which:	27.0	36.2	7.1	2 153	23.6	32.8	7.7	2 706	20.0	28.3	8.3	3 326
Sub-Saharan Africa	42.0	46.0	5.7	229	40.4	46.5	5.7	305	36.8	44.9	5.7	412
Arab States	36.8	43.3	6.2	105	30.8	41.2	6.2	143	26.6	35.0	6.4	192
Latin America/Caribbean	27.7	37.8	7.8	229	22.3	32.5	8.3	292	18.3	26.8	9.1	358
Eastern Asia/Oceania	20.1	31.9	7.6	968	17.4	25.8	8.5	1 176	13.6	21.6	9.6	1 362
of which: China	17.4	29.6	8.0	690	15.5	23.5	9.0	824	11.6	19.3	10.3	936
Southern Asia	30.8	38.0	6.8	607	26.1	36.9	7.2	771	21.5	30.2	7.7	983
of which: India	28.5	35.8	7.2	448	23.8	34.0	7.6	562	19.2	28.0	8.3	696
Least developed countries	40.1	45.6	5.8	234	36.8	46.1	5.8	307	33.5	40.8	5.6	415

1. Percentage ratio of the population in each age-group to the population aged 15–64.

Source: United Nations Population Division database (1996 revision).

Table 2
Estimated illiterate population (millions) aged 15 and over, 1985–2005

	1985			1995			2005		
	MF	F	%F	MF	F	%F	MF	F	%F
WORLD TOTAL	885.9	560.1	63.2	884.7	564.7	63.8	869.5	558.2	64.2
More developed regions and countries in transition	22.5	15.6	69.3	12.9	7.9	61.6	8.6	5.0	58.4
Less developed regions of which:	863.3	544.4	63.1	871.8	556.7	63.9	860.9	553.2	64.3
Sub-Saharan Africa	132.0	80.6	61.1	140.5	87.1	62.0	145.4	91.0	62.5
Arab States	59.8	37.1	62.0	65.5	41.2	62.9	69.4	44.1	63.5
Latin America/Caribbean	43.8	24.5	56.0	42.9	23.4	54.7	41.2	21.9	53.3
Eastern Asia/Oceania	258.5	177.8	68.8	209.9	149.5	71.2	152.9	112.7	73.7
of which: China	205.4	141.6	68.9	166.2	119.5	71.9	118.4	89.1	75.3
Southern Asia	370.4	224.3	60.6	415.5	256.1	61.6	456.1	285.0	62.5
of which: India	265.9	164.0	61.7	290.7	182.7	62.8	308.8	196.6	63.7
Least developed countries	144.7	87.0	60.2	165.9	100.8	60.7	188.1	115.1	61.2

Source: *Compendium of Statistics on Illiteracy.* Paris, UNESCO, 1995. (Statistical Reports and Studies, 35).

Table 3
Estimated adult literacy rates (percentages),[1] 1985–2005

	1985			1995			2005		
	MF	M	F	MF	M	F	MF	M	F
WORLD TOTAL	72.5	79.7	65.4	77.4	83.6	71.2	81.4	86.7	76.1
More developed regions and countries in transition	97.5	98.4	96.7	98.7	98.9	98.4	99.2	99.3	99.1
Less developed regions of which:	62.9	73.0	52.5	70.4	78.9	61.7	76.4	83.3	69.3
Sub-Saharan Africa	45.6	56.7	34.9	56.8	66.6	47.3	66.9	74.9	59.2
Arab States	46.4	59.9	32.2	56.6	68.4	44.2	65.9	75.6	55.9
Latin America/Caribbean	82.4	84.3	80.5	86.6	87.7	85.5	89.6	90.1	89.1
Eastern Asia/Oceania	75.2	84.7	65.3	83.6	90.6	76.3	89.8	94.7	84.7
of which: China	72.5	83.4	60.9	81.5	89.9	72.7	88.5	94.5	82.3
Southern Asia	42.9	56.3	28.5	50.2	62.9	36.6	57.2	68.8	44.9
of which: India	44.6	58.9	29.3	52.0	65.5	37.7	59.3	71.3	46.4
Least developed countries	40.5	51.9	29.2	48.8	59.5	38.1	56.7	66.3	47.0

1. Percentage of literate adults in the population aged 15 years and over. The population data utilized are those of the United Nations Population Division database (1994 revision).

Source: Compendium of Statistics on Illiteracy. Paris, UNESCO, 1995. (Statistical Reports and Studies, 35).

Table 4
Culture and communication indicators, 1985 and 1995

	Consumption of newsprint and other printing and writing paper (kgs per inhabitant)		Circulation of daily newspapers (copies per thousand inhabitants)		Radio receivers (per thousand inhabitants)		Television receivers (per thousand inhabitants)		Telephone main lines (per thousand inhabitants)	
	1985	1995	1985	1995	1985	1995	1985	1995	1985	1995
WORLD TOTAL	16.5	20.7	105	96	345	362	154	204	83	120
More developed regions of which:	80.0	110.4	310	286	1 179	1 287	559	625	401	534
North America	123.5	148.0	255	213	1 954	1 990	762	796	488	614
Asia/Oceania	61.2	108.2	519	520	828	948	552	643	375	489
Europe	55.7	82.2	268	250	754	878	415	485	347	490
Countries in transition	10.5	6.1	315	114	568	403	291	318	93	158
Less developed regions of which:	3.4	5.1	39	43	143	185	54	114	14	39
Sub-Saharan Africa	1.6	1.5	12	12	139	169	16	33	8	11
Arab States	3.3	2.7	33	37	215	251	81	109	26	46
Latin America/Caribbean	8.8	10.7	85	80	315	387	139	192	50	90
Eastern Asia/Oceania	3.9	7.3	49	57	141	199	62	170	10	44
of which: China	3.6	5.5	36	43	112	185	65	205	3	34
Southern Asia	1.4	1.9	22	27	72	88	14	43	5	15
of which: India	1.4	1.9	26	32	65	81	13	51	4	13
Least developed countries	0.4	0.4	6	7	87	115	5	11	2	3

Table 5
Enrolment (millions) and gross enrolment ratios in pre-primary education, 1985 and 1995

	Enrolment						Gross enrolment ratio (%)					
	1985			1995			1985			1995		
	MF	*F*	*%F*	*MF*	*F*	*%F*	*MF*	*M*	*F*	*MF*	*M*	*F*
WORLD TOTAL	72.5	34.7	48	95.3	45.4	48	26.7	27.2	26.3	30.1	30.6	29.5
More developed regions of which:	19.7	9.6	49	21.6	10.4	48	65.0	64.8	65.2	69.9	70.5	69.3
North America	6.7	3.3	49	8.8	4.2	48	59.4	58.8	60.0	68.1	69.5	66.6
Asia/Oceania	2.6	1.3	49	2.4	1.2	49	49.7	49.6	49.9	53.3	52.9	53.8
Europe	10.4	5.0	49	10.3	5.0	49	75.5	75.6	75.4	77.3	77.4	77.2
Countries in transition	16.3	7.9	49	13.3	6.3	47	64.1	64.9	63.4	54.0	55.7	52.4
Less developed regions of which:	36.5	17.2	47	60.4	28.6	47	16.9	17.4	16.4	23.1	23.5	22.6
Sub-Saharan Africa	1.8	0.9	47	3.1	1.5	47	7.1	7.5	6.7	9.2	9.7	8.7
Arab States	1.6	0.6	38	2.4	1.0	41	14.8	18.0	11.4	15.4	17.7	12.9
Latin America/Caribbean	9.4	4.6	49	14.2	7.0	49	35.4	35.8	35.1	51.1	50.7	51.5
Eastern Asia/Oceania	19.7	9.4	48	34.7	16.5	48	20.1	20.3	19.9	28.9	29.0	28.8
of which: China	14.8	7.0	47	27.1	12.7	47	20.0	20.4	19.5	28.7	29.0	28.2
Southern Asia	4.1	1.7	43	6.2	2.8	44	7.6	8.4	6.7	9.8	10.6	9.0
of which: India	1.2	0.6	45	2.1	1.0	46	3.2	3.3	3.0	4.8	5.0	4.5
Least developed countries	2.6	1.1	45	3.9	1.8	45	9.8	10.6	8.8	10.8	11.9	9.8

Table 6
Enrolment (millions) and gross enrolment ratios in primary education, 1985 and 1995

	Enrolment						Gross enrolment ratio (%)					
	1985			1995			1985			1995		
	MF	*F*	*%F*	*MF*	*F*	*%F*	*MF*	*M*	*F*	*MF*	*M*	*F*
WORLD TOTAL	567.2	256.5	45	650.2	299.9	46	99.1	106.0	91.8	99.6	104.8	94.2
More developed regions of which:	61.8	30.1	49	62.7	30.5	49	101.7	101.9	101.5	104.5	104.8	104.2
North America	22.5	10.9	49	26.9	13.0	49	99.5	99.8	99.3	103.3	103.8	102.7
Asia/Oceania	13.7	6.7	49	11.0	5.4	49	102.1	102.0	102.2	102.9	102.8	103.0
Europe	25.6	12.4	49	24.9	12.1	49	103.4	103.7	103.1	106.7	106.9	106.4
Countries in transition	29.8	14.5	49	28.9	14.0	49	98.7	99.0	98.4	98.1	98.6	97.6
Less developed regions of which:	475.7	211.9	45	558.6	255.4	46	98.7	106.9	90.1	99.1	105.0	92.9
Sub-Saharan Africa	57.9	25.8	45	76.5	34.6	45	76.1	84.0	68.2	73.9	80.7	67.1
Arab States	25.7	10.8	42	36.1	16.0	44	80.4	90.9	69.5	83.8	91.7	75.6
Latin America/Caribbean	70.2	34.0	48	81.7	39.5	48	105.1	107.2	103.0	110.4	112.0	108.8
Eastern Asia/Oceania	203.2	93.2	46	206.1	98.2	48	117.8	124.3	111.0	114.5	115.8	113.0
of which: China	133.7	59.9	45	132.0	62.4	47	123.2	132.0	113.9	118.3	119.4	117.1
Southern Asia	114.0	45.6	40	155.4	65.6	42	85.1	98.2	70.8	94.2	105.5	82.1
of which: India	87.4	35.2	40	109.7	47.4	43	96.0	110.5	80.3	100.3	110.1	89.8
Least developed countries	45.9	19.2	42	65.3	28.2	43	65.9	75.6	56.0	69.5	78.2	60.7

Table 7
Enrolment (millions) and gross enrolment ratios in secondary education, 1985 and 1995

| | Enrolment | | | | | | Gross enrolment ratio (%) | | | | | |
| | 1985 | | | 1995 | | | 1985 | | | 1995 | | |
	MF	F	%F	MF	F	%F	MF	M	F	MF	M	F
WORLD TOTAL	291.6	126.5	43	372.0	168.7	45	48.5	53.5	43.2	58.1	62.5	53.4
More developed regions of which:	72.3	35.5	49	75.3	37.1	49	92.3	91.7	92.9	105.8	104.8	106.9
North America	22.9	11.2	49	23.7	11.6	49	97.4	97.4	97.5	97.0	96.5	97.4
Asia/Oceania	12.9	6.4	49	13.0	6.4	49	93.0	92.0	94.1	107.8	107.3	108.3
Europe	36.4	17.9	49	38.6	19.1	49	89.1	88.3	89.9	111.4	109.8	113.1
Countries in transition	36.0	17.7	49	40.7	20.3	50	94.6	94.6	94.7	86.9	85.4	88.4
Less developed regions of which:	183.3	73.4	40	256.1	111.3	43	37.7	44.0	31.0	48.8	53.9	43.6
Sub-Saharan Africa	12.3	5.0	40	18.8	8.4	44	21.7	25.8	17.6	24.3	26.9	21.6
Arab States	12.1	4.8	40	16.9	7.5	44	44.8	52.7	36.6	53.7	58.4	48.8
Latin America/Caribbean	20.5	10.4	51	25.8	13.3	52	50.2	48.8	51.7	56.6	53.9	59.3
Eastern Asia/Oceania	80.0	33.6	42	100.7	46.4	46	41.5	47.0	35.8	61.5	64.5	58.3
of which: China	51.7	20.6	40	63.8	28.8	45	39.7	46.3	32.6	66.6	70.5	62.4
Southern Asia	56.0	18.7	33	89.2	33.8	38	33.8	43.2	23.6	44.5	53.4	35.0
of which: India	44.5	14.8	33	66.6	24.9	37	37.7	48.2	26.3	48.7	58.7	38.0
Least developed countries	10.2	3.5	34	14.6	5.5	38	16.3	21.3	11.2	18.4	22.5	14.1

Table 8
Enrolment (millions) and gross enrolment ratios in tertiary education, 1985 and 1995

| | Enrolment | | | | | | Gross enrolment ratio (%) | | | | | |
| | 1985 | | | 1995 | | | 1985 | | | 1995 | | |
	MF	F	% F	MF	F	% F	MF	M	F	MF	M	F
WORLD TOTAL	60.3	26.8	44	81.7	38.4	47	12.9	14.0	11.7	16.2	16.8	15.6
More developed regions of which:	25.1	12.2	49	34.3	17.8	52	39.3	39.4	39.2	59.6	56.0	63.3
North America	13.9	7.3	53	16.4	9.0	55	61.2	56.9	65.7	84.0	74.6	93.8
Asia/Oceania	2.9	1.1	37	5.3	2.4	46	28.1	34.5	21.4	45.3	47.9	42.6
Europe	8.2	3.8	47	12.6	6.4	51	26.9	28.2	25.6	47.8	45.9	49.8
Countries in transition	10.9	5.9	54	10.8	5.8	54	36.5	33.1	40.0	34.2	30.7	37.7
Less developed regions of which:	24.4	8.7	36	36.6	14.7	40	6.5	8.1	4.8	8.8	10.3	7.3
Sub-Saharan Africa	0.9	0.2	25	1.9	0.7	35	2.2	3.4	1.1	3.5	4.6	2.5
Arab States	2.0	0.7	33	3.1	1.3	41	10.7	14.0	7.2	12.5	14.5	10.5
Latin America/Caribbean	6.4	2.8	45	8.1	4.0	49	15.8	17.4	14.2	17.3	17.6	17.0
Eastern Asia/Oceania	9.1	3.3	36	14.3	5.7	40	5.4	6.8	3.9	8.9	10.5	7.2
of which: China	3.5	1.0	29	5.6	1.9	33	2.9	3.9	1.7	5.3	6.8	3.6
Southern Asia	5.5	1.6	29	8.0	2.7	34	5.3	7.3	3.2	6.5	8.2	4.6
of which: India	4.5	1.3	30	5.6	2.0	36	6.0	8.1	3.8	6.4	7.9	4.8
Least developed countries	1.0	0.3	26	1.7	0.5	27	2.5	3.7	1.3	3.2	4.6	1.7

Table 9
Number of teachers (thousands), by level of education, 1985 and 1995

	1985					1995				
	Pre-primary	Pri-mary	Sec-ondary	Ter-tiary	All levels	Pre-primary	Pri-mary	Sec-ondary	Ter-tiary	All levels
WORLD TOTAL	3 869	20 841	16 844	4 332	45 887	4 729	24 330	21 670	5 919	56 648
More developed regions of which:	988	3 699	5 099	1 667	11 453	1 059	3 883	5 567	2 415	12 924
North America	277	1 560	1 441	751	4 030	316	1 667	1 504	983	4 469
Asia/Oceania	126	621	775	294	1 816	138	621	962	488	2 209
Europe	585	1 518	2 882	622	5 607	605	1 595	3 101	945	6 246
Countries in transition	1 538	1 369	2 420	905	6 232	1 429	1 552	3 404	976	7 361
Less developed regions of which:	1 343	15 773	9 326	1 760	28 202	2 241	18 895	12 699	2 528	36 363
Sub-Saharan Africa	55	1 510	510	65	2 140	101	1 981	762	118	2 962
Arab States	68	970	636	108	1 782	110	1 548	1 058	167	2 882
Latin America/Caribbean	366	2 601	1 338	506	4 811	652	3 386	1 699	728	6 466
Eastern Asia/Oceania	747	7 882	4 410	698	13 736	1 215	8 418	5 975	969	16 577
of which: China	550	5 377	3 039	432	9 398	875	5 664	4 038	540	11 117
Southern Asia	107	2 657	2 315	362	5 440	165	3 429	2 998	505	7 097
of which: India	20	1 868	1 724	303	3 914	35	2 352	2 090	375	4 852
Least developed countries	70	1 097	413	50	1 629	111	1 462	630	94	2 297

Table 10
Number of teachers (all levels) per thousand population in the age-group 15–64
and percentage of female teachers by level of education, 1985 and 1995

	Number of teachers (all levels)[1] per thousand population in the age-group 15–64		Percentage of female teachers					
			1985			1995		
	1985	1995	Pre-primary	Pri-mary	Sec-ondary	Pre-primary	Pri-mary	Sec-ondary
WORLD TOTAL	16	16	94.5	54.5	43.0	94.0	57.8	47.2
More developed regions of which:	22	23	92.4	76.6	48.3	92.9	78.9	52.4
North America	23	23	94.4	83.5	53.5	93.6	84.7	56.6
Asia/Oceania	19	21	89.5	60.1	32.3	90.3	64.8	38.8
Europe	23	24	92.1	76.2	50.0	93.1	78.3	54.6
Countries in transition	24	27	99.8	84.8	63.6	99.7	88.3	66.5
Less developed regions of which:	13	13	90.0	46.7	34.7	90.8	51.0	39.7
Sub-Saharan Africa	9	10	86.5	38.0	33.3	86.8	41.7	32.9
Arab States	17	20	49.9	47.8	35.4	68.4	53.0	41.7
Latin America/Caribbean	21	22	97.1	76.9	47.9	96.8	76.7	46.2
Eastern Asia/Oceania	14	14	96.2	44.1	32.8	95.1	50.5	39.5
of which: China	14	13	95.9	39.6	28.1	94.6	46.6	34.9
Southern Asia	9	9	46.7	29.8	30.7	48.7	31.8	37.2
of which: India	9	9	93.3	27.5	30.9	93.5	29.3	37.9
Least developed countries	7	8	42.0	29.8	25.4	40.2	34.2	27.4

1. Including tertiary education.

Table 11
Foreign students by host region and region of origin, 1995

Region of origin	WORLD	More developed regions	Countries in transition	Less developed regions	Sub-Saharan Africa	Arab States	Latin America/ Caribbean	Eastern Asia/ Oceania	Southern Asia
					Host region[1]				
WORLD	1 502 040	1 224 016	134 753	143 271	12 625	67 568	16 922	29 646	...
More developed regions of which:	439 725	403 474	15 157	21 094	3 607	248	574	14 895	...
North America	56 029	52 256	507	3 266	–	66	–	3 155	...
Asia/Oceania	82 946	70 803	2 377	9 766	–	50	3	9 557	...
Europe	300 750	280 415	12 273	8 062	3 607	132	571	2 183	...
Countries in transition	152 189	59 804	84 299	8 086	–	397	–	425	...
Less developed regions of which:	854 542	713 625	35 186	105 731	9 018	62 108	13 727	13 761	...
Sub-Saharan Africa	97 141	75 891	7 331	13 919	7 701	2 272	3 259	370	...
Arab States	177 527	104 930	13 603	58 994	–	56 677	241	596	...
Latin America/Caribbean	90 903	78 116	1 808	10 979	495	53	10 172	253	...
Eastern Asia/Oceania	348 353	330 578	3 885	13 890	822	1 953	47	10 867	...
Southern Asia	93 620	82 621	6 813	4 186	–	910	8	1 636	...
Least developed countries	37 596	27 309	5 689	4 598	911	1 511	1 752	252	...
Unspecified	55 584	47 113	111	8 360	–	4 815	2 621	565	...

– Magnitude nil. ... Data not available.
1. Refers to fifty major host countries for which data are available and does not include major host countries such as Brazil and India. Only one host country (South Africa) is covered in sub-Saharan Africa and only two (Argentina and Cuba) in Latin America/Caribbean.

Table 12
Estimated public expenditure on education, 1980–95

	US$ (billions)				Percentage of GNP			
	1980	1985	1990	1995	1980	1985	1990	1995
WORLD TOTAL	566.3	607.3	1 062.0	1 403.3	4.9	4.9	4.9	4.9
More developed regions of which:	407.8	446.4	816.4	1 109.9	5.2	5.0	5.0	5.1
North America	155.1	221.6	330.2	408.9	5.2	5.1	5.4	5.5
Asia/Oceania	63.3	69.5	133.3	224.7	5.0	4.5	4.0	4.0
Europe	189.4	155.3	352.9	476.3	5.2	5.2	5.1	5.4
Countries in transition	61.1	62.2	90.0	45.7	6.4	6.3	7.5	5.2
Less developed regions of which:	97.4	98.7	155.6	247.7	3.8	3.9	3.9	4.1
Sub-Saharan Africa	15.8	11.3	14.8	18.8	5.1	4.8	5.1	5.6
Arab States	18.0	23.7	24.4	27.5	4.1	5.8	5.2	5.2
Latin America/Caribbean	33.5	27.9	44.6	72.8	3.8	3.9	4.1	4.5
Eastern Asia/Oceania	16.0	20.1	32.0	59.9	2.8	3.1	3.0	3.0
of which: China	7.6	7.7	9.1	15.6	2.5	2.5	2.3	2.3
Southern Asia	12.8	14.7	35.8	62.6	4.1	3.3	3.9	4.3
of which: India	4.8	7.1	11.9	11.7	2.8	3.4	3.9	3.5
Least developed countries	3.5	3.1	4.3	5.3	2.9	3.0	2.7	2.5

Table 13
Estimated public current expenditure per pupil, by level of education, 1985 and 1995

	Number of countries		All levels		Pre-primary + primary		Secondary		Pre-primary + primary + secondary		Tertiary	
			US$	% of GNP per capita	US$	% of GNP per capita	US$	% of GNP per capita	US$	% of GNP per capita	US$	% of GNP per capita
WORLD TOTAL	113	1985	683	22.4	...	...	...	...	532	17.5	2 011	66.1
		1995	1 273	22.0	...	...	...	...	1 052	18.2	3 370	58.2
More developed regions	22	1985	2 344	20.5	...	...	...	...	1 982	17.3	3 498	30.5
		1995	4 979	21.4	...	...	...	...	4 636	19.9	5 936	25.5
of which:												
North America	2	1985	3 107	19.0	...	...	...	...	2 900	17.8	3 761	23.0
		1995	5 150	22.0	...	...	...	...	5 021	21.5	5 596	23.9
Asia/Oceania	4	1985	2 131	19.7	...	...	...	...	1 823	16.9	3 720	34.4
		1995	5 727	18.3	...	...	...	...	5 390	17.2	5 488	17.5
Europe	16	1985	1 803	22.1	...	...	...	...	1 385	16.9	2 975	36.4
		1995	4 552	22.7	...	...	...	...	4 062	20.3	6 585	32.9
Countries in transition	26	1985	571	22.7	...	...	...	...	473	18.8	666	26.5
		1995	432	20.5	...	...	...	...	377	17.9	457	21.7
Less developed regions	65	1985	101	17.5	...	...	...	...	74	12.8	602	103.9
		1995	217	17.7	...	...	...	...	165	13.5	967	78.9
of which:												
Sub-Saharan Africa	23	1985	92	29.0	52	16.4	183	57.5	72	22.6	1 531	481.5
		1995	87	30.4	49	17.0	165	57.6	66	23.2	1 241	433.9
Arab States	9	1985	476	24.9	...	...	...	...	364	19.0	2 211	115.6
		1995	444	20.5	...	...	...	...	360	16.6	1 588	73.5
Latin America/Caribbean	18	1985	211	11.7	106	5.9	266	14.8	153	8.5	548	30.4
		1995	444	12.9	312	9.1	451	13.1	352	10.2	937	27.2
Eastern Asia/Oceania	8	1985	60	13.8	31	7.2	79	18.1	44	10.1	406	93.1
		1995	155	15.3	89	8.8	182	18.1	116	11.5	709	70.3
Southern Asia	5	1985	77	17.8	46	10.7	76	17.7	56	13.0	333	77.6
		1995	223	18.8	121	10.2	253	21.3	168	14.1	1 058	89.1
Least developed countries	17	1985	34	17.7	19	9.7	50	26.0	25	12.9	299	153.9
		1995	33	16.6	19	9.2	59	29.2	26	12.8	252	125.6

Table 14
Expenditure on educational development co-operation by bilateral and multilateral agencies, 1980–95[1] (millions of current US dollars)

Agency	1980	1985	1988	1990	1991	1992	1993	1994	1995
I. Bilateral[2]	3 395	2 301	3 516	3 642	3 589	3 465	3 740	4 419	4 450
II. Multilateral banks and funds[3]	668	1 394	1 212	2 083	2 640	2 852	3 222	3 265	2 717
African Development Bank	27	116	48	148	177	310	127	14	+
Arab Multilateral[4]	17	49	20	2	+	+	55	1	1
Asian Development Bank	65	67	180	291	182	236	387	88	358
Caribbean Development Bank	1	1	3	3	2	10	5	1	20
European Development Fund[5]	34	30	81	43	3	89	106	124	53
Inter-American Development Bank	67	126	22	61	195	261	495	969	107
Islamic Development Bank	17	45	18	43	23	32	26	53	55
OPEC[6] Fund	+	32	8	5	56	30	15	7	66
World Bank	440	928	832	1 487	2 002	1 884	2 006	2 008	2 057
III. United Nations programmes and funds									
UNDP[7]	31	16	17	18	16	12	10	7	7
UNFPA[8]	3	4	5	8	8	5	4	6	7
UNICEF[9]	34	33	37	57	48	72	72	87	85
WFP[10]	...	...	99	129	125	133	119	79	106
UNESCO[11]	78	88	78	73	73	82	82	100	100
Memo Item:									
World GDP deflator (1990=100)[12]	21	42	63	100	117	137	165	198	215

+ Amount less than US$0.5 million.
.... Data not available.

1. Financial year for each agency.
2. Official Development Assistance (ODA, as defined by OECD), by OECD donor countries, members of the Development Assistance Committee (DAC). The Members of the Development Assistance Committee are Australia, Austria, Belgium, Canada, Denmark, Finland, France, Germany, Ireland, Italy, Japan, Luxembourg, Netherlands, New Zealand, Norway, Portugal, Spain, Sweden, Switzerland, United Kingdom of Great Britain and Northern Ireland, United States of America, and the Commission of the European Communities.
3. New loan, credit or grant approvals, net of cancellation of previous loans or credits.
4. Includes Arab Fund for Economic and Social Development (AFESD) and Arab Gulf Programme for United Nations Development Organizations (AGFUND).
5. Figures refer to technical and financial co-operation by the European Development Fund (EDF) outside the European Union in the African, Caribbean and Pacific (ACP) countries.
6. Organization of the Petroleum Exporting Countries.
7. United Nations Development Programme; figures refer to expenditure by UNESCO on account of education projects financed by UNDP.
8. United Nations Population Fund; figures refer to education projects implemented by UNESCO.
9. United Nations Children's Fund.
10. World Food Programme.
11. Approved programme and budget for education.
12. Taken from *International Financial Statistics,* Washington, D.C., International Monetary Fund, 1997.

Source: Annual reports of the various agencies.

III. World education indicators

THIS APPENDIX contains eleven tables of statistical indicators relating to selected aspects of education and its demographic, socio-economic, cultural and communications setting in 190 countries and territories.

The particular selection of indicators shown in this and previous editions of the *World Education Report* basically represents a compromise between the demands of a wide range of users on the one hand and the availability of data on the other. The majority of the indicators are updated in each edition of the report; a minority are new (indicated by * in the Explanatory notes below), being selected for their particular relevance to the themes of the report, or, in a few cases, because new data have become available. An important consideration in selecting any particular indicator is that the relevant data should be available for a number of countries belonging to all major regions of the world, and not just for countries in only one or two regions.

Improvement of the comparability, scope and depth of coverage of the world education indicators, and of international educational statistics generally, is a long term task; the main constraints were evoked in the *World Education Report 1993* (pp. 108–9).

During the biennium 1996–1997, the Organization's efforts to improve international educational statistics were concentrated on the revision of the International Standard Classification of Education (ISCED), in collaboration with the Organisation for Economic Co-operation and Development (OECD) and the statistical office of the European Union (EUROSTAT). The revised ISCED terminology for the levels of education – 'primary', 'secondary', and 'tertiary' – is used in the present report in place of the old terms 'first', 'second', and 'third', although the data reported for each level are based on the previous ISCED criteria.

Explanatory notes

General notes

Data refer to the year indicated or to the nearest year for which data are available. For educational indicators the year indicated is that in which the school year begins; e.g. 1995 refers to the school year 1995/96. Expenditure indicators refer to the financial year.

Certain indicators such as enrolment ratios, dependency ratios and illiteracy rates were not calculated for some countries because of inconsistencies between enrolment and population data and/or the unavailability of population data by age.

Due to the more comprehensive definition of the scope of education used in the recent common UNESCO/OECD/EUROSTAT surveys, 1995 data for OECD countries are not strictly comparable with those for 1985, particularly as regards secondary and tertiary education.

Enrolment data for Cyprus do not include Turkish schools.

Data provided for the Democratic Republic of the Congo refer to former Zaire.

Data presented for Jordan, with the exception of data on population in Table 1, refer to the East Bank only.

The following symbols are used:

–	Magnitude nil.
0 or 0.0	Magnitude less than half the unit employed.
...	Data not available.
.	Category not applicable.
♦ or #	The explanation of these symbols is given below for each specific indicator.
./.	Data included elsewhere with another category.

Table notes

Table 1. Population and GNP

Total population. Estimates of 1995 population, in thousands.

Population growth rate. Average annual percentage growth rate of total population between 1985 and 1995.

Dependency ratios. Populations in the age-groups 0–14 and 65 years and over, expressed as percentages of the population in the age-group 15–64.

Urban population. Number of persons living in urban

areas, expressed as a percentage of the total population. 'Urban areas' are defined according to national criteria, which affects the comparability between countries.

Life expectancy at birth. The average number of years a newborn infant would live if prevailing patterns of mortality at the time of its birth were to stay the same throughout its life.

Total fertility rate. The average number of children that would be born alive to a woman during her lifetime if she were to bear children at each age in accord with prevailing age-specific fertility rates.

Infant mortality rate. The number of deaths of infants under 1 year of age per 1,000 live births in a given year. More specifically, the probability of dying between birth and exactly 1 year of age times 1,000.

GNP per capita. Gross national product per capita in 1995 US dollars, the average annual growth rate of GNP per capita between 1985 and 1995 in constant prices, and estimates of GNP per capita based on purchasing power parities (PPP). The figures are extracted from the World Development Indicators 1997 of the World Bank.

Table 2. Literacy, culture and communication

Estimated number of adult illiterates. Estimated number of adult illiterates (15 years and over), in thousands, and the percentage of female illiterates, 1985 and 1995.

Estimated adult illiteracy rate. Estimated number of adult illiterates (15 years and over) expressed as a percentage of the population in the corresponding age-group.

Number of volumes in public libraries. Number of books and bound periodicals in public libraries per 1,000 inhabitants.

Daily newspapers. Estimated circulation of daily newspapers, expressed in number of copies per 1,000 inhabitants.

Radio and television receivers. Number of radio and television receivers per 1,000 inhabitants. The indicators are based on estimates of the number of receivers in use.

Main telephone lines. Number of telephone lines per

1,000 inhabitants connecting a customer's equipment to the switched network and which have a dedicated port on a telephone exchange.

Table 3. Enrolment in pre-primary education and access to schooling

Age-group in pre-primary education. Population age-group that according to the national regulations can be enrolled at this level of education.

The symbol ♦ is shown when there has been a change in the duration of pre-primary school between 1985 and 1995.

Gross enrolment ratio, pre-primary. Total enrolment in education preceding primary education, regardless of age, expressed as a percentage of the population age-group corresponding to the national regulations for this level of education.

Apparent intake rate, primary education. Number of new entrants into first grade of primary education, regardless of age, expressed as a percentage of the population of official admission age to primary education.

The symbol ♦ is shown when enrolment data including repeaters are used instead of new entrants.

School life expectancy. The school life expectancy, or expected number of years of formal education, is the number of years a child is expected to remain at school, or university, including years spent on repetition. It is the sum of the age-specific enrolment ratios for primary, secondary and tertiary education.

Table 4. Primary education: duration, population and enrolment ratios

Duration of compulsory education. Number of years of compulsory education, according to the regulations in force in each country.

Duration of primary education. Number of grades (years) in primary education, according to the education system in force in each country in 1995.

The symbol ♦ is shown when there has been a change in the duration between 1985 and 1995.

School-age population. Population, in thousands, of the

age-group which officially corresponds to primary schooling.

Gross enrolment ratio/Net enrolment ratio. The gross enrolment ratio is the total enrolment in primary education, regardless of age, divided by the population of the age-group which officially corresponds to primary schooling. The net enrolment ratio only includes enrolment for the age-group corresponding to the official school age of primary education. All ratios are expressed as percentages.

Table 5. Primary education: internal efficiency

Percentage of repeaters. Total number of pupils who are enrolled in the same grade as the previous year, expressed as a percentage of the total enrolment in primary education.

Percentage of a cohort reaching Grade 2 and Grade 5. Percentage of children starting primary school who eventually attain Grade 2 or Grade 5 (Grade 4, if the duration of primary education is four years). The estimate is based on the Reconstructed Cohort Method, which uses data on enrolment and repeaters for two consecutive years. (See Birger Fredriksen, *Statistics of Education in Developing Countries: An Introduction to their Collection and Analysis,* Paris, UNESCO, 1983. (Training Seminars on Education Statistics, Basic Background Material, Book 3.) (Document ST-83/WS/1.))

The symbol ♦ is shown when data on repeaters are missing for the year shown and the Apparent Cohort Method was used for estimating survival. When repetition rates are relatively high and vary between grades this method may overestimate or underestimate the survival rate.

Table 6. Secondary education: duration, population and enrolment ratios

Duration of secondary general education, lower and upper. Number of grades (years) in secondary general education, according to the education system in force in each country in 1995.

The symbol ♦ is shown when there has been a change in the duration between 1985 and 1995.

School-age population. Population, in thousands, of the age-group which officially corresponds to secondary general education.

Gross enrolment ratio/Net enrolment ratio. The gross enrolment ratio is the total enrolment in secondary education, regardless of age, divided by the population of the age-group which officially corresponds to secondary schooling. The net enrolment ratio only includes enrolment for the age-group corresponding to the official school age of secondary education. All ratios are expressed as percentages.

Table 7. Teaching staff in pre-primary, primary and secondary education

Pupil-teacher ratio. This ratio represents the average number of pupils per teacher at the level of education specified. Since teaching staff includes in principle both full- and part-time teachers, comparability of these ratios may be affected as the proportion of part-time teachers varies from one country to another. For secondary education the ratio refers to general education only.

Percentage of female teachers. The number of female teachers, at the level specified, expressed as a percentage of the total number of teachers at the same level. For secondary education, the data refer to general education only.

*Teachers per 1,000 non-agricultural labour force *.* Total number of teachers in pre-primary, primary, secondary and tertiary education expressed as per 1,000 of the economically active population engaged in non-agricultural activities. The economically active population refers to the adult population and covers all employed and unemployed persons.

Table 8. Tertiary education: enrolment and breakdown by ISCED level

Number of students per 100,000 inhabitants. Number of students enrolled in tertiary education (or higher education) per 100,000 inhabitants.

*Gross enrolment ratios *.* Total enrolment in tertiary education regardless of age, expressed as a percentage of the population in the five-year age-group following on from the secondary-school leaving age.

Percentage of students by ISCED level. Enrolment in higher education at each ISCED level as a percentage of total enrolment.

Percentage of female students in each ISCED level. Female enrolment as a percentage of total (male and female) enrolment at the level specified.

Definitions of ISCED level categories within higher education:

Level 5: first stage of tertiary education, of the type that leads to an award not equivalent to a first university degree.

Level 6: first stage of tertiary education, of the type that leads to a first university degree or equivalent.

Level 7: second stage of tertiary education, of the type that leads to a postgraduate degree or equivalent.

When the symbol ♦ is shown, data refer to universities only.

When the symbol ./. is shown, data are included with level 6.

When the symbol # is shown, data do not include students at ISCED level 7, for which registration is not required.

Table 9. Tertiary education: students and graduates by broad field of study, 1995

Percentage of students and graduates by field of study. Enrolment in tertiary education, in the broad field of study specified, expressed as a percentage of the total enrolment in tertiary education. Figures in parentheses refer to graduates. The total may not add to 100 per cent due to 'other' or 'unspecified' fields. The distribution is shown only for countries where the percentage of students in 'other' or 'unspecified' fields is less than 25 per cent.

Percentage of female students in each field of study. Number of female students in each broad field of study, expressed as a percentage of the total (male and female) enrolment in the field specified.

Gender segregation index. This index is defined as the percentage of all persons enrolled in tertiary edu-

cation who would need to change their field of study if the ratio of females to males were to be the same in all fields of study, assuming that in each field of study there is no change in the total enrolment. The index shown in this table is calculated on the basis of enrolments in the five broad fields of study mentioned below, plus the residual field 'other'. The index is calculated only for countries where the percentage of students in 'other' is less than 25 per cent.

For an explanation of the calculation of this index, see Appendix I of the *World Education Report 1995.*

ISCED fields of study are grouped into the following broad fields of study:

Education: education science and teacher training.

Humanities: humanities; fine and applied arts; religion and theology. When the symbol ./. is shown, humanities are included with education.

Law and social sciences: law; social and behavioural sciences; commercial and business administration; home economics; mass communication and documentation; service trades.

Natural sciences, engineering and agriculture: natural sciences; engineering; mathematics and computer sciences; architecture and town planning; transport and communications; trade, craft and industrial programmes; agriculture, forestry and fisheries.

Medical sciences: medical and health related sciences.

When the symbol ♦ is shown, data refer to universities only.

When the symbol # is shown, data do not include students at ISCED level 7, for which registration is not required.

Table 10. Private enrolment and public expenditure on education

Private enrolment as percentage of total enrolment. Enrolment in private schools, at the level specified, expressed as a percentage of the total enrolment at the same level. Government-aided schools are considered as private if they are privately managed. For secondary education, data refer to general education only.

Public expenditure on education as percentage of GNP. Total public expenditure on education expressed as a percentage of the Gross National Product (for Cuba as a percentage of Global Social Product).

The symbol ♦ is shown when total public expenditure on education refers to expenditure of the Ministry of Education only.

Public expenditure on education as percentage of government expenditure. Total public expenditure on education expressed as a percentage of total government expenditure.

The symbol ♦ is shown when total public expenditure on education refers to expenditure of the Ministry of Education only.

Average annual growth rate of public expenditure on education. The average annual growth rate between 1985 and 1995 refers to the growth of total public expenditure on education in constant prices (data are deflated by using the implicit gross domestic product (GDP) deflator); it has been computed by fitting a trend line to the logarithmic values of data on expenditure (actual or estimated) for each year of the period.

Current expenditure as percentage of total. Public current expenditure on education, expressed as a percentage of total public expenditure on education.

Table 11. Public current expenditure on education

Teachers' emoluments as percentage of total current expenditure. Expenditure on emoluments of teaching staff expressed as a percentage of total public current expenditure on education.

The symbol ♦ is shown when the indicator refers to the emoluments of total personnel (administrative staff, teaching staff and other personnel).

Percentage distribution of current expenditure by level. Public current expenditure by level, expressed as a percentage of total public current expenditure on education. The total may not add to 100 due to expenditure on 'other types of education' and/or expenditure not distributed by level of education.

Current expenditure per pupil/student as a percentage of GNP per capita. Public current expenditure per pupil/student, at each level of education, expressed as a percentage of GNP per capita.

When the symbol ./. is shown, data are included with pre-primary and primary education.

Data sources

Population and demographic indicators: United Nations Population Division database (1996 revision).

GNP and GNP per capita: World Bank, World Development Indicators 1997.

Illiteracy: Estimates and projections by the UNESCO Division of Statistics based on actual country data supplied by the United Nations Statistical Division or drawn from national publications.

Education, culture and communication: UNESCO Division of Statistics.

Main telephone lines: International Telecommunication Union, World Telecommunication Indicators 1996.

Non-agricultural, economically active population: Food and Agriculture Organization of the United Nations (FAO) (1997 revision).

Table 1
Population and GNP

Country or territory	Population							Life expectancy at birth (years)	Total fertility rate (births per woman)	Infant mortality rate (per 1,000 live births)	GNP per capita		
	Total (000)	Average annual growth rate (%)	Dependency ratio				Percentage urban				Average annual growth rate		PPP (International dollars)
			Age 0–14		Age 65 and over						US$	rate (%)	
	1995	1985–95	1985	1995	1985	1995	1995	1995	1995	1995	1995	1985–95	1995
Africa													
Algeria	28 109	2.5	85	68	8	6	56	69	3.8	44	1 600	−2.6	5 300
Angola	10 816	3.1	90	96	6	6	31	47	6.7	124	410	−6.1	1 310
Benin	5 409	3.0	94	100	7	6	38	55	5.8	84	370	−0.4	1 760
Botswana	1 450	3.0	92	80	4	4	60	50	4.5	56	3 020	6.0	5 580
Burkina Faso	10 479	2.9	95	95	6	5	16	46	6.6	97	230	−0.1	780
Burundi	6 064	2.5	86	92	7	6	8	47	6.3	114	160	−1.3	630
Cameroon	13 192	2.8	87	85	7	7	45	56	5.3	58	650	−7.0	2 110
Cape Verde	386	2.2	88	77	11	8	54	67	3.6	41	960	2.1	1 870
Central African Republic	3 273	2.3	79	78	8	7	39	49	5.0	96	340	−2.0	1 070
Chad	6 335	2.4	78	83	7	7	22	48	5.5	115	180	0.5	700
Comoros	612	3.2	96	91	5	5	30	58	5.5	82	470	−1.4	1 320
Congo	2 593	3.0	88	89	7	7	58	51	5.9	90	680	−3.2	2 050
Côte d'Ivoire	13 694	3.3	95	85	5	5	43	51	5.1	86	660	−4.3	1 580
Dem. Rep. of the Congo	45 453	3.7	93	94	6	6	29	53	6.2	89	120	−8.5	490
Djibouti	601	4.4	81	74	5	5	82	50	5.4	106	...	...	...
Egypt	62 096	2.2	70	66	7	7	45	66	3.4	54	790	1.1	3 820
Equatorial Guinea	400	2.5	76	82	8	8	42	50	5.5	107	380	2.3	...
Eritrea	3 171	1.6	82	83	5	6	17	51	5.3	98	...	...	...
Ethiopia	56 404	3.2	87	90	6	6	15	50	7.0	107	100	−0.5	450
Gabon	1 076	3.0	61	68	10	11	50	56	5.4	85	3 490	−1.6	...
Gambia	1 111	4.1	81	73	5	5	29	47	5.2	122	320	0.3	930
Ghana	17 338	3.1	87	86	5	6	36	58	5.3	73	390	1.5	1 990
Guinea	7 349	4.0	91	94	5	5	29	47	6.6	124	550	1.4	...
Guinea-Bissau	1 069	2.0	72	78	7	8	22	44	5.4	132	250	1.8	790
Kenya	27 150	3.2	107	90	7	6	29	55	4.9	65	280	0.1	1 380
Lesotho	2 027	2.6	81	78	8	7	24	59	4.9	72	770	1.5	1 780
Liberia	2 123	−0.4	86	79	7	7	45	52	6.3	153	...	...	...
Libyan Arab Jamahiriya	5 407	3.6	91	87	5	5	85	66	5.9	56	...	...	...
Madagascar	14 874	3.4	91	93	5	5	26	59	5.7	77	230	−2.0	640
Malawi	9 673	2.9	93	93	5	5	13	41	6.7	142	170	−0.7	750
Mali	10 795	3.2	92	95	5	5	27	48	6.6	149	250	0.6	550
Mauritania	2 274	2.6	87	80	6	6	51	54	5.0	92	460	0.5	1 540
Mauritius	1 117	1.0	50	42	7	9	41	72	2.3	15	3 380	5.7	13 210
Morocco	26 524	2.1	76	61	7	7	52	67	3.1	51	1 110	0.8	3 340
Mozambique	17 260	2.5	82	87	6	6	34	47	6.1	110	80	3.6	810
Namibia	1 536	2.7	81	79	7	7	36	56	4.9	60	2 000	2.8	4 150
Niger	9 151	3.3	94	98	5	5	18	49	7.1	114	220	−2.1	750
Nigeria	111 721	3.0	86	88	5	5	40	52	6.0	77	260	1.2	1 220
Rwanda	5 184	−1.5	99	91	5	4	6	42	6.0	125	180	−5.0	540
Sao Tome and Principe	133	2.3	...	...	...	...	43	...	...	...	350	−2.1	...
Senegal	8 312	2.7	89	85	6	6	44	51	5.6	62	600	−1.2	1 780
Seychelles	73	1.2	...	...	...	...	54	...	...	...	6 620	4.2	...
Sierra Leone	4 195	1.6	81	83	6	6	33	38	6.1	169	180	−3.4	580
Somalia	9 491	1.9	92	95	6	5	26	49	7.0	112	...	...	...
South Africa	41 465	2.3	72	64	7	8	49	65	3.8	48	3 160	−1.0	5 030
Sudan	26 707	2.2	86	74	5	5	31	55	4.6	71	...	0.6	...
Swaziland	857	2.8	97	79	7	5	31	60	4.5	65	1 170	0.6	2 880
Togo	4 085	3.0	87	90	6	6	31	50	6.1	86	310	−2.8	1 130
Tunisia	8 987	2.1	70	58	7	7	62	70	2.9	37	1 820	1.8	5 000

Country or territory	Population							Life expectancy at birth (years)	Total fertility rate (births per woman)	Infant mortality rate (per 1,000 live births)	GNP per capita		
	Total (000)	Average annual growth rate (%)	Dependency ratio				Percentage urban				Average annual growth rate		PPP (International dollars)
			Age 0–14		Age 65 and over						US$	(%)	
	1995	1985–95	1985	1995	1985	1995	1995	1995	1995	1995	1995	1985–95	1995
Uganda	19 689	2.9	96	99	5	5	13	41	7.1	113	240	2.8	1 470
United Rep. of Tanzania	30 026	3.3	93	89	5	5	24	51	5.5	80	120	0.9	640
Zambia	8 081	2.3	103	97	5	5	43	43	5.5	103	400	−1.0	930
Zimbabwe	11 190	2.9	90	84	5	5	32	49	4.7	68	540	−0.6	2 030
America, North													
Antigua and Barbuda	66	0.6	...	...	...	...	36	...	...	...	...	2.7	...
Bahamas	279	1.9	59	44	7	8	86	74	2.0	14	11 940	−1.0	14 710
Barbados	261	0.3	44	36	19	18	47	76	1.7	9	6 560	−0.2	10 620
Belize	213	2.5	92	77	8	8	47	75	3.7	30	2 630	4.4	5 400
British Virgin Islands	19	3.1	...	...	...	...	56	...	...	...	...	...	...
Canada	29 402	1.3	31	30	15	18	77	79	1.6	6	19 380	0.4	21 130
Costa Rica	3 424	2.6	62	58	7	8	49	77	3.0	12	2 610	2.9	5 850
Cuba	10 964	0.8	41	33	13	13	76	76	1.6	9	...	...	...
Dominica	71	−0.1	...	...	...	...	69	...	...	...	2 990	4.0	...
Dominican Republic	7 823	2.1	68	58	6	7	62	71	2.8	34	1 460	2.1	3 870
El Salvador	5 662	1.9	86	64	7	7	45	70	3.1	39	1 610	2.9	2 610
Grenada	92	0.2	...	...	...	...	36	...	...	...	2 980	...	...
Guatemala	10 621	2.9	90	85	6	7	39	67	4.9	40	1 340	0.3	3 340
Haiti	7 124	2.0	73	72	8	7	32	54	4.6	82	250	−5.2	910
Honduras	5 654	3.1	91	83	6	6	44	70	4.3	35	600	0.2	1 900
Jamaica	2 468	0.7	65	51	13	11	54	75	2.4	12	1 510	3.7	3 540
Mexico	91 145	1.9	78	59	7	7	73	73	2.8	31	3 320	0.1	6 400
Netherlands Antilles	194	0.6	43	40	11	12	69	76	2.1	10	...	...	...
Nicaragua	4 123	2.6	95	82	5	6	62	68	3.9	44	380	−5.8	2 000
Panama	2 631	2.0	65	54	8	9	56	74	2.6	21	2 750	−0.4	5 980
Saint Kitts and Nevis	41	−0.5	...	...	...	...	34	...	...	...	5 170	4.6	9 410
Saint Lucia	142	1.4	...	...	...	...	37	...	...	...	3 370	3.9	...
Saint Vincent and the Grenadines	107	0.5	...	...	...	...	48	...	...	...	2 280	3.9	...
Trinidad and Tobago	1 287	0.9	55	48	9	10	72	74	2.1	14	3 770	−1.6	8 610
United States	267 115	1.0	33	34	18	19	76	77	2.0	7	26 980	1.4	26 980
America, South													
Argentina	34 768	1.4	51	47	14	15	88	73	76.8	22	8 030	1.9	8 310
Bolivia	7 414	2.3	78	73	7	7	61	62	4.4	66	800	1.7	2 540
Brazil	159 015	1.6	62	50	7	7	78	67	2.2	42	3 640	−0.7	5 400
Chile	14 210	1.7	49	46	9	10	84	75	2.4	13	4 160	6.1	9 520
Colombia	35 814	2.0	62	56	7	7	73	71	2.7	24	1 910	2.8	6 130
Ecuador	11 460	2.3	75	61	7	7	59	70	3.1	46	1 390	0.8	4 220
Guyana	830	0.5	62	51	6	6	35	64	2.3	58	590	0.8	2 420
Paraguay	4 828	3.0	78	76	8	6	52	70	4.2	39	1 690	1.1	3 650
Peru	23 532	1.9	72	60	7	7	71	68	3.0	45	2 310	−1.6	3 770
Suriname	427	1.3	63	58	7	8	49	72	2.4	24	880	0.7	2 250
Uruguay	3 186	0.6	43	39	18	19	90	73	2.3	17	5 170	3.3	6 630
Venezuela	21 844	2.5	68	61	6	7	86	73	3.0	21	3 020	0.5	7 900
Asia													
Afghanistan	19 661	3.1	75	73	5	5	20	46	6.9	154	...	...	...
Armenia	3 632	0.8	47	45	8	12	69	71	1.7	25	730	−15.1	2 260
Azerbaijan	7 531	1.2	53	52	8	9	56	71	2.3	33	480	−16.3	1 460
Bahrain	557	3.0	48	48	3	4	90	73	3.0	18	7 840	0.6	13 400

World education report

Table 1 (continued)

Country or territory	Total (000) 1995	Average annual growth rate (%) 1985–95	Dependency ratio Age 0–14 1985	Age 0–14 1995	Age 65 and over 1985	Age 65 and over 1995	Percentage urban 1995	Life expectancy at birth (years) 1995	Total fertility rate (births per woman) 1995	Infant mortality rate (per 1,000 live births) 1995	US$ 1995	Average annual growth rate (%) 1985–95	PPP (International dollars) 1995
						Population					GNP per capita		
Bangladesh	118 229	1.8	86	75	6	6	18	58	3.1	78	240	2.1	1 380
Bhutan	1 770	2.0	76	79	6	6	6	53	5.9	104	420	4.0	1 260
Brunei Darussalam	293	2.8	63	53	5	4	69	76	2.7	9	...	...	...
Cambodia	10 024	3.1	69	78	5	5	20	54	4.5	102	270	2.0	...
China	1 220 224	1.3	47	39	8	9	30	70	1.8	38	620	8.0	2 920
Cyprus	745	1.4	39	40	17	17	54	78	2.3	7	...	4.6	...
Dem. People's Rep. of Korea	22 097	1.6	49	39	6	7	61	72	2.1	22	...	...	...
Georgia	5 450	0.3	38	37	13	18	58	73	1.9	23	440	–17.0	1 470
Hong Kong	6 123	1.2	34	28	11	14	95	79	1.3	5	22 990	4.8	22 950
India	929 005	1.9	64	58	7	8	27	62	3.1	72	340	3.1	1 400
Indonesia	197 460	1.7	67	53	6	7	35	65	2.6	48	980	6.0	3 800
Iran, Islamic Republic of	68 365	3.4	88	86	6	7	59	69	4.8	39	...	0.5	5 470
Iraq	20 095	2.8	87	79	5	5	75	62	5.3	95	...	...	...
Israel	5 525	2.7	56	48	15	15	91	78	2.8	7	15 920	2.5	16 490
Japan	125 068	0.3	32	23	15	20	78	80	1.5	4	39 640	2.9	22 110
Jordan	5 373	3.4	92	80	6	5	71	70	5.1	30	1 510	–2.8	4 060
Kazakhstan	16 817	0.6	51	47	9	11	60	68	2.3	34	1 330	–8.6	3 010
Kuwait	1 691	–0.2	60	65	2	3	97	76	2.8	14	17 390	0.9	23 790
Kyrgyzstan	4 460	1.1	64	64	9	10	39	68	3.2	39	700	–6.9	1 800
Lao People's Dem. Rep.	4 882	3.1	78	86	5	6	21	54	6.7	86	350	2.7	...
Lebanon	3 009	1.2	65	56	9	9	88	70	2.8	29	2 660	2.7	...
Macau	430	3.5	37	38	10	10	99	78	1.6	8	...	...	...
Malaysia	20 140	2.5	67	65	6	7	54	72	3.2	11	3 890	5.7	9 020
Maldives	254	3.3	89	94	6	7	27	65	6.8	49	990	6.7	3 080
Mongolia	2 463	2.6	77	68	6	7	61	66	3.3	52	310	–3.8	1 950
Myanmar	45 106	1.9	69	59	7	7	26	60	3.3	78	...	...	...
Nepal	21 456	2.7	80	81	5	7	10	57	5.0	82	200	2.4	1 170
Oman	2 207	4.5	86	94	5	5	76	71	7.2	25	4 820	0.3	8 140
Pakistan	136 257	3.0	79	79	5	6	34	64	5.0	74	460	1.2	2 230
Palestinian Auton. Territories	...	.	.	...	.	...	...	...	...	...	...	.	...
Gaza Strip	792	4.2	101	113	5	6	94	68	8.0	37	...	...	...
West Bank	...	...	...	...	...	...	...	...	...	...	...	...	...
Philippines	67 839	2.2	73	66	5	6	54	68	3.6	35	1 050	1.5	2 850
Qatar	548	4.3	39	38	2	2	91	72	3.8	17	11 600	–2.6	17 690
Republic of Korea	44 909	1.0	46	33	7	8	81	72	1.7	9	9 700	7.6	11 450
Saudi Arabia	18 255	3.7	79	75	5	5	83	71	5.9	23	7 040	–1.9	8 820
Singapore	3 327	2.1	34	31	7	9	100	77	1.8	5	26 730	6.2	22 770
Sri Lanka	17 928	1.1	57	46	8	9	22	73	2.1	15	700	2.7	3 250
Syrian Arab Republic	14 203	3.2	99	86	6	6	52	69	4.0	33	1 120	1.0	5 320
Tajikistan	5 828	2.5	80	78	7	8	32	67	3.9	56	340	–13.0	920
Thailand	58 242	1.3	59	42	6	7	20	69	1.7	30	2 740	8.4	7 540
Turkey	60 838	1.9	61	49	7	8	69	69	2.5	44	2 780	2.2	5 580
Turkmenistan	4 075	2.4	73	70	7	7	45	65	3.6	57	920	–9.6	...
United Arab Emirates	2 210	3.6	40	45	2	3	84	75	3.5	15	17 400	–3.5	16 470
Uzbekistan	22 762	2.3	73	71	8	8	41	68	3.5	43	970	–3.9	2 370
Viet Nam	73 793	2.1	74	64	8	8	19	67	3.0	37	240	4.2	...
Yemen	15 027	4.5	102	95	5	5	34	58	7.6	80	260	...	...
Europe													
Albania	3 383	1.3	57	50	9	9	37	71	2.6	32	670	...	...
Austria	8 045	0.6	27	26	21	22	64	77	1.4	6	26 890	1.9	21 250

Country or territory	Population								Life expect-ancy at birth (years)	Total fertility rate (births per woman)	Infant mortality rate (per 1,000 live births)	GNP per capita		
	Total (000)	Average annual growth rate (%)	Dependency ratio				Per-centage urban					Average annual growth		PPP (Inter-national dollars)
			Age 0–14		Age 65 and over							US$	rate (%)	
	1995	1985–95	1985	1995	1985	1995	1995	1995	1995	1995	1995	1985–95	1995
Belarus	10 352	0.3	34	33	15	19	71	70	1.4	15	2 070	−5.2	4 220
Belgium	10 127	0.3	28	27	21	24	97	77	1.6	7	24 710	2.2	21 660
Bosnia and Herzegovina	3 569	−1.4	36	31	8	11	41	73	1.4	13	...	...	...
Bulgaria	8 509	−0.5	32	28	17	22	68	71	1.5	16	1 330	−2.2	4 480
Croatia	4 505	0.0	31	28	15	19	56	72	1.6	10	3 250	...	...
Czech Republic	10 263	−0.0	36	28	18	18	65	73	1.4	9	3 870	−1.8	9 770
Denmark	5 223	0.2	28	26	23	22	85	76	1.8	7	29 890	1.5	21 230
Estonia	1 488	−0.2	34	31	17	19	73	69	1.3	12	2 860	−4.3	4 220
Finland	5 107	0.4	29	28	18	21	63	77	1.8	5	20 580	−0.2	17 760
France	58 104	0.5	32	30	20	23	75	79	1.6	7	24 990	1.5	21 030
Germany	81 594	0.5	23	23	21	22	87	77	1.3	6	27 510	...	20 070
Greece	10 454	0.5	33	25	20	24	59	78	1.4	8	8 210	1.2	11 710
Hungary	10 106	−0.5	32	27	19	21	65	69	1.4	14	4 120	−1.0	6 410
Iceland	269	1.1	42	37	16	17	92	79	2.2	5	24 950	0.3	20 460
Ireland	3 546	−0.0	50	37	18	18	58	77	1.8	6	14 710	5.2	15 680
Italy	57 204	0.0	29	22	19	23	67	78	1.2	7	19 020	1.7	19 870
Latvia	2 536	−0.2	32	31	18	20	73	68	1.4	16	2 270	−6.6	3 370
Lithuania	3 736	0.5	35	33	15	18	72	70	1.5	13	1 900	−11.7	4 120
Luxembourg	407	1.0	25	26	19	20	89	76	1.8	6	41 210	1.0	37 930
Malta	367	0.6	37	33	15	16	89	77	2.1	8	...	5.1	...
Monaco	32	1.3	...	...	...	...	100	...	...	...	...	...	...
Netherlands	15 482	0.7	28	27	18	19	89	78	1.6	6	24 000	1.8	19 950
Norway	4 332	0.4	31	30	24	25	73	78	1.9	5	31 250	1.6	21 940
Poland	38 557	0.4	39	35	14	17	64	71	1.7	13	2 790	−0.4	5 400
Portugal	9 815	−0.0	36	26	19	22	36	75	1.5	8	9 740	3.7	12 670
Republic of Moldova	4 437	0.5	42	41	12	14	52	68	1.8	26	920	−8.2	...
Romania	22 728	0.0	37	30	14	17	56	70	1.4	24	1 480	−4.0	4 360
Russian Federation	148 460	0.4	34	31	14	18	76	64	1.4	19	2 240	−5.1	4 480
San Marino	25	1.3	...	...	...	...	94	...	...	...	...	...	...
Slovakia	5 338	0.4	41	34	14	16	59	71	1.5	12	2 950	−2.6	3 610
Slovenia	1 925	0.2	34	26	15	18	51	74	1.3	7	8 200	...	...
Spain	39 627	0.3	36	24	18	22	76	78	1.2	7	13 580	2.6	14 520
Sweden	8 788	0.5	27	29	28	27	83	79	1.8	5	23 750	−0.1	18 540
Switzerland	7 166	0.9	26	26	21	21	61	79	1.5	5	40 630	0.2	25 860
The FYR of Macedonia	2 156	1.2	42	37	10	12	60	73	1.9	23	860	...	...
Ukraine	51 757	0.2	32	31	17	21	70	69	1.4	18	1 630	−9.2	2 400
United Kingdom	58 079	0.3	29	30	23	24	89	77	1.7	6	18 700	1.4	19 260
Yugoslavia	10 251	0.4	36	33	13	17	57	73	1.8	19	...	...	...
Oceania													
Australia	17 866	1.3	36	32	15	18	85	78	1.9	6	18 720	1.4	18 940
Cook Islands	19	1.1	...	...	...	...	60	...	...	...	...	...	...
Fiji	784	1.2	65	56	5	6	41	73	2.8	20	2 440	2.3	5 780
Kiribati	78	1.5	...	...	...	...	36	...	...	...	920	−0.3	...
New Zealand	3 561	0.9	37	35	16	17	86	77	2.0	7	14 340	0.6	16 360
Papua New Guinea	4 301	2.3	74	69	3	5	16	58	4.7	61	1 160	2.1	2 420
Samoa	165	0.5	77	67	6	7	21	69	3.8	58	...	...	...
Solomon Islands	378	3.4	94	84	4	6	17	72	5.0	23	910	2.2	2 190
Tonga	98	0.7	...	...	...	...	41	...	...	...	1 630	0.2	...
Tuvalu	10	2.3	...	...	...	...	47	...	...	...	...	...	...
Vanuatu	169	2.5	86	81	6	7	19	67	4.4	38	1 200	−1.1	2 290

Table 2
Literacy, culture and communication

Country or territory	Estimated number of adult illiterates 1985 Total (000)	%F	1995 Total (000)	%F	Estimated adult illiteracy rate (%) 1995 Total	Male	Female	Number of volumes in public libraries (per 1,000 inhabitants) 1985	1995	Daily newspapers (number of copies per 1,000 inhabitants) 1985	1995	Radio receivers (per 1,000 inhabitants) 1985	1995	Television receivers (per 1,000 inhabitants) 1985	1995	Main telephone lines (per 1,000 inhabitants) 1985	1995
Africa																	
Algeria	6 483	63	6 582	66	38.4	26.1	51.0	...	...	26	51	219	238	69	89	25	42
Angola	...	...	...	...	...	...	...	...	...	13	11	27	34	5	7	6	6
Benin	1 632	58	1 792	60	63.0	51.3	74.2	...	7	0	1	75	92	4	6	3	5
Botswana	224	69	255	69	30.2	19.5	40.1	...	...	17	31	107	131	–	19	10	41
Burkina Faso	3 818	56	4 597	57	80.8	70.5	90.8	...	...	0	1	19	28	5	6	1	3
Burundi	1 907	62	2 221	62	64.7	50.7	77.5	...	...	0	3	53	68	0	2	1	3
Cameroon	2 723	65	2 712	67	36.6	25.0	47.9	...	...	4	6	120	152	–	24	3	4
Cape Verde	72	71	64	71	28.4	18.6	36.2	...	...	–	–	161	179	–	4	7	55
Central African Republic	908	61	760	63	40.0	31.5	47.6	...	...	–	1	58	75	2	5	1	2
Chad	1 806	63	1 868	64	51.9	37.9	65.3	0	...	0	0	229	248	–	1	0	0
Comoros	115	58	143	58	42.7	35.8	49.6	...	...	–	–	125	137	–	1	4	9
Congo	422	66	354	68	25.1	16.9	32.8	7	...	4	8	72	116	3	8	5	8
Côte d'Ivoire	3 712	55	4 339	57	59.9	50.1	70.0	...	...	5	15	131	153	51	62	6	8
Dem. Rep. of the Congo	5 740	71	5 184	73	22.7	13.4	32.3	...	...	2	3	88	98	0	2	0	0
Djibouti	141	62	181	64	53.8	39.7	67.3	...	...	–	–	77	80	31	43	10	13
Egypt	16 921	62	18 954	62	48.6	36.4	61.2	...	...	48	43	241	312	78	110	18	46
Equatorial Guinea	60	74	49	76	21.5	10.4	31.9	...	...	5	5	410	425	7	10	3	6
Eritrea	...	...	...	...	...	...	...	...	...	–	–	...	98	...	0	...	5
Ethiopia	16 577	57	19 052	57	64.5	54.5	74.7	3	...	1	2	194	193	2	4	2	2
Gabon	334	63	295	65	36.8	26.3	46.7	...	...	25	28	164	181	27	47	14	24
Gambia	301	60	403	62	61.4	47.2	75.1	119	78	6	1	141	164	–	3	3	17
Ghana	3 422	65	3 387	67	35.5	24.1	46.5	...	...	40	18	195	231	12	92	3	4
Guinea	1 970	59	2 272	61	64.1	50.1	78.1	...	...	–	–	36	44	2	9	3	2
Guinea-Bissau	292	64	282	65	45.1	32.0	57.5	...	...	7	6	34	42	...	...	6	9
Kenya	3 439	68	3 237	69	21.9	13.7	30.0	...	22	14	17	81	96	5	18	6	9
Lesotho	342	68	340	68	28.7	18.9	37.7	...	...	30	7	28	37	0	12	5	9
Liberia	864	60	1 014	62	61.7	46.1	77.6	...	...	13	16	216	318	16	26	4	2
Libyan Arab Jamahiriya	765	70	702	73	23.8	12.1	37.0	...	...	17	13	211	231	62	102	37	59
Madagascar	...	...	...	...	...	...	...	...	...	6	4	183	192	9	20	2	2
Malawi	1 973	69	2 587	69	43.6	28.1	58.2	4	25	2	3	207	256	–	–	3	4
Mali	3 420	56	3 917	57	69.0	60.6	76.9	...	...	1	4	32	46	0	2	0	2
Mauritania	651	60	806	60	62.3	50.4	73.7	...	...	–	1	142	150	0	25	2	4
Mauritius	157	64	138	62	17.1	12.9	21.2	17	...	69	112	330	367	138	222	39	131
Morocco	8 484	61	9 730	62	56.3	43.4	69.0	...	...	15	15	178	226	63	94	11	43
Mozambique	5 359	63	5 298	65	59.9	42.3	76.7	...	...	6	8	33	38	1	4	3	3
Namibia	...	...	...	...	...	...	...	...	...	17	100	127	140	14	25	38	51
Niger	3 146	55	4 081	55	86.4	79.1	93.4	...	...	1	0	45	68	2	11	1	1
Nigeria	26 626	61	26 075	63	42.9	32.7	52.7	9	5	17	17	175	197	12	55	2	4
Rwanda	1 616	62	1 695	63	39.5	30.2	48.4	...	...	1	1	55	101	–	–	0	2
Sao Tome and Principe	...	...	...	...	...	...	...	...	...	–	–	255	271	–	162	18	19
Senegal	2 602	57	3 084	58	66.9	57.0	76.8	...	2	8	6	110	120	31	38	3	10
Seychelles	...	...	...	...	...	...	...	589	...	46	41	385	548	31	137	91	178
Sierra Leone	1 569	59	1 727	61	68.6	54.6	81.8	...	...	3	5	216	250	8	12	3	4
Somalia	...	...	...	...	...	...	...	...	...	1	1	25	42	0	13	1	2
South Africa	4 373	53	4 731	51	18.2	18.1	18.3	...	...	44	31	303	316	91	109	68	95
Sudan	7 672	60	8 507	61	53.9	42.3	65.4	...	...	12	24	250	270	51	84	3	3
Swaziland	114	58	114	56	23.3	22.0	24.4	...	...	15	18	156	163	12	21	12	21
Togo	1 013	64	1 085	67	48.3	33.0	63.0	...	13	4	2	208	215	5	12	3	5
Tunisia	2 044	64	1 930	68	33.3	21.4	45.4	...	...	38	45	162	200	55	89	26	58

Country or territory	Estimated number of adult illiterates				Estimated adult illiteracy rate (%)			Culture and communication										
	1985		1995		1995			Number of volumes in public libraries (per 1,000 inhabitants)		Daily newspapers (number of copies per 1,000 inhabitants)		Radio receivers (per 1,000 inhabitants)		Television receivers (per 1,000 inhabitants)		Main telephone lines (per 1,000 inhabitants)	
	Total (000)	%F	Total (000)	%F	Total	Male	Female	1985	1995	1985	1995	1985	1995	1985	1995	1985	1995
Uganda	3 810	65	4 172	66	38.2	26.3	49.8	...	...	2	2	85	117	6	13	2	2
United Rep. of Tanzania	5 089	68	5 171	69	32.2	20.6	43.2	...	...	5	12	17	276	0	2	2	3
Zambia	1 148	67	1 082	68	21.8	14.4	28.7	...	...	15	13	78	99	14	32	6	8
Zimbabwe	947	67	940	68	14.9	9.6	20.1	...	...	24	17	60	89	21	29	12	14
America, North																	
Antigua and Barbuda	...	...	...	...	...	...	...	...	...	97	91	339	439	306	424	113	308
Bahamas	4	62	3	60	1.8	1.5	2.0	...	...	168	125	517	735	220	229	179	283
Barbados	7	67	5	65	2.6	2.0	3.2	...	668	158	157	791	900	237	284	225	345
Belize	...	...	...	...	...	...	...	633	713	18	–	530	587	–	178	42	134
British Virgin Islands	...	...	...	...	...	...	...	...	...	–	–	486	474	201	211	...	...
Canada	...	...	...	...	...	...	...	2 192	2 383	215	166	896	1053	541	714	481	590
Costa Rica	118	50	115	49	5.2	5.3	5.0	121	114	106	88	246	263	76	143	79	164
Cuba	587	58	364	55	4.3	3.8	4.7	336	575	119	119	324	351	158	228	27	32
Dominica	...	...	...	...	...	...	...	...	507	...	...	528	634	–	70	67	251
Dominican Republic	879	50	908	49	17.9	18.0	17.8	...	90	34	34	160	176	78	93	23	73
El Salvador	882	56	975	56	28.5	26.5	30.2	...	...	52	49	406	459	75	689	19	53
Grenada	...	...	...	...	...	...	...	...	...	–	–	500	598	–	348	16	27
Guatemala	2 520	58	2 627	58	44.4	37.5	51.4	...	...	31	23	57	71	26	56	43	255
Haiti	2 215	55	2 360	54	55.0	52.0	57.8	...	...	9	6	24	53	4	5	5	8
Honduras	763	52	869	50	27.3	27.4	27.3	...	...	70	42	382	409	67	88	11	29
Jamaica	279	40	254	37	15.0	19.2	10.9	...	...	60	65	398	438	93	162	33	116
Mexico	6 622	61	6 246	61	10.4	8.2	12.6	45	265	132	115	199	263	113	219	50	96
Netherlands Antilles	...	...	...	...	...	...	...	...	...	297	273	1 044	1 093	319	345	260	374
Nicaragua	634	52	822	52	34.3	35.4	33.4	...	...	50	32	250	280	59	73	13	23
Panama	170	52	161	53	9.2	8.6	9.8	...	...	113	61	185	228	162	175	78	114
Saint Kitts and Nevis	...	...	...	...	...	...	...	...	...	–	–	488	668	116	244	69	351
Saint Lucia	...	...	...	...	...	...	...	...	...	–	–	738	765	135	211	61	184
Saint Vincent and the Grenadines	...	...	...	...	...	...	...	...	2 232	–	–	539	670	59	158	53	164
Trinidad and Tobago	30	71	19	72	2.1	1.2	3.0	...	...	147	186	424	505	272	322	102	160
United States	...	...	...	...	...	...	...	...	...	260	218	2 067	2 093	786	805	494	626
America, South																	
Argentina	1 045	53	935	52	3.8	3.8	3.8	...	388	130	135	594	676	214	219	90	160
Bolivia	872	70	745	73	16.9	9.5	24.0	...	7	49	67	623	672	71	115	26	47
Brazil	18 521	53	18 331	51	16.7	16.7	16.8	...	...	48	45	362	399	185	220	48	75
Chile	585	54	485	54	4.8	4.6	5.0	78	79	108	99	332	348	145	215	44	132
Colombia	2 204	53	2 046	51	8.7	8.8	8.6	81	...	61	42	136	564	93	117	57	100
Ecuador	790	60	719	60	9.9	8.0	11.8	...	...	88	70	313	332	66	96	30	65
Guyana	19	67	11	66	1.9	1.4	2.5	...	...	98	47	448	494	–	48	23	53
Paraguay	242	61	235	59	7.9	6.5	9.4	...	...	47	41	166	180	24	93	21	34
Peru	1 935	73	1 736	76	11.3	5.5	17.0	298	...	82	85	205	259	77	106	21	47
Suriname	24	67	19	66	7.0	4.9	9.0	...	...	146	101	610	679	119	141	73	130
Uruguay	108	47	65	45	2.7	3.1	2.3	...	...	226	235	585	609	166	235	96	196
Venezuela	1 366	56	1 244	54	8.9	8.2	9.7	...	151	158	206	408	458	131	169	71	111
Asia																	
Afghanistan	6 493	58	8 169	60	68.5	52.8	85.0	24	...	8	10	100	122	7	10	2	1
Armenia	...	...	...	...	...	...	...	...	3 950	...	23	...	5	...	224	127	155
Azerbaijan	...	...	...	...	...	...	...	...	4 245	...	28	...	20	...	33	71	85
Bahrain	64	55	56	55	14.8	10.9	20.6	496	...	45	126	507	575	411	467	167	242

Table 2 (continued)

Country or territory	Estimated number of adult illiterates				Estimated adult illiteracy rate (%) 1995			Culture and communication										
	1985		1995					Number of volumes in public libraries (per 1,000 inhabitants)		Daily newspapers (number of copies per 1,000 inhabitants)		Radio receivers (per 1,000 inhabitants)		Television receivers (per 1,000 inhabitants)		Main telephone lines (per 1,000 inhabitants)	
	Total (000)	%F	Total (000)	%F	Total	Male	Female	1985	1995	1985	1995	1985	1995	1985	1995	1985	1995
Bangladesh	36 818	57	45 082	58	61.9	50.6	73.9	4	...	6	6	40	47	3	6	2	2
Bhutan	554	60	558	62	57.8	43.8	71.9	...	...	–	–	12	17	–	6	1	6
Brunei Darussalam	26	66	22	67	11.8	7.4	16.6	...	...	–	68	247	273	202	239	92	240
Cambodia	...	...	...	...	...	...	...	...	...	–	–	108	112	7	9	0	0
China	205 352	69	166 173	72	18.5	10.1	27.3	239	257	36	...	112	185	65	205	3	34
Cyprus	...	...	...	...	...	...	...	...	525	128	101	294	309	142	322	205	474
Dem. People's Rep. of Korea	...	...	...	...	...	...	...	...	...	238	226	106	136	11	48	30	46
Georgia	...	...	...	...	...	...	...	...	5 735	...	...	...	551	...	468	80	103
Hong Kong	479	77	370	74	7.8	4.0	11.8	...	811	751	735	596	668	234	286	323	530
India	265 857	62	290 705	63	48.0	34.5	62.3	...	...	26	...	65	81	13	51	4	13
Indonesia	26 251	67	21 507	68	16.2	10.4	22.0	...	...	18	24	128	149	38	66	4	17
Iran, Islamic Republic of	...	...	...	...	...	...	...	...	234	26	17	204	228	53	63	27	76
Iraq	4 513	63	4 848	65	42.0	29.3	55.0	...	...	39	26	196	224	59	80	31	33
Israel	...	...	...	...	...	...	...	...	2 035	260	271	425	489	260	290	279	418
Japan	...	...	...	...	...	...	...	1 030	...	565	576	786	916	579	684	375	488
Jordan	486	73	414	75	13.4	6.6	20.6	37	...	40	47	206	251	63	80	56	73
Kazakhstan	...	...	...	...	...	...	...	...	5 642	...	...	...	384	...	256	58	118
Kuwait	313	48	200	59	21.4	17.8	25.1	185	...	221	387	311	473	262	370	129	226
Kyrgyzstan	...	...	...	...	...	...	...	...	3 134	...	12	...	114	...	34	54	76
Lao People's Dem. Rep.	1 098	63	1 170	66	43.4	30.6	55.6	...	...	4	3	120	129	–	9	2	4
Lebanon	191	68	151	67	7.6	5.3	9.7	...	...	112	110	768	891	300	366	98	82
Macau	...	...	...	...	...	...	...	...	...	817	581	320	337	–	105	134	361
Malaysia	2 345	67	2 057	67	16.5	10.9	21.9	225	541	96	139	421	432	115	164	61	166
Maldives	9	47	9	49	6.8	6.7	7.0	...	...	8	12	103	118	17	26	12	57
Mongolia	261	67	256	67	17.1	11.4	22.8	...	...	93	81	105	134	24	45	26	32
Myanmar	4 770	69	4 913	67	16.9	11.3	22.3	0	0	14	22	67	89	1	5	1	3
Nepal	7 404	57	9 149	59	72.5	59.1	86.0	...	...	8	7	27	36	1	5	1	4
Oman	...	...	...	...	...	...	...	...	5	36	29	561	580	632	657	30	79
Pakistan	40 036	57	48 693	58	62.2	50.0	75.6	...	4	11	21	84	92	13	20	5	16
Palestinian Auton. Territories	.	.	...	...	...	...	...	.	...	...	...	.	...	.	...	.	...
Gaza Strip	...	...	...	...	...	...	...	...	...	...	...	...	...	...	...	...	...
West Bank	...	...	...	...	...	...	...	...	...	...	...	...	...	...	...	...	...
Philippines	2 715	54	2 234	53	5.4	5.0	5.7	...	...	40	62	91	147	27	49	9	21
Qatar	66	30	82	27	20.6	20.8	20.1	380	252	168	146	419	438	335	401	194	223
Republic of Korea	1 246	82	697	82	2.0	0.7	3.3	92	304	245	394	946	1 024	189	334	160	415
Saudi Arabia	3 323	54	3 871	55	37.2	28.5	49.8	50	...	33	58	280	291	243	257	72	96
Singapore	257	76	196	77	8.9	4.1	13.7	...	977	261	301	572	601	314	361	315	478
Sri Lanka	1 363	68	1 241	67	9.8	6.6	12.8	...	...	24	25	159	206	28	51	5	11
Syrian Arab Republic	2 136	72	2 259	75	29.2	14.3	44.2	...	...	16	19	212	264	58	67	43	63
Tajikistan	...	...	...	...	...	...	...	...	...	...	14	...	...	...	...	39	45
Thailand	3 564	70	2 613	68	6.2	4.0	8.4	...	...	85	46	156	189	81	189	12	59
Turkey	7 580	74	7 231	76	17.7	8.3	27.6	130	184	60	118	139	164	159	189	44	212
Turkmenistan	...	...	...	...	...	...	...	...	...	...	...	...	81	...	180	50	71
United Arab Emirates	270	31	272	29	20.8	21.1	20.2	...	...	187	136	245	271	84	104	150	283
Uzbekistan	...	...	...	...	...	...	...	...	...	...	6	...	81	...	191	51	76
Viet Nam	4 332	73	2 916	73	6.3	3.5	8.8	374	173	9	8	100	106	33	43	1	11
Yemen	...	...	...	...	...	...	...	...	...	...	15	...	43	...	28	7	12
Europe																	
Albania	...	...	...	...	...	...	...	...	...	46	53	166	207	78	103	11	12
Austria	...	...	...	...	...	...	...	912	1 352	361	298	553	620	431	497	361	465

Country or territory	Estimated number of adult illiterates 1985 Total (000)	%F	1995 Total (000)	%F	Estimated adult illiteracy rate (%) 1995 Total	Male	Female	Number of volumes in public libraries (per 1,000 inhabitants) 1985	1995	Daily newspapers (number of copies per 1,000 inhabitants) 1985	1995	Radio receivers (per 1,000 inhabitants) 1985	1995	Television receivers (per 1,000 inhabitants) 1985	1995	Main telephone lines (per 1,000 inhabitants) 1985	1995
Belarus	203	87	38	73	0.5	0.3	0.6	...	5 887	245	174	245	285	250	227	101	190
Belgium	...	...	...	...	...	...	...	...	2 945	220	316	756	790	401	454	308	457
Bosnia and Herzegovina	...	...	...	...	...	...	...	...	...	...	146	...	235	...	0	...	54
Bulgaria	207	70	125	69	1.7	1.1	2.3	6 254	...	293	212	419	471	248	378	167	306
Croatia	125	66	87	64	2.4	1.8	2.9	944	...	55	50	240	266	218	255	130	269
Czech Republic	...	...	...	...	...	...	...	...	3 678	...	296	427	638	...	482	129	236
Denmark	...	...	...	...	...	...	...	6 783	6 191	363	308	953	1 034	523	574	497	613
Estonia	5	76	3	56	0.2	0.2	0.2	8 848	6 921	...	...	...	491	...	383	176	277
Finland	...	...	...	...	...	...	...	6 215	7 226	543	468	985	1 008	469	519	447	550
France	...	...	...	...	...	...	...	...	1 635	193	234	870	895	390	589	417	558
Germany	...	...	...	...	...	...	...	...	1 511	391	313	...	944	...	564	416	493
Greece	496	78	283	74	3.3	1.7	4.7	835	914	122	153	403	430	191	220	314	493
Hungary	88	62	69	62	0.8	0.7	1.0	4 670	4 479	257	169	581	643	402	433	70	185
Iceland	...	...	...	...	...	...	...	6 450	7 017	467	...	768	799	311	353	426	555
Ireland	...	...	...	...	...	...	...	3 058	3 271	193	154	577	649	256	409	199	365
Italy	1 296	64	931	64	1.9	1.4	2.4	284	...	97	100	652	822	416	446	305	434
Latvia	15	82	5	64	0.3	0.2	0.3	10 409	6 478	...	233	...	678	...	477	203	280
Lithuania	55	78	16	67	0.5	0.4	0.7	...	6 562	...	134	...	401	...	415	152	254
Luxembourg	...	...	...	...	...	...	...	1 672	...	381	332	624	639	251	381	413	565
Malta	...	...	...	...	...	...	...	851	731	163	174	517	545	683	749	246	459
Monaco	...	...	...	...	...	...	...	...	469	357	250	1 007	1 019	679	750	...	...
Netherlands	...	...	...	...	...	...	...	2 674	...	310	329	828	937	462	497	402	525
Norway	...	...	...	...	...	...	...	4 235	4 712	510	596	778	808	395	433	423	556
Poland	...	...	...	...	...	...	...	3 217	3 545	207	140	329	454	280	311	67	148
Portugal	1 251	65	827	66	10.4	7.5	13.0	...	1 264	42	41	202	245	178	326	145	361
Republic of Moldova	88	62	34	27	1.1	1.6	0.5	...	4 275	...	24	...	699	...	273	73	131
Romania	623	77	388	75	2.1	1.1	3.1	2 965	2 042	158	299	180	211	193	220	88	131
Russian Federation	2 903	89	543	73	0.5	0.3	0.6	7 850	6 624	...	122	...	340	...	377	103	170
San Marino	...	...	...	...	...	...	...	...	...	45	40	527	600	314	360	...	...
Slovakia	...	...	...	...	...	...	...	...	3 571	...	244	...	570	...	476	105	208
Slovenia	...	...	...	...	...	...	...	...	3 089	115	203	346	384	266	327	149	309
Spain	1 665	72	957	70	2.9	1.8	3.9	512	1 611	80	102	294	314	270	404	243	385
Sweden	...	...	...	...	...	...	...	5 353	5 027	526	460	868	882	464	478	628	681
Switzerland	...	...	...	...	...	...	...	3 648	...	492	371	830	851	390	419	502	613
The FYR of Macedonia	...	...	...	...	...	...	...	...	...	36	25	...	183	161	167	121	165
Ukraine	...	...	...	...	...	...	...	8 233	6 506	...	50	715	856	298	339	102	161
United Kingdom	...	...	...	...	...	...	...	...	2 232	397	344	1 007	1 433	433	448	374	502
Yugoslavia	...	...	...	...	...	...	...	1 393	1 363	43	83	...	141	174	190	118	191

Oceania

Australia	...	...	...	...	...	...	...	...	...	275	257	1 247	1 304	448	495	392	510
Cook Islands	...	...	...	...	...	...	...	...	...	117	105	612	705	–	184	...	...
Fiji	57	62	43	63	8.4	6.2	10.7	102	...	97	45	529	612	–	18	44	83
Kiribati	...	...	...	...	...	...	...	...	...	–	–	195	212	–	9	10	26
New Zealand	...	...	...	...	...	...	...	...	...	326	239	909	997	430	514	396	479
Papua New Guinea	731	63	724	65	27.8	19.0	37.3	...	...	13	15	67	77	–	4	9	10
Samoa	...	...	...	...	...	...	...	...	...	–	–	433	485	32	41	...	...
Solomon Islands	...	...	...	...	...	...	...	81	...	–	–	100	122	–	6	8	17
Tonga	...	...	...	...	...	...	...	...	...	–	71	330	571	–	16	29	67
Tuvalu	...	...	...	...	...	...	...	...	...	–	–	238	320	–	–	...	...
Vanuatu	...	...	...	...	...	...	...	...	...	–	–	269	296	–	13	12	25

Table 3
Enrolment in pre-primary education and access to schooling

Country or territory	Age-group	Pre-primary education							Access to schooling					
		Gross enrolment ratio (%)				Apparent intake rate in primary education (%)			School life expectancy (expected number of years of formal schooling)					
		Total	Total	Male	Female	Total	Male	Female	Total		Male		Female	
	1995	1985	1995			1995			1985	1995	1985	1995	1985	1995
Africa														
Algeria	4–5	–	2	2	2	103	106	101	9.1	10.5	10.3	11.1	7.9	9.9
Angola	5	...	...	...	...	...	...	...	...	...	...	...	...	...
Benin	3–5	3	3	3	3	78	93	63	...	...	...	...	...	...
Botswana	–	–	–	–	–	118	120	115	8.5	10.6	8.1	10.5	8.9	10.7
Burkina Faso	4–6	0	...	...	...	34	41	26	1.9	2.7	2.4	3.3	1.3	2.0
Burundi	4–6	0	...	...	...	...	...	...	3.3	4.6	3.9	5.1	2.7	4.0
Cameroon	4–5	11	11	11	11	...	...	...	...	...	...	...	...	...
Cape Verde	5–6	23	...	...	...	135	136	134	7.5	8.8	7.8	9.0	7.2	8.6
Central African Republic	3–5	5	...	...	...	...	...	...	...	...	...	...	...	...
Chad	3–5	...	1	1	1	67	86	49	...	...	...	...	...	...
Comoros	4–6	...	...	...	...	♦100	109	89	...	...	...	...	...	...
Congo	3–5	3	1	1	1	86	90	82	...	...	...	...	...	...
Côte d'Ivoire	3–5	1	2	2	2	69	77	61	...	...	...	...	...	...
Dem. Rep. of the Congo	3–5	...	1	1	1	69	78	61	5.8	5.6	7.1	6.8	4.6	4.4
Djibouti	4–5	1	0	0	0	♦41	47	35	3.2	...	3.7	...	2.6	...
Egypt	4–5	5	8	8	8	99	105	92	...	9.9	...	10.8	...	8.8
Equatorial Guinea	3–5	...	...	...	...	...	...	...	...	...	...	...	...	...
Eritrea	5–6	...	4	4	4	50	56	44	...	4.1	...	4.6	...	3.5
Ethiopia	4–6	2	1	1	1	61	79	42	...	...	...	...	...	...
Gabon	3–5	...	...	...	...	128	129	128	...	...	...	...	...	...
Gambia	5–6	...	...	...	...	...	...	...	4.8	5.0	6.1	6.1	3.5	4.0
Ghana	4–5	25	...	...	...	...	...	...	...	...	...	...	...	...
Guinea	4–6	...	9	...	...	49	58	40	3.0	...	4.2	...	1.8	...
Guinea-Bissau	4–6	2	...	...	...	...	...	...	4.3	...	5.6	...	2.6	...
Kenya	3–5	26	36	36	35	♦107	110	105	...	...	...	...	...	...
Lesotho	–	–	–	–	–	102	101	103	9.1	8.3	8.0	7.6	10.2	9.0
Liberia	4–6	35	...	...	...	...	...	...	...	...	...	...	...	...
Libyan Arab Jamahiriya	4–5	6	...	...	...	...	...	...	...	...	...	...	...	...
Madagascar	3–5	...	...	...	...	80	81	79	...	...	...	...	...	...
Malawi	–	–	–	–	–	...	...	...	...	10.6	...	11.0	...	9.9
Mali	5–6	...	3	3	2	30	35	26	...	...	...	...	...	...
Mauritania	3–5	...	0	0	0	99	105	93	...	.	...	...	...	...
Mauritius	3–4	...	85	86	85	109	110	108	...	...	...	...	...	...
Morocco	5–6	57	63	85	40	88	96	80	...	...	...	...	...	...
Mozambique	–	–	–	–	–	69	77	61	...	3.4	...	4.0	...	2.8
Namibia	6	13	11	10	11	125	126	125	...	12.3	...	...	...	...
Niger	4–6	1	1	1	1	31	39	24	...	...	...	...	...	...
Nigeria	3–5	...	...	...	...	♦99	109	89	...	...	...	...	...	...
Rwanda	4–6	1	...	...	...	...	...	...	...	...	...	...	...	...
Sao Tome and Principe	3–6	...	...	...	...	...	...	...	...	...	...	...	...	...
Senegal	4–6	2	2	2	2	77	81	72	4.4	...	5.4	...	3.4	...
Seychelles	...	...	...	...	...	...	...	...	...	...	...	...	...	...
Sierra Leone	3–4	...	...	...	...	...	...	...	...	...	...	...	...	...
Somalia	4–5	0	...	...	...	...	...	...	1.3	...	1.8	...	0.9	...
South Africa	5	10	28	28	28	♦157	165	149	...	13.1	...	13.0	...	13.2
Sudan	♦4–5	17	37	42	33	...	...	...	...	...	...	...	...	...
Swaziland	3–5	...	26	...	...	126	128	124	...	11.2	...	11.5	...	10.8
Togo	3–5	3	3	3	3	109	122	97	...	...	...	...	...	...
Tunisia	3–5	...	11	11	11	93	93	93	9.3	...	10.4	...	8.2	...

Country or territory	Age-group 1995	Pre-primary education Gross enrolment ratio (%) Total 1985	Total 1995	Male 1995	Female 1995	Apparent intake rate in primary education (%) Total 1995	Male 1995	Female 1995	Access to schooling School life expectancy (expected number of years of formal schooling) Total 1985	Total 1995	Male 1985	Male 1995	Female 1985	Female 1995
Uganda	...	...	...	...	...	♦99	109	90	...	...	...	...	...	...
United Rep. of Tanzania	4–6	...	...	...	...	75	76	73	...	...	...	...	...	...
Zambia	3–6	...	...	...	...	♦92	92	92	...	7.3	...	7.9	...	6.8
Zimbabwe	5	...	...	...	...	...	...	...	...	...	...	...	...	...
America, North														
Antigua and Barbuda	3–4	...	...	...	...	...	...	...	...	...	...	...	...	...
Bahamas	3–4	...	8	8	8	110	...	...	11.9	12.6	11.6	12.1	12.2	13.2
Barbados	3–4	...	...	...	...	...	...	...	...	...	...	...	...	...
Belize	3–4	19	27	26	28	143	143	144	...	10.5	...	10.6	...	10.4
British Virgin Islands	3–5	...	...	...	...	...	...	...	...	...	...	...	...	...
Canada	4–5	57	63	64	63	♦125	127	123	15.6	17.5	15.3	17.2	16.0	17.8
Costa Rica	5	52	70	70	70	104	104	103	8.7	10.3	8.8	...	8.6	...
Cuba	5	79	92	105	79	♦101	102	100	12.7	11.3	12.6	10.9	12.8	11.7
Dominica	...	...	...	...	...	...	...	...	...	...	...	...	...	...
Dominican Republic	♦3–5	10	20	19	20	♦193	206	179	...	11.2	...	11.1	...	11.3
El Salvador	4–6	...	31	30	32	126	128	125	7.7	9.7	7.6	9.6	7.7	9.9
Grenada	3–5	...	...	...	...	...	...	...	...	...	...	...	...	...
Guatemala	5–6	26	32	33	32	♦152	160	145	...	...	...	...	...	...
Haiti	3–5	...	...	...	...	...	...	...	...	...	...	...	...	...
Honduras	4–6	12	14	13	14	133	135	131	8.1	...	8.1	...	8.1	...
Jamaica	3–5	76	81	85	78	...	...	...	10.3	11.0	10.1	10.8	10.5	11.1
Mexico	4–5	56	71	70	72	117	117	116	10.9	...	...	...	...	...
Netherlands Antilles	4–5	...	...	...	...	...	...	...	...	...	...	...	...	...
Nicaragua	3–6	14	20	20	21	140	141	138	8.1	9.1	7.2	8.9	9.1	9.4
Panama	5	51	76	...	...	...	...	...	11.2	...	11.0	...	11.5	...
Saint Kitts and Nevis	...	...	...	...	...	...	...	...	...	...	...	...	...	...
Saint Lucia	...	...	...	...	...	...	...	...	...	...	...	...	...	...
Saint Vincent and the Grenadines	...	...	...	...	...	...	...	...	...	...	...	...	...	...
Trinidad and Tobago	3–4	8	10	9	10	86	82	90	10.8	10.8	10.7	10.1	11.0	11.3
United States	3–5	60	68	70	67	♦106	105	106	14.7	15.8	14.5	15.4	14.9	16.2
America, South														
Argentina	♦3–5	50	54	53	56	...	...	...	...	...	...	...	...	...
Bolivia	4–5	38	...	...	...	...	...	...	10.0	...	10.9	...	9.0	...
Brazil	4–6	36	56	...	...	147	...	...	9.4	11.1	...	...	...	...
Chile	5	82	96	96	96	100	100	99	11.6	11.8	11.7	11.8	11.5	11.7
Colombia	3–5	12	28	...	...	142	145	138	9.3	10.5	...	...	...	...
Ecuador	5	36	49	48	19	129	130	128	...	...	...	...	...	...
Guyana	4–5	71	85	84	85	99	98	101	...	9.5	...	9.4	...	9.7
Paraguay	♦5	19	38	37	38	129	130	127	8.1	9.1	8.3	9.2	7.8	9.1
Peru	3–5	21	36	36	37	124	124	123	11.3	12.4	...	12.9	...	11.8
Suriname	4–5	...	...	...	...	...	...	...	11.5	...	11.2	...	11.7	...
Uruguay	2–5	25	33	33	34	105	104	106	11.8	...	...	...	...	...
Venezuela	♦3–5	39	43	42	43	...	...	...	10.1	10.5	9.9	10.2	10.4	10.7
Asia														
Afghanistan	3–6	1	...	...	...	28	42	14	...	...	...	...	...	...
Armenia	3–6	54	22	...	...	♦83	82	84	...	...	...	...	...	...
Azerbaijan	♦3–5	21	20	22	19	106	105	106	...	...	...	...	...	...
Bahrain	3–5	27	33	34	33	104	104	104	12.7	13.0	12.3	12.6	13.0	13.3

Table 3 (continued)

Country or territory	Age-group 1995	Pre-primary education Gross enrolment ratio (%)				Apparent intake rate in primary education (%)			Access to schooling School life expectancy (expected number of years of formal schooling)					
		Total	Total	Male	Female	Total	Male	Female	Total		Male		Female	
		1985		1995			1995		1985	1995	1985	1995	1985	1995
Bangladesh	5	...	...	...	...	...	...	...	4.5	...	5.5	...	3.4	...
Bhutan	...	...	...	...	...	18	19	16	...	...	...	...	...	...
Brunei Darussalam	3–5	44	51	51	51	♦110	113	107	11.0	12.0	10.9	11.8	11.0	12.1
Cambodia	3–5	...	5	5	5	116	122	110	...	...	...	...	...	...
China	3–6	20	29	29	28	108	107	109	...	...	...	...	...	...
Cyprus	2–5	...	60	60	60	...	...	...	...	...	...	...	...	...
Dem. People's Rep. of Korea	4–5	...	...	...	...	...	...	...	...	...	...	...	...	...
Georgia	3–5	...	32	...	...	♦81	81	81	...	10.2	...	10.1	...	10.4
Hong Kong	3–5	92	84	83	84	♦102	101	103	12.1	12.6	12.2	12.6	12.1	12.7
India	4–5	3	5	5	5	♦131	141	119	...	...	...	...	...	...
Indonesia	5–6	15	19	18	19	109	112	106	9.8	10.0	10.3	10.4	9.2	9.5
Iran, Islamic Republic of	5	7	7	7	7	84	85	84	...	...	...	...	...	...
Iraq	4–5	8	8	8	7	...	...	...	9.9	8.3	11.2	9.4	8.5	7.1
Israel	2–5	77	71	...	...	♦96	96	96	...	...	...	...	...	...
Japan	3–5	46	49	49	50	102	102	102	12.9	14.0	...	14.2	...	13.8
Jordan	4–5	...	25	27	24	...	...	...	...	...	...	...	...	...
Kazakhstan	3–6	70	29	30	28	98	99	98	...	...	...	...	...	...
Kuwait	4–5	46	52	52	51	72	73	70	...	9.0	...	8.9	...	9.1
Kyrgyzstan	3–6	30	8	9	6	♦106	107	105	...	...	...	...	...	...
Lao People's Dem. Rep.	3–5	6	7	6	7	118	133	104	...	6.9	...	8.2	...	5.7
Lebanon	3–5	...	74	76	73	...	...	...	...	...	...	...	...	...
Macau	3–5	...	87	89	86	...	...	...	...	...	...	...	...	...
Malaysia	4–5	37	...	...	...	97	97	97	...	...	...	...	...	...
Maldives	4–5	...	59	59	59	♦134	138	131	...	...	...	...	...	...
Mongolia	4–7	28	23	21	25	95	95	95	...	7.2	...	6.2	...	8.1
Myanmar	4	...	...	...	...	♦158	...	...	...	...	...	...	...	...
Nepal	3–5	...	...	...	...	...	...	...	5.1	...	6.8	...	2.9	...
Oman	4–5	2	3	4	3	67	68	66	...	8.6	...	8.8	...	8.1
Pakistan	3–4	...	...	...	...	...	...	...	...	...	...	...	...	...
Palestinian Auton. Territories	4–5	.	...	...	...	...	...	...	.	...	.	...	.	...
Gaza Strip	4–5	...	...	...	...	♦112	115	109	...	...	...	...	...	...
West Bank	4–5	...	...	...	...	...	...	...	...	...	...	...	...	...
Philippines	5–6	6	13	...	...	♦168	...	...	10.0	11.0	9.9	11.0	10.1	11.0
Qatar	4–5	33	31	32	29	53	51	56	11.7	11.1	10.9	10.6	12.4	11.6
Republic of Korea	5	42	85	85	85	99	98	99	13.2	14.5	13.8	15.1	12.5	13.9
Saudi Arabia	4–5	6	8	...	...	75	74	76	6.7	8.7	7.7	9.0	5.7	8.4
Singapore	4–5	20	...	...	...	...	...	...	...	...	...	...	...	...
Sri Lanka	4	...	...	...	...	♦113	114	112	...	...	...	...	...	...
Syrian Arab Republic	3–5	6	7	7	6	97	101	93	10.2	9.2	11.4	9.8	8.9	8.5
Tajikistan	3–6	...	10	...	...	101	...	...	...	...	...	...	...	...
Thailand	♦3–5	18	58	...	...	♦93	...	...	...	...	...	...	...	...
Turkey	4–5	5	6	7	6	106	109	102	8.4	9.7	...	10.6	...	8.7
Turkmenistan	3–6	...	...	...	...	...	...	...	...	...	...	...	...	...
United Arab Emirates	4–5	56	57	59	56	94	96	92	...	10.0	...	9.8	...	10.3
Uzbekistan	3–5	70	54	56	53	♦99	100	97	...	...	...	...	...	...
Viet Nam	3–5	33	35	...	...	...	...	...	...	...	...	...	...	...
Yemen	3–5	...	1	1	1	...	...	...	...	...	...	...	...	...
Europe														
Albania	3–5	52	38	37	39	94	93	95	...	...	...	...	...	...
Austria	3–5	71	76	76	76	♦103	104	103	...	14.3	...	14.4	...	14.2

Country or territory	Pre-primary education							Access to schooling					
	Age-group	Gross enrolment ratio (%)				Apparent intake rate in primary education (%)			School life expectancy (expected number of years of formal schooling)					
		Total	Total	Male	Female	Total	Male	Female	Total		Male		Female	
	1995	1985	1995			1995			1985	1995	1985	1995	1985	1995
Belarus	♦3–5	66	80	85	75	99	101	96	...	...	...	...	...	...
Belgium	3–5	110	116	116	116	♦114	117	111	13.9	15.5	13.9	15.6	13.8	15.4
Bosnia and Herzegovina	...	...	...	...	...	...	...	...	...	...	...	...	...	...
Bulgaria	♦3–6	93	62	62	61	102	103	100	11.5	12.1	11.5	11.8	11.6	12.5
Croatia	3–6	...	31	31	30	...	...	...	...	11.6	...	11.5	...	11.7
Czech Republic	3–5	...	91	90	92	105	105	105	...	13.1	...	13.1	...	13.1
Denmark	♦3–6	94	81	81	81	99	99	99	14.0	14.6	14.0	14.5	14.0	14.8
Estonia	3–6	...	73	74	73	97	97	97	...	12.5	...	12.2	...	12.9
Finland	3–6	28	39	39	39	96	96	96	...	15.5	...	15.0	...	16.0
France	2–5	89	84	84	84	♦109	110	107	13.3	15.4	13.1	15.2	13.6	15.6
Germany	3–5	...	84	85	82	104	104	104	...	15.1	...	15.4	...	14.8
Greece	4–5	57	61	61	62	...	...	...	12.9	13.8	13.0	13.9	12.8	13.6
Hungary	3–5	91	111	112	109	♦104	105	104	11.3	12.5	11.2	12.3	11.3	12.6
Iceland	5–6	55	53	54	52	103	103	103	...	...	...	...	...	...
Ireland	4–5	106	107	108	107	104	104	104	12.0	13.6	11.8	13.5	12.1	13.8
Italy	3–5	85	96	96	95	98	99	97	12.3	...	12.4	...	12.1	...
Latvia	3–6	67	44	45	43	♦98	101	95	...	11.4	...	11.1	...	11.7
Lithuania	3–6	64	36	37	36	94	94	93	...	...	...	...	...	...
Luxembourg	4–5	95	99	...	...	...	...	...	11.1	...	11.1	...	11.0	...
Malta	♦3–4	139	105	106	103	110	110	111	11.8	13.4	12.2	13.7	11.4	13.1
Monaco	3–5	...	...	...	...	...	...	...	...	...	...	...	...	...
Netherlands	4–5	106	100	100	99	...	...	...	15.0	15.5	15.3	15.7	14.5	15.2
Norway	4–6	66	98	96	101	97	98	97	13.5	14.9	13.3	14.7	13.8	15.2
Poland	3–6	51	45	45	45	♦97	97	96	11.5	13.1	11.4	13.0	11.7	13.3
Portugal	3–5	30	58	58	57	♦112	112	111	...	14.3	...	13.9	...	14.7
Republic of Moldova	3–6	66	45	47	43	97	98	97	...	...	...	...	...	...
Romania	♦3–6	75	53	52	53	♦105	107	104	...	11.4	...	11.5	...	11.4
Russian Federation	3–6	73	63	65	60	101	103	100	...	...	...	...	...	...
San Marino	3–5	...	...	...	...	...	...	...	...	...	...	...	...	...
Slovakia	3–5	87	71	...	...	99	99	99	...	...	...	...	...	...
Slovenia	3–6	...	66	68	64	♦109	111	108	...	...	...	...	...	...
Spain	2–5	51	69	68	69	100	99	102	...	15.5	...	15.1	...	15.9
Sweden	3–6	62	60	59	62	102	102	102	...	14.3	...	13.9	...	14.5
Switzerland	♦5–6	57	94	65	93	94	93	96	13.6	14.0	14.2	14.5	12.9	13.5
The FYR of Macedonia	3–6	...	24	24	24	94	96	92	...	10.3	...	10.3	...	10.3
Ukraine	3–6	65	54	56	51	99	100	98	...	...	...	...	...	...
United Kingdom	3–4	49	...	...	...	...	...	...	13.4	16.3	13.4	16.1	13.4	16.6
Yugoslavia	3–6	...	31	31	31	...	...	...	...	...	...	...	...	...
Oceania														
Australia	5	71	73	74	73	♦104	104	103	12.5	16.2	12.5	16.3	12.5	16.1
Cook Islands	...	...	...	...	...	...	...	...	...	...	...	...	...	...
Fiji	3–5	7	15	15	16	...	...	...	...	...	...	...	...	...
Kiribati	...	...	...	...	...	...	...	...	...	...	...	...	...	...
New Zealand	♦2–4	91	77	78	77	♦102	103	102	13.7	16.4	13.8	16.0	13.6	16.7
Papua New Guinea	5–6	...	1	1	1	104	110	97	...	...	...	...	...	...
Samoa	...	...	...	...	...	113	114	112	...	11.5	...	11.4	...	11.7
Solomon Islands	...	...	...	...	...	♦116	121	111	...	...	...	...	...	...
Tonga	...	...	...	...	...	...	...	...	...	...	...	...	...	...
Tuvalu	...	...	...	...	...	...	...	...	...	...	...	...	...	...
Vanuatu	...	...	...	...	...	...	...	...	...	...	...	...	...	...

Table 4
Primary education: duration, population and enrolment ratios

Country or territory	Duration in years — Compulsory education	Duration in years — Primary education	School-age population (000) 1985	School-age population (000) 1995	Gross enrolment ratio (%) Total 1985	Gross enrolment ratio (%) Total 1995	Gross enrolment ratio (%) Male 1985	Gross enrolment ratio (%) Male 1995	Gross enrolment ratio (%) Female 1985	Gross enrolment ratio (%) Female 1995	Net enrolment ratio (%) Total 1985	Net enrolment ratio (%) Total 1995	Net enrolment ratio (%) Male 1985	Net enrolment ratio (%) Male 1995	Net enrolment ratio (%) Female 1985	Net enrolment ratio (%) Female 1995
Africa																
Algeria	9	6	3 720	4 336	94	107	103	112	83	100	86	95	94	99	78	91
Angola	8	4	917	...	106	...	117	...	96	...	...	...	...	...	...	...
Benin	6	6	656	1 003	68	72	90	92	45	52	53	59	71	74	36	43
Botswana	–	7	213	269	105	115	100	114	111	117	89	96	84	94	94	99
Burkina Faso	6	6	1 303	1 721	27	38	34	46	20	30	23	31	29	37	17	24
Burundi	6	6	735	933	52	70	61	77	44	63	41	52	47	56	35	48
Cameroon	6	6	1 662	2 144	103	88	111	93	94	84	...	...	...	...	...	...
Cape Verde	6	6	49	60	117	131	120	132	114	129	96	100	98	100	95	100
Central African Republic	6	6	413	...	75	...	93	...	57	...	61	...	74	...	47	...
Chad	8	6	776	998	43	55	63	74	24	36	...	...	...	...	...	...
Comoros	9	◆6	79	99	84	78	93	85	73	71	62	53	...	58	...	48
Congo	10	6	323	437	147	114	154	119	141	109	...	...	...	...	...	...
Côte d'Ivoire	6	6	1 697	2 420	72	69	84	79	59	58	...	...	...	...	...	...
Dem. Rep. of the Congo	6	6	5 378	7 522	86	72	105	86	68	59	...	61	...	71	...	50
Djibouti	6	6	63	94	40	38	47	44	33	33	31	32	37	37	26	28
Egypt	8	◆5	7 280	8 128	85	100	94	107	76	93	...	...	...	...	...	...
Equatorial Guinea	5	5	...	...	...	...	...	...	...	...	...	...	...	...	...	...
Eritrea	7	5	...	427	...	57	...	63	...	51	...	31	...	33	...	30
Ethiopia	6	6	6 540	8 677	37	31	44	39	30	24	...	24	...	28	...	19
Gabon	10	6	...	...	...	...	...	...	...	...	...	...	...	...	...	...
Gambia	–	◆6	107	156	68	73	84	78	52	67	62	...	77	...	48	...
Ghana	9	6	2 182	...	72	...	81	...	62	...	...	...	...	...	...	...
Guinea	6	6	802	1 207	34	48	47	63	22	34	27	...	36	...	18	...
Guinea-Bissau	6	6	125	157	62	64	81	81	43	47	46	...	60	...	33	...
Kenya	8	8	4 761	6 508	99	85	102	85	96	85	...	...	...	...	...	...
Lesotho	7	7	285	371	110	99	97	92	123	105	71	65	61	60	81	71
Liberia	9	6	334	...	40	...	51	...	28	...	...	...	...	...	...	...
Libyan Arab Jamahiriya	9	9	932	1 189	109	106	113	107	104	104	...	97	...	98	...	96
Madagascar	5	5	1 488	2 104	109	72	113	73	106	70	...	...	...	...	...	...
Malawi	8	8	1 573	2 116	60	135	68	142	52	128	43	100	46	100	41	100
Mali	9	6	1 255	1 715	23	32	30	39	17	25	18	25	22	30	13	19
Mauritania	6	6	292	369	48	78	58	85	39	72	...	60	...	64	...	55
Mauritius	7	6	129	115	110	107	110	107	109	106	100	96	100	96	100	96
Morocco	6	◆6	2 955	3 743	77	83	93	94	60	71	61	72	73	81	48	62
Mozambique	7	◆5	1 429	2 347	87	60	99	70	76	50	51	40	56	45	47	35
Namibia	10	7	217	277	135	133	...	132	...	134	...	92	...	...	...	...
Niger	8	6	1 081	1 521	26	29	33	36	18	22	25	...	32	...	17	...
Nigeria	6	6	13 593	18 157	96	89	107	100	85	79	...	...	...	...	...	...
Rwanda	7	◆7	1 329	...	63	...	65	...	61	...	60	...	61	...	58	...
Sao Tome and Principe	4	4	...	...	...	...	...	...	...	...	...	...	...	...	...	...
Senegal	6	6	1 034	1 352	56	65	67	72	46	57	48	54	57	60	39	48
Seychelles	9	6	...	...	...	...	...	...	...	...	...	...	...	...	...	...
Sierra Leone	–	7	673	...	63	...	...	...	...	...	...	...	...	...	...	...
Somalia	8	8	1 713	...	11	...	15	...	8	...	8	...	11	...	6	...
South Africa	10	7	6 030	6 796	103	117	103	119	103	115	...	96	...	95	...	96
Sudan	8	◆8	3 476	5 642	50	54	59	59	41	48	...	...	...	...	...	...
Swaziland	7	7	137	158	102	122	104	125	100	119	79	95	78	95	80	96
Togo	6	6	499	696	93	118	114	140	71	97	...	85	...	98	...	72
Tunisia	9	6	1 122	1 271	115	116	124	119	105	112	93	97	99	98	87	95

Country or territory	Duration in years		School-age population (000)		Gross enrolment ratio (%)						Net enrolment ratio (%)					
	Com-pulsory edu-cation	Pri-mary edu-cation			Total		Male		Female		Total		Male		Female	
			1985	1995	1985	1995	1985	1995	1985	1995	1985	1995	1985	1995	1985	1995
Uganda	–	7	3 024	3 991	74	73	81	79	67	67	57	...	60	...	53	...
United Rep. of Tanzania	7	7	4 232	5 786	75	67	76	68	74	66	56	48	55	47	56	48
Zambia	3	7	1 326	1 686	104	89	109	92	98	86	88	75	90	76	85	75
Zimbabwe	5	7	1 669	2 149	136	116	139	117	132	114	100	...	100	...	100	...
America, North																
Antigua and Barbuda	11	7	...	...	...	...	...	...	...	...	...	...	...	...	...	...
Bahamas	10	6	33	35	100	94	100	95	99	94	100	...	100	...	99	...
Barbados	12	7	...	...	...	...	...	...	...	...	...	...	...			
Belize	10	8	40	45	103	121	106	124	100	118	87	99	89	100	85	98
British Virgin Islands	7	7	...	...	...	...	...	...	...	...	...	...	...	...	...	...
Canada	10	6	2 183	2 366	103	102	104	103	102	101	95	95	95	96	95	94
Costa Rica	9	6	374	476	97	107	98	107	96	106	84	92	83	...	84	...
Cuba	6	6	1 062	1 023	101	105	105	107	98	103	91	99	91	99	91	99
Dominica	10	7	...	...	...	...	...	...	...	...	...	...	...	...	...	...
Dominican Republic	9	♦8	968	1 414	126	103	123	103	129	104	70	81	70	79	69	83
El Salvador	9	9	...	1 205	...	88	...	88	...	89	...	79	...	78	...	80
Grenada	11	7	...	...	...	...	...	...	...	...	...	...	...	...	...	...
Guatemala	6	6	1 329	1 749	76	84	83	90	70	78	...	...	...	...	...	...
Haiti	6	6	898	...	97	...	103	...	91	...	56	...	57	...	54	...
Honduras	6	6	728	887	111	112	110	111	113	112	92	90	89	89	94	91
Jamaica	6	6	340	305	100	109	99	110	101	109	94	100	92	100	95	100
Mexico	6	6	12 864	12 695	118	115	119	116	116	113	100	100	...	...	...	...
Netherlands Antilles	–	6	...	...	...	...	...	...	...	...	...	...	...	...	...	...
Nicaragua	6	6	554	694	101	110	97	109	106	112	76	83	74	82	79	85
Panama	6	6	319	349	106	106	109	...	104	...	90	...	90	...	90	...
Saint Kitts and Nevis	12	7	...	...	...	...	...	...	...	...	...	...	...	...	...	...
Saint Lucia	10	7	...	...	...	...	...	...	...	...	...	...	...	...	...	...
Saint Vincent and the Grenadines	...	7	...	...	...	...	...	...	...	...	...	...	...	...	...	...
Trinidad and Tobago	7	7	175	193	96	96	96	91	97	102	92	88	91	83	92	94
United States	10	6	20 391	22 987	99	101	99	101	99	101	93	96	92	96	93	97
America, South																
Argentina	7	7	4 369	4 634	105	113	105	114	105	113	...	...	...	...	...	...
Bolivia	8	8	1 271	...	95	...	100	...	89	...	86	...	90	...	82	...
Brazil	8	8	24 861	27 875	100	112	...	...	...	...	81	90	...	...	...	...
Chile	8	8	1 969	2 175	104	99	105	100	102	98	89	86	...	87	...	85
Colombia	5	5	3 588	4 102	113	114	111	115	114	114	72	85	...	...	...	...
Ecuador	6	6	1 461	1 637	119	109	120	109	118	108	...	92	...	91	...	92
Guyana	10	6	111	106	103	94	104	95	101	93	...	90	...	90	...	89
Paraguay	6	6	542	768	105	109	108	110	102	107	89	89	90	89	89	89
Peru	6	6	3 081	3 361	120	123	123	125	118	121	96	91	...	91	...	90
Suriname	11	6	...	...	...	...	...	...	...	...	...	...	...	...	...	...
Uruguay	6	6	331	307	106	111	106	112	105	110	87	95	87	95	87	95
Venezuela	10	9	3 666	4 469	97	94	95	93	98	96	84	...	...	...	...	...
Asia																
Afghanistan	6	♦6	2 898	2 703	20	49	27	64	13	32	17	...	23	...	11	...
Armenia	9	♦4	...	304	...	82	...	...	...	...	...	...	...	...	...	...
Azerbaijan	11	♦4	412	671	118	104	...	100	...	108	...	...	...	...	...	...
Bahrain	12	6	51	67	112	108	109	107	116	109	96	100	94	99	98	100

Table 4 (continued)

Country or territory	Duration in years		School-age population (000)		Gross enrolment ratio (%)						Net enrolment ratio (%)					
	Com-pulsory edu-cation	Pri-mary edu-cation			Total		Male		Female		Total		Male		Female	
			1985	1995	1985	1995	1985	1995	1985	1995	1985	1995	1985	1995	1985	1995
Bangladesh	5	5	14 140	...	63	...	72	...	53	...	57	...	64	...	48	...
Bhutan	−	7	...	...	...	...	...	...	...	...	...	...	...	...	...	...
Brunei Darussalam	12	6	32	38	107	110	109	113	104	107	78	91	78	91	78	91
Cambodia	6	5	...	1 400	...	122	...	134	...	109	...	...	...	...	...	...
China	9	5	108 482	111 521	123	118	132	119	114	117	...	99	...	99	...	98
Cyprus	9	6	...	...	103	100	103	100	102	100	98	96	99	96	98	96
Dem. People's Rep. of Korea	10	4	...	...	...	...	...	...	...	...	...	...	...	...	...	...
Georgia	9	4	...	353	...	82	...	81	...	82	...	82	...	81	...	82
Hong Kong	9	6	506	489	106	96	107	95	105	97	96	91	96	90	96	92
India	8	5	91 102	109 383	96	100	111	110	80	90	...	...	...	...	...	...
Indonesia	6	6	25 548	25 970	117	114	120	117	114	112	98	97	100	99	95	95
Iran, Islamic Republic of	5	5	7 098	9 800	96	99	106	103	85	96	79	...	85	...	72	...
Iraq	6	6	2 615	...	108	...	116	...	99	...	93	...	99	...	87	...
Israel	11	♦6	722	640	97	99	95	...	98	...	...	...	...	...	...	...
Japan	9	6	10 913	8 619	102	102	102	102	102	102	100	100	100	100	100	100
Jordan	10	♦10	...	...	...	94	...	94	...	95	...	89	...	89	...	89
Kazakhstan	11	4	1 310	1 424	88	96	...	96	...	96	...	...	...	...	...	...
Kuwait	8	4	168	195	103	73	104	73	102	72	87	65	88	65	85	65
Kyrgyzstan	10	♦4	280	444	122	107	123	108	122	105	...	97	...	99	...	95
Lao People's Dem. Rep.	5	5	473	637	111	107	121	123	100	91	...	68	...	75	...	61
Lebanon	−	5	...	336	...	109	...	111	...	108	...	...	...	...	...	...
Macau	5	6	...	41	...	98	...	100	...	97	...	...	...	...	...	...
Malaysia	11	6	2 184	3 068	101	91	101	91	100	92	...	91	...	91	...	92
Maldives	−	5	...	36	...	134	...	136	...	132	...	...	...	...	...	...
Mongolia	8	3	146	199	103	88	102	87	104	90	...	80	...	78	...	81
Myanmar	5	5	4 782	5 346	98	103	101	105	96	102	...	...	...	...	...	...
Nepal	5	5	2 267	2 822	80	110	108	129	50	89	...	...	...	...	...	...
Oman	−	6	233	386	76	80	85	82	68	78	66	71	70	72	63	70
Pakistan	−	5	14 109	18 426	44	74	56	101	30	45	...	...	...	...	...	...
Palestinian Auton. Territories	10	10	.	...	.	...	.	...	.	...	.	...	.	...	.	...
Gaza Strip	.	.	...	...	...	...	...	...	...	...	...	...	...	...	...	...
West Bank	.	.	...	...	...	...	...	...	...	...	...	...	...	...	...	...
Philippines	6	6	8 313	9 987	107	116	108	...	107	...	96	100	97	...	96	...
Qatar	−	6	37	58	109	89	110	92	107	87	91	80	88	81	94	80
Republic of Korea	9	6	5 006	4 310	97	101	96	100	98	101	94	99	94	98	95	99
Saudi Arabia	−	6	2 078	2 890	65	78	73	79	57	76	51	62	60	63	42	61
Singapore	−	6	260	...	111	...	113	...	109	...	99	...	99	...	99	...
Sri Lanka	11	♦5	2 240	1 736	103	113	104	114	102	112	100	...	100	...	100	...
Syrian Arab Republic	6	6	1 853	2 655	110	101	117	106	102	95	98	91	100	95	92	87
Tajikistan	9	4	...	663	...	89	...	91	...	88	...	...	...	...	...	...
Thailand	6	6	7 451	6 819	96	87	...	...	...	...	...	...	...	...	...	...
Turkey	5	5	5 856	6 175	113	105	117	107	110	102	98	96	...	98	...	94
Turkmenistan	...	4	...	...	...	...	...	...	...	...	...	...	...	...	...	...
United Arab Emirates	6	6	156	279	98	94	98	96	97	92	77	83	76	84	77	82
Uzbekistan	...	4	1 863	2 477	87	77	88	78	85	76	...	...	...	...	...	...
Viet Nam	5	5	7 891	8 957	103	114	106	...	100	...	...	...	...	...	...	...
Yemen	9	9	...	3 374	...	79	...	113	...	45	...	...	...	...	...	...
Europe																
Albania	8	8	527	553	103	101	104	100	102	102	...	96	...	95	...	97
Austria	9	4	343	378	100	101	101	101	99	101	...	100	...	100	...	100

Country or territory	Duration in years Compulsory education	Primary education	School-age population (000) 1985	1995	Gross enrolment ratio (%) Total 1985	1995	Male 1985	1995	Female 1985	1995	Net enrolment ratio (%) Total 1985	1995	Male 1985	1995	Female 1985	1995
Belarus	9	♦4	735	655	108	97	...	98	...	95	...	97	...	98	...	95
Belgium	12	6	738	718	99	103	99	103	99	102	94	98	94	98	95	98
Bosnia and Herzegovina	...	...	...	...	...	...	...	...	...	...	...	...	...	...	...	...
Bulgaria	8	♦4	1 057	448	102	97	103	98	102	96	...	97	...	98	...	96
Croatia	8	♦4	493	241	105	86	105	87	106	86	...	...	...	...	...	...
Czech Republic	9	4	700	525	99	103	...	103	...	102	...	98	...	98	...	98
Denmark	9	6	409	334	99	99	99	98	98	99	99	99	99	98	98	99
Estonia	9	♦5	135	116	98	109	97	110	99	108	...	94	...	93	...	94
Finland	9	6	370	388	102	100	103	100	102	100	...	99	...	99	...	99
France	10	5	3 792	3 849	109	106	110	107	107	105	97	99	97	99	97	99
Germany	12	4	...	3 668	...	102	...	102	...	101	...	100	...	100	...	100
Greece	9	6	852	...	104	...	104	...	104	...	99	...	99	...	99	...
Hungary	10	8	1 310	1 016	99	97	99	97	99	97	97	93	97	92	98	94
Iceland	8	6	25	25	99	97	99	99	99	95	...	...	...	...	...	...
Ireland	9	6	421	368	100	104	100	104	100	103	100	100	100	100	100	100
Italy	8	5	3 978	2 876	98	98	98	99	98	97	97	97	96	...	97	...
Latvia	9	4	141	157	80	89	80	91	80	86	...	84	...	86	...	82
Lithuania	9	4	214	233	80	96	80	97	81	95	...	...	...	...	...	...
Luxembourg	9	6	25	27	89	104	88	...	89	...	81	...	80	...	82	...
Malta	10	6	34	32	107	108	109	111	104	105	97	100	97	100	96	99
Monaco	10	5	...	...	...	...	...	...	...	...	...	...	...	...	...	...
Netherlands	11	6	1 119	1 109	99	107	98	108	100	106	92	99	91	99	94	99
Norway	9	6	346	317	97	99	97	99	97	99	96	99	96	99	96	99
Poland	8	8	4 749	5 286	101	98	102	99	100	98	99	97	100	97	99	96
Portugal	9	6	960	728	129	128	132	131	125	124	100	100	100	100	100	100
Republic of Moldova	11	4	294	340	84	94	85	95	84	93	...	...	...	...	...	...
Romania	8	♦4	3 094	1 393	98	100	98	101	98	99	...	92	...	92	...	92
Russian Federation	9	3	6 350	7 298	104	108	103	108	104	107	...	100	...	100	...	100
San Marino	8	5	...	...	...	...	...	...	...	...	...	...	...	...	...	...
Slovakia	9	4	...	330	...	100	...	100	...	100	...	...	...	...	...	...
Slovenia	8	4	...	98	...	103	...	103	...	103	...	100	...	100	...	99
Spain	10	5	3 166	2 251	110	105	111	105	109	105	100	100	100	100	100	100
Sweden	9	6	612	615	98	105	98	104	98	105	...	100	...	100	...	100
Switzerland	9	6	456	474	95	107	94	108	95	107	95	100	94	100	95	100
The FYR of Macedonia	8	8	271	297	101	89	...	90	...	87	...	85	...	86	...	84
Ukraine	8	♦4	3 630	3 071	103	87	...	87	...	86	...	...	...	...	...	...
United Kingdom	11	6	4 124	4 549	104	115	104	114	105	115	100	100	100	100	100	100
Yugoslavia	8	4	...	625	...	72	...	71	...	72	...	...	...	...	...	...
Oceania																
Australia	10	6	1 444	1 527	107	108	107	108	106	108	98	98	98	98	98	98
Cook Islands	10	6	...	...	...	...	...	...	...	...	...	...	...	...	...	...
Fiji	–	6	104	114	122	128	122	128	122	127	97	99	97	99	97	100
Kiribati	9	7	...	...	...	...	...	...	...	...	...	...	...	...	...	...
New Zealand	11	6	308	331	107	104	108	105	106	104	100	100	100	100	100	100
Papua New Guinea	–	6	554	643	67	80	73	87	62	74	...	...	...	...	...	...
Samoa	8	8	30	31	104	116	101	117	108	115	...	99	...	100	...	99
Solomon Islands	–	6	49	62	79	97	...	104	...	90	...	...	...	...	...	...
Tonga	8	6	...	...	...	...	...	...	...	...	...	...	...	...	...	...
Tuvalu	9	8	...	...	...	...	...	...	...	...	...	...	...	...	...	...
Vanuatu	6	6	23	27	100	106	...	105	...	107	...	...	...	...	...	...

Table 5
Primary education: internal efficiency

Country or territory	Percentage of repeaters						Percentage of 1994 cohort reaching					
	Total		Male		Female		Grade 2			Grade 5		
	1985	1995	1985	1995	1985	1995	Total	Male	Female	Total	Male	Female
Africa												
Algeria	8	9	9	11	6	6	100	100	100	95	94	95
Angola	...	...	...	...	...	...	...	...	...	...	...	...
Benin	27	25	26	25	28	25	87	89	84	61	63	57
Botswana	6	3	6	3	6	2	94	92	95	89	86	92
Burkina Faso	16	16	15	16	16	17	99	98	100	79	78	80
Burundi	18	24	18	24	18	23	...	...	...	...	...	...
Cameroon	29	...	30	...	28	...	...	...	...	...	...	...
Cape Verde	28	17	29	18	26	16	...	...	...	...	...	...
Central African Republic	29	...	30	...	29	...	...	...	...	...	...	...
Chad	32	35	31	34	35	35	70	73	66	28	33	21
Comoros	33	36	32	...	33	...	90	...	...	78	...	...
Congo	30	33	31	35	29	32	93	...	...	54	...	...
Côte d'Ivoire	28	27	29	28	28	25	90	91	90	73	76	68
Dem. Rep. of the Congo	19	5	19	7	19	3	83	86	81	64	73	54
Djibouti	12	12	...	...	...	...	♦99	100	100	94	97	98
Egypt	2	5	2	6	1	4	100	100	100	98	98	97
Equatorial Guinea	...	25	...	25	...	25	...	...	...	...	...	...
Eritrea	...	19	...	15	...	23	93	92	93	79	78	79
Ethiopia	10	9	8	7	11	11	60	60	60	51	51	51
Gabon	36	39	37	40	35	38	...	...	...	...	...	...
Gambia	17	14	18	15	16	14	...	...	...	...	...	...
Ghana	...	...	...	...	...	...	...	...	...	...	...	...
Guinea	27	22	25	21	31	24	97	98	95	80	82	75
Guinea-Bissau	41	...	40	...	42	...	...	...	...	...	...	...
Kenya	...	...	...	...	...	...	♦87	...	...	68	...	...
Lesotho	23	18	25	21	21	16	89	87	90	79	72	87
Liberia	...	...	...	...	...	...	...	...	...	...	...	...
Libyan Arab Jamahiriya	...	...	...	...	...	...	...	...	...	...	...	...
Madagascar	33	32	35	34	31	31	66	66	67	28	26	30
Malawi	18	18	18	17	17	19	...	...	...	...	...	...
Mali	30	28	30	28	30	28	96	98	94	72	75	70
Mauritania	18	16	17	15	20	17	90	88	92	63	68	62
Mauritius	6	6	6	6	6	5	100	100	100	99	99	99
Morocco	20	12	21	13	18	10	93	94	92	78	80	77
Mozambique	24	26	23	25	24	27	86	90	79	47	52	39
Namibia	...	23	...	24	...	21	91	90	92	82	79	84
Niger	15	16	15	19	15	12	99	99	98	77	76	78
Nigeria	...	...	...	...	...	...	♦89	...	...	80	...	...
Rwanda	12	...	12	...	12	...	...	...	...	...	...	...
Sao Tome and Principe	35	...	35	...	35	...	...	...	...	...	...	...
Senegal	16	14	16	14	17	14	93	...	...	81	...	...
Seychelles	–	–	–	–	–	–	98	...	...	97	...	...
Sierra Leone	...	...	...	...	...	...	...	...	...	...	...	...
Somalia	...	...	...	...	...	...	...	...	...	...	...	...
South Africa	...	...	...	...	...	...	♦78	...	...	65	...	...
Sudan	–	–	–	–	–	–	100	...	...	94	...	...
Swaziland	14	15	16	17	12	13	92	92	93	78	76	82
Togo	35	24	34	24	36	25	89	91	87	71	79	60
Tunisia	20	17	21	19	19	16	99	99	98	92	92	93

| Country or territory | Percentage of repeaters | | | | | | Percentage of 1994 cohort reaching | | | | | |
| | Total | | Male | | Female | | Grade 2 | | | Grade 5 | | |
	1985	1995	1985	1995	1985	1995	Total	Male	Female	Total	Male	Female
Uganda	14	...	14	...	14	...	...	...	...	...	...	...
United Rep. of Tanzania	0	3	0	3	0	3	94	93	94	83	81	86
Zambia	2	3	2	3	2	3	♦97	98	96	84	87	80
Zimbabwe	–	–	–	–	–	–	88	...	...	76	...	...
America, North												
Antigua and Barbuda	...	...	...	...	...	...	...	...	...	...	...	...
Bahamas	–	–	–	–	–	–	♦90	...	...	78	...	...
Barbados	...	...	...	...	...	...	...	...	...	...	...	...
Belize	...	10	...	12	...	9	77	77	76	70	71	70
British Virgin Islands	10	7	11	8	8	5	...	...	...	...	...	...
Canada	...	...	...	...	...	...	♦99	99	99	99	99	99
Costa Rica	11	9	12	11	9	8	97	95	98	89	87	90
Cuba	3	3	...	...	...	...	99	...	...	94	...	...
Dominica	5	...	6	...	5	...	♦91	89	93	84	81	87
Dominican Republic	17	...	...	...	...	...	♦67	66	68	58	50	65
El Salvador	8	6	9	7	8	5	76	75	77	58	58	59
Grenada	7	...	8	...	5	...	...	...	...	...	...	...
Guatemala	13	16	...	17	...	16	...	...	...	...	...	...
Haiti	9	13	9	13	9	13	...	...	...	...	...	...
Honduras	15	12	16	13	15	11	♦84	73	76	60	44	51
Jamaica	4	3	4	4	3	3	...	...	...	...	...	...
Mexico	10	7	...	8	...	6	94	94	94	84	85	84
Netherlands Antilles	...	...	...	...	...	...	...	...	...	...	...	...
Nicaragua	15	15	16	16	15	14	79	79	80	54	52	56
Panama	13	...	15	...	11	...	...	...	...	...	...	...
Saint Kitts and Nevis	–	–	–	–	–	–	...	...	...	...	...	...
Saint Lucia	7	–	7	–	6	–	♦100	100	100	95	91	97
Saint Vincent and the Grenadines	...	...	...	...	...	...	...	...	...	...	...	...
Trinidad and Tobago	5	6	4	6	5	5	100	100	100	95	95	95
United States	...	...	...	...	...	...	...	...	...	...	...	...
America, South												
Argentina	...	...	...	...	...	...	...	...	...	...	...	...
Bolivia	...	...	...	...	...	...	...	...	...	...	...	...
Brazil	20	18	...	...	...	...	86	...	...	71	...	...
Chile	7	6	8	7	6	5	97	97	97	92	92	91
Colombia	17	9	17	10	17	9	76	75	77	58	55	61
Ecuador	7	4	7	5	6	4	86	85	86	77	76	78
Guyana	6	4	7	5	5	3	...	...	...	...	...	...
Paraguay	11	8	12	9	9	7	91	91	91	71	70	73
Peru	14	15	...	16	...	15	...	...	...	...	...	...
Suriname	22	...	24	...	20	...	...	...	...	...	...	...
Uruguay	11	10	13	11	9	8	98	98	99	94	93	96
Venezuela	10	11	...	13	...	9	92	91	93	78	75	82
Asia												
Afghanistan	6	9	6	9	6	9	...	...	...	...	...	...
Armenia	...	0	...	...	...	...	...	...	...	...	...	...
Azerbaijan	...	0	...	0	...	0	94	95	93	...	...	...
Bahrain	9	5	8	6	9	5	98	99	98	94	90	94

Table 5 (continued)

Country or territory	Percentage of repeaters						Percentage of 1994 cohort reaching					
	Total		Male		Female		Grade 2			Grade 5		
	1985	1995	1985	1995	1985	1995	Total	Male	Female	Total	Male	Female
Bangladesh	...	...	...	...	...	...	...	...	...	...	...	...
Bhutan	17	19	...	20	...	18	96	94	98	82	81	84
Brunei Darussalam	9	9	11	...	6	...	99	...	...	95	...	...
Cambodia	...	30	...	31	...	30	83	84	81	50	56	42
China	7	2	...	2	...	2	99	99	99	92	92	92
Cyprus	0	0	0	0	0	0	100	100	100	100	100	100
Dem. People's Rep. of Korea	...	...	...	...	...	...	...	...	...	...	...	...
Georgia	...	0	...	...	...	...	100	...	...	98	...	...
Hong Kong	2	1	2	...	2	...	100	...	...	100	...	...
India	4	...	4	...	4	...	♦81	81	81	62	65	59
Indonesia	11	8	...	8	...	7	97	100	94	90	96	81
Iran, Islamic Republic of	12	7	13	9	9	6	96	97	96	90	92	89
Iraq	21	...	22	...	19	...	...	...	...	...	...	...
Israel	...	...	...	...	...	...	♦100	100	100	100	100	100
Japan	–	–	–	–	–	–	100	100	100	100	100	100
Jordan	6	1	6	1	6	1	99	99	99	98	98	99
Kazakhstan	...	0	...	0	...	0	...	...	...	...	...	...
Kuwait	5	3	5	3	5	4	99	99	99	99	98	99
Kyrgyzstan	...	0	...	...	...	...	97	...	...	92	...	...
Lao People's Dem. Rep.	27	26	...	27	...	25	73	74	72	53	55	51
Lebanon	...	...	...	...	...	...	...	...	...	...	...	...
Macau	...	7	...	5	...	8	100	100	100	97	94	96
Malaysia	–	–	–	–	–	–	95	95	95	94	94	94
Maldives	...	...	...	...	...	...	♦95	94	96	93	91	94
Mongolia	...	1	...	1	...	0	96	95	96	...	...	...
Myanmar	...	...	...	...	...	...	...	...	...	...	...	...
Nepal	21	27	...	28	...	24	65	68	62	52	52	52
Oman	12	8	13	10	9	7	99	99	99	96	96	96
Pakistan	...	...	...	...	...	...	...	...	...	...	...	...
Palestinian Auton. Territories	.	4	.	5	.	4	100	100	100	98	98	98
Gaza Strip	...	...	...	...	...	...	...	...	...	...	...	...
West Bank	...	...	...	...	...	...	...	...	...	...	...	...
Philippines	2	...	2	...	2	...	♦84	...	...	70	...	...
Qatar	11	5	13	7	8	3	♦99	99	99	95	92	98
Republic of Korea	–	–	–	–	–	–	100	100	100	100	100	100
Saudi Arabia	12	8	15	11	9	5	97	98	97	94	95	93
Singapore	1	...	1	...	1	...	...	...	...	...	...	...
Sri Lanka	8	...	8	...	9	...	♦100	100	100	98	98	99
Syrian Arab Republic	7	7	8	8	7	6	99	99	98	91	92	90
Tajikistan	...	0	...	...	...	...	...	...	...	...	...	...
Thailand	...	...	...	...	...	...	...	...	...	...	...	...
Turkey	8	5	8	4	8	5	97	97	98	89	88	90
Turkmenistan	...	...	...	...	...	...	...	...	...	...	...	...
United Arab Emirates	6	5	6	6	5	4	99	99	99	98	97	98
Uzbekistan	...	0	...	...	...	...	100	...	...	...	...	...
Viet Nam	...	...	...	...	...	...	...	...	...	...	...	...
Yemen	...	...	...	...	...	...	...	...	...	...	...	...
Europe												
Albania	...	5	...	7	...	4	93	93	93	82	81	83
Austria	...	...	...	...	...	...	♦99	99	99	99	99	99

Country or territory	Percentage of repeaters						Percentage of 1994 cohort reaching					
	Total		Male		Female		Grade 2			Grade 5		
	1985	1995	1985	1995	1985	1995	Total	Male	Female	Total	Male	Female
Belarus	0	1	...	1	...	1	100	100	99	100	100	98
Belgium	17	...	18	...	15	...	...	...	...	...	...	...
Bosnia and Herzegovina	...	...	...	...	...	...	...	...	...	...	...	...
Bulgaria	2	4	3	4	0	3	95	95	95	95	95	94
Croatia	...	0	...	0	...	0	99	99	99	98	98	98
Czech Republic	...	1	...	1	...	1	100	100	100	100	100	100
Denmark	−	−	−	−	−	−	100	100	100	100	100	100
Estonia	...	3	...	4	...	1	100	100	100	100	100	98
Finland	0	0	0	0	0	0	100	100	100	100	100	100
France	8	...	...	...	...	...	♦100	100	100	99	99	99
Germany	...	2	...	2	...	2	100	100	100	100	99	100
Greece	0	...	0	...	0	...	...	...	...	...	...	...
Hungary	3	2	4	...	2	...	98	...	...	98	...	...
Iceland	...	...	...	...	...	...	...	...	...	...	...	...
Ireland	...	2	...	2	...	2	100	100	100	100	100	100
Italy	1	0	1	0	0	0	100	100	100	100	100	100
Latvia	...	3	...	...	...	...	98	...	...	...	...	...
Lithuania	...	1	...	2	...	0	...	...	...	...	...	...
Luxembourg	...	...	...	...	...	...	...	...	...	...	...	...
Malta	3	2	3	2	2	1	100	100	98	97	...	...
Monaco	...	...	...	...	...	...	♦99	99	99	98	99	95
Netherlands	2	...	3	...	2	...	...	...	...	...	...	...
Norway	−	−	−	−	−	−	♦100	100	100	100	100	100
Poland	3	1	...	2	...	1	99	...	...	98	...	...
Portugal	17	...	19	...	15	...	...	...	...	...	...	...
Republic of Moldova	...	1	...	1	...	1	99	99	99	...	...	...
Romania	...	3	...	3	...	2	99	100	97	99	100	96
Russian Federation	...	2	...	2	...	2	99	99	99	...	...	...
San Marino	0	0	...	0	...	−	100	...	...	100	...	...
Slovakia	...	2	...	2	...	2	98	97	98	97	96	97
Slovenia	...	0	...	...	...	...	100	...	...	98	...	...
Spain	5	3	6	3	4	2	100	100	100	98	99	99
Sweden	−	−	−	−	−	−	99	98	99	98	97	98
Switzerland	2	2	2	2	2	1	100	100	100	100	100	100
The FYR of Macedonia	...	1	...	2	...	0	99	99	99	...	...	...
Ukraine	0	0	...	0	...	0	98	96	100	...	...	...
United Kingdom	−	−	−	−	−	−	...	...	...	...	...	...
Yugoslavia	...	1	...	...	...	...	100	...	...	100	...	...
Oceania												
Australia	...	...	...	...	...	...	♦99	99	99	99	99	99
Cook Islands	...	...	...	...	...	...	...	...	...	...	...	...
Fiji	3	...	4	...	2	...	92	94	90	87	88	84
Kiribati	3	0	3	0	3	0	91	90	93	90	85	92
New Zealand	3	4	3	4	3	4	96	95	96	96	95	96
Papua New Guinea	−	−	−	−	−	−	84	84	84	59	59	60
Samoa	...	2	...	...	...	...	...	...	...	...	...	...
Solomon Islands	7	9	8	...	7	...	92	...	...	81	...	...
Tonga	8	8	8	8	7	8	95	95	95	...	...	...
Tuvalu	−	−	−	−	−	−	100	95	100	96	89	98
Vanuatu	...	13	...	14	...	11	92	93	91	61	62	60

Table 6
Secondary education: duration, population and enrolment ratios

Country or territory	Duration in years of secondary general education		School-age population (000)		Gross enrolment ratio (%)						Net enrolment ratio (%)					
					Total		Male		Female		Total		Male		Female	
	Lower	Upper	1985	1995	1985	1995	1985	1995	1985	1995	1985	1995	1985	1995	1985	1995
Africa																
Algeria	3	3	3 547	4 076	51	62	59	66	44	59	45	56	51	59	38	53
Angola	4	3	1 285	...	14	...	...	...	...	...	...	...	...	...	...	...
Benin	4	3	600	832	17	16	24	23	10	10	13	...	19	...	8	...
Botswana	2	3	125	166	29	56	27	54	31	58	23	45	21	42	25	48
Burkina Faso	4	3	1 202	1 508	4	8	6	11	3	6	3	7	5	9	2	5
Burundi	4	3	730	832	4	7	5	8	2	5	3	5	3	6	2	4
Cameroon	4	3	1 507	2 044	23	27	28	32	18	22	...	...	...	...	...	...
Cape Verde	♦3	3	40	51	14	27	16	28	13	26	9	22	10	22	9	22
Central African Republic	4	3	372	...	16	...	24	...	8	...	...	...	...	...	...	...
Chad	4	3	...	929	...	9	...	15	...	4	...	...	...	...	...	...
Comoros	4	3	73	91	29	19	34	21	23	17	...	...	...	...	...	...
Congo	4	3	297	405	75	53	86	62	64	45	...	...	...	...	...	...
Côte d'Ivoire	4	3	1 457	2 281	20	23	27	30	12	15	...	...	...	...	...	...
Dem. Rep. of the Congo	2	4	4 235	5 909	23	26	32	32	13	19	...	23	...	29	...	18
Djibouti	4	3	60	92	12	13	14	15	9	11	11	...	13	...	8	...
Egypt	3	3	6 235	8 668	61	74	72	80	50	68	...	...	...	...	...	...
Equatorial Guinea	4	3	...	...	...	...	...	...	...	...	...	...	...	...	...	...
Eritrea	2	4	...	416	...	19	...	22	...	16	...	15	...	16	...	14
Ethiopia	2	4	5 326	6 925	13	11	15	12	10	10	...	...	...	...	...	...
Gabon	4	3	105	...	...	...	...	...	...	...	...	...	...	...	...	...
Gambia	♦5	2	98	145	16	22	23	28	10	15	13	...	19	...	8	...
Ghana	4	3	2 064	...	39	...	49	...	31	...	...	...	...	...	...	...
Guinea	4	3	757	1 103	13	12	18	18	7	6	9	...	13	...	5	...
Guinea-Bissau	3	2	88	...	7	...	11	...	4	...	...	...	...	...	...	...
Kenya	♦.	4	2 161	2 759	21	24	26	26	16	22	...	...	...	...	...	...
Lesotho	3	2	162	223	23	28	19	22	28	34	13	16	9	10	18	21
Liberia	3	3	273	...	17	...	...	...	...	...	...	...	...	...	...	...
Libyan Arab Jamahiriya	.	3	243	320	59	97	61	...	57	...	...	...	...	...	...	...
Madagascar	4	3	1 677	2 296	29	14	32	14	27	14	...	...	...	...	...	...
Malawi	2	2	630	854	4	6	6	7	3	4	...	2	...	2	...	2
Mali	3	3	1 062	1 363	6	9	9	12	4	6	...	...	...	...	...	...
Mauritania	3	3	236	318	15	15	22	19	8	11	...	...	...	...	...	...
Mauritius	3	4	149	151	49	62	51	60	46	64	...	...	...	...	...	...
Morocco	♦3	3	3 527	3 660	35	39	42	44	28	33	...	...	...	...	...	...
Mozambique	2	5	2 094	2 627	7	7	10	9	5	5	...	6	...	7	...	5
Namibia	.	5	128	166	39	62	...	57	...	67	...	36	...	...	...	...
Niger	4	3	989	1 375	5	7	8	9	3	4	...	...	...	...	...	...
Nigeria	♦3	3	9 173	14 605	33	30	38	33	27	28	...	...	...	...	...	...
Rwanda	♦.	6	752	...	6	...	7	...	5	...	...	...	...	...	...	...
Sao Tome and Principe	5	2	...	...	...	...	...	...	...	...	...	...	...	...	...	...
Senegal	4	3	940	1 297	14	16	18	20	9	12	...	...	...	...	...	...
Seychelles	.	5	...	...	...	...	...	...	...	...	...	...	...	...	...	...
Sierra Leone	5	2	532	632	18	...	...	...	...	...	...	...	...	...	...	...
Somalia	.	4	680	...	7	...	9	...	5	...	3	...	4	...	2	...
South Africa	3	2	3 610	4 372	55	82	52	76	59	88	...	52	...	47	...	57
Sudan	♦.	3	2 753	1 919	20	13	23	14	17	12	...	...	...	...	...	...
Swaziland	3	2	79	102	39	52	40	53	38	51	...	...	...	...	...	...
Togo	4	3	462	637	21	27	32	41	10	14	...	...	...	...	...	...
Tunisia	3	4	1 176	1 387	39	61	46	63	32	59	...	...	...	...	...	...

Country or territory	Duration in years of secondary general education		School-age population (000)		Gross enrolment ratio (%)						Net enrolment ratio (%)					
					Total		Male		Female		Total		Male		Female	
	Lower	Upper	1985	1995	1985	1995	1985	1995	1985	1995	1985	1995	1985	1995	1985	1995
Uganda	4	2	2 006	2 718	13	12	17	15	9	9	...	...	...	...	...	...
United Rep. of Tanzania	4	2	2 859	3 931	3	5	4	6	2	5	...	...	...	...	...	...
Zambia	2	3	727	942	19	28	25	34	14	21	...	16	...	19	...	14
Zimbabwe	.	6	1 162	1 450	41	44	50	49	33	39	...	...	...	...	...	...
America, North																
Antigua and Barbuda	3	2	...	...	...	...	...	...	...	...	...	...	...	...	...	...
Bahamas	3	3	32	32	87	90	82	88	91	91	83	...	79	...	87	...
Barbados	5	1	...	...	...	...	...	...	...	...	...	...	...	...	...	...
Belize	.	4	17	21	42	49	39	47	46	52	...	...	...	...	...	...
British Virgin Islands	3	2	...	...	...	...	...	...	...	...	...	...	...	...	...	...
Canada	3	3	2 279	2 336	99	106	99	106	99	105	88	92	88	92	89	91
Costa Rica	3	2	280	358	40	50	38	48	42	52	34	43	32	...	36	...
Cuba	3	3	1 402	883	82	80	80	78	85	82	67	...	63	...	71	...
Dominica	.	5	...	...	...	...	...	...	...	...	...	...	...	...	...	...
Dominican Republic	♦.	4	918	648	51	41	44	34	57	47	...	22	...	18	...	26
El Salvador	.	3	...	445	...	32	...	30	...	34	...	21	...	19	...	22
Grenada	.	5	...	...	...	...	...	...	...	...	...	...	...	...	...	...
Guatemala	3	3	1 068	1 473	19	25	...	26	...	24	...	...	...	...	...	...
Haiti	3	3	801	...	18	...	19	...	17	...	...	...	...	...	...	...
Honduras	3	2	494	627	37	32	...	...	...	...	...	...	...	...	...	...
Jamaica	3	4	402	358	59	66	56	62	62	70	57	64	54	61	60	68
Mexico	3	3	11 584	12 462	57	58	58	58	55	59	46	...	...	...	...	...
Netherlands Antilles	.	5	...	...	...	...	...	...	...	...	...	...	...	...	...	...
Nicaragua	3	2	379	512	34	47	22	43	46	50	19	...	14	...	24	...
Panama	3	3	307	320	60	68	57	...	63	...	48	...	45	...	51	...
Saint Kitts and Nevis	4	2	...	...	...	...	...	...	...	...	...	...	...	...	...	...
Saint Lucia	3	2	...	...	...	...	...	...	...	...	...	...	...	...	...	...
Saint Vincent and the Grenadines	5	2	...	...	...	...	...	...	...	...	...	...	...	...	...	...
Trinidad and Tobago	3	2	117	144	83	72	82	66	84	79	71	...	70	...	72	...
United States	3	3	21 204	21 372	97	99	97	99	97	98	91	89	91	89	92	89
America, South																
Argentina	3	2	2 565	3 378	70	77	66	73	74	81	...	...	...	...	...	...
Bolivia	.	4	540	...	39	...	42	...	36	...	27	...	29	...	25	...
Brazil	.	3	8 528	10 012	35	45	...	...	...	...	14	19	...	...	...	...
Chile	2	2	998	977	67	69	64	66	70	73	...	55	...	52	...	57
Colombia	4	2	4 018	4 512	48	67	48	62	49	72	...	50	...	47	...	53
Ecuador	3	3	1 266	1 536	58	50	57	50	59	50	...	...	...	...	...	...
Guyana	3	2	101	83	76	76	73	68	78	85	...	...	...	...	...	...
Paraguay	3	3	479	627	31	38	32	38	31	39	...	33	...	32	...	34
Peru	2	3	2 271	2 672	63	70	66	72	60	67	49	53	...	54	...	52
Suriname	4	3	...	...	...	...	...	...	...	...	...	...	...	...	...	...
Uruguay	3	3	293	322	71	82	...	74	...	89	56	...	...	...	...	...
Venezuela	♦2	2	1 119	859	24	35	21	29	27	41	16	20	14	16	18	24
Asia																
Afghanistan	♦.	6	1 280	2 344	8	22	11	32	5	11	...	...	...	...	...	...
Armenia	♦4	2	...	413	...	79	...	...	...	...	...	...	...	...	...	...
Azerbaijan	5	2	962	1 043	95	78	...	76	...	80	...	...	...	...	...	...
Bahrain	3	3	40	57	97	99	98	97	97	100	77	85	76	84	77	87

Table 6 (continued)

Country or territory	Duration in years of secondary general education		School-age population (000)		Gross enrolment ratio (%)						Net enrolment ratio (%)					
					Total		Male		Female		Total		Male		Female	
	Lower	Upper	1985	1995	1985	1995	1985	1995	1985	1995	1985	1995	1985	1995	1985	1995
Bangladesh	5	2	17 113	...	18	...	26	...	10	...	17	...	...	...	...	...
Bhutan	2	2	...	...	...	...	...	...	...	...	...	...	...	...	...	...
Brunei Darussalam	5	2	31	37	64	78	61	75	67	81	51	68	48	64	55	71
Cambodia	3	3	...	1 156	...	27	...	34	...	20	...	...	...	...	...	...
China	3	2	130 175	95 852	40	67	46	70	33	62	...	...	...	...	...	...
Cyprus	3	3	...	...	94	97	93	96	95	99	85	93	84	91	86	94
Dem. People's Rep. of Korea	.	6	...	...	...	...	...	...	...	...	...	...	...	...	...	...
Georgia	5	2	...	606	...	73	...	74	...	72	...	71	...	71	...	70
Hong Kong	5	2	651	633	70	75	67	73	72	77	65	71	63	69	68	73
India	3	4	117 915	136 705	38	49	48	59	26	38	...	...	...	...	...	...
Indonesia	3	3	22 963	25 376	41	48	...	52	...	44	...	42	...	45	...	39
Iran, Islamic Republic of	3	4	7 800	11 017	44	69	52	76	35	62	...	...	...	...	...	...
Iraq	3	3	2 133	...	53	...	67	...	38	...	44	...	55	...	32	...
Israel	♦3	3	313	612	80	89	76	...	85	...	...	...	...	...	...	...
Japan	3	3	11 589	10 362	95	98	94	98	96	99	95	96	...	96	...	97
Jordan	♦2	2	...	...	...	...	...	...	...	...	...	...	...	...	...	...
Kazakhstan	5	2	2 118	2 245	103	83	...	82	...	83	...	...	...	...	...	...
Kuwait	4	4	264	324	91	64	95	64	87	64	...	...	...	...	...	...
Kyrgyzstan	5	2	603	657	109	81	111	76	107	85	...	...	...	...	...	...
Lao People's Dem. Rep.	3	3	484	617	23	25	27	31	19	19	...	18	...	21	...	15
Lebanon	4	3	...	421	...	81	...	77	...	84	...	...	...	...	...	...
Macau	.	6	...	29	...	71	...	66	...	76	...	...	...	...	...	...
Malaysia	3	4	2 446	2 848	53	57	53	55	53	59	...	...	...	...	...	...
Maldives	5	2	...	39	...	49	...	49	...	49	...	...	...	...	...	...
Mongolia	5	2	304	399	90	59	85	50	96	68	...	57	...	48	...	65
Myanmar	4	2	5 516	5 919	23	30	24	29	22	30	...	...	...	...	...	...
Nepal	2	3	1 968	2 288	25	37	37	49	12	25	...	...	...	...	...	...
Oman	3	3	178	293	27	66	36	68	17	64	...	56	...	58	...	55
Pakistan	3	4	17 020	...	17	...	24	...	10	...	...	...	...	...	...	...
Palestinian Auton. Territories	.	2	.	...	.	...	.	...	.	...	.	...	.	...	.	...
Gaza Strip	.	.	...	...	...	...	...	...	...	...	...	...	...	...	...	...
West Bank	.	.	...	...	...	...	...	...	...	...	...	...	...	...	...	...
Philippines	.	4	4 991	6 071	64	79	64	...	65	...	50	60	49	...	50	...
Qatar	3	3	27	44	82	83	78	83	86	84	66	70	63	69	69	71
Republic of Korea	3	3	5 385	4 670	92	101	93	101	91	101	84	96	85	96	84	96
Saudi Arabia	3	3	1 504	2 463	40	58	48	62	31	54	27	48	32	54	22	41
Singapore	4	3	341	...	59	...	58	...	60	...	...	...	...	...	...	...
Sri Lanka	♦6	2	2 325	3 103	63	75	60	71	66	78	...	...	...	...	...	...
Syrian Arab Republic	3	3	1 496	2 161	58	44	68	47	48	40	51	39	59	41	42	37
Tajikistan	5	2	...	887	...	82	...	86	...	77	...	...	...	...	...	...
Thailand	3	3	7 379	6 951	30	55	...	...	...	...	...	...	...	...	...	...
Turkey	3	3	7 046	8 373	42	56	52	67	30	45	36	50	...	58	...	41
Turkmenistan	5	2	...	...	...	...	...	...	...	...	...	...	...	...	...	...
United Arab Emirates	3	3	114	200	55	80	54	76	55	84	...	71	...	67	...	75
Uzbekistan	5	2	2 919	3 566	107	93	117	99	97	87	...	...	...	...	...	...
Viet Nam	4	3	9 951	11 705	43	47	44	...	41	...	...	...	...	...	...	...
Yemen	.	3	...	926	...	23	...	36	...	8	...	...	...	...	...	...
Europe																
Albania	.	4	248	256	72	35	75	35	68	35	...	...	...	...	...	...
Austria	4	4	859	752	99	104	103	107	94	102	...	90	...	90	...	90

Country or territory	Duration in years of secondary general education		School-age population (000)		Gross enrolment ratio (%)						Net enrolment ratio (%)					
					Total		Male		Female		Total		Male		Female	
	Lower	Upper	1985	1995	1985	1995	1985	1995	1985	1995	1985	1995	1985	1995	1985	1995
Belarus	♦5	2	724	1 125	99	94	...	92	...	96	...	...	...	...	...	...
Belgium	2	4	813	731	102	144	101	140	102	148	89	98	87	98	90	98
Bosnia and Herzegovina	...	...	...	...	...	...	...	...	...	...	...	...	...	...	...	...
Bulgaria	♦4	4	368	970	102	78	101	78	102	77	...	75	...	...	...	...
Croatia	♦4	4	...	510	...	82	...	81	...	83	...	...	...	...	...	...
Czech Republic	4	4	...	1 248	...	96	...	94	...	97	...	88	...	87	...	89
Denmark	3	3	462	378	105	118	106	116	105	120	83	86	83	85	84	88
Estonia	♦3	3	106	131	117	86	111	82	124	90	...	77	...	74	...	81
Finland	3	3	401	393	106	116	98	108	114	124	...	93	...	92	...	93
France	4	3	5 961	5 434	90	110	86	110	94	110	82	92	78	92	85	93
Germany	6	3	...	7 915	...	103	...	104	...	102	...	88	...	88	...	88
Greece	3	3	899	899	90	95	92	97	89	92	81	84	81	84	81	83
Hungary	.	4	586	646	72	81	72	79	72	83	70	73	69	71	70	76
Iceland	3	4	30	29	91	103	95	104	87	102	...	...	...	...	...	...
Ireland	3	2	346	343	98	114	93	111	103	117	81	85	79	83	84	87
Italy	3	5	7 407	5 575	72	88	73	87	72	88	69	...	69	...	69	...
Latvia	5	3	280	282	103	85	...	83	...	87	...	78	...	77	...	78
Lithuania	5	3	445	434	105	84	...	83	...	86	...	...	...	...	...	...
Luxembourg	3	4	34	31	75	74	76	72	74	76	66	...	66	...	67	...
Malta	2	5	36	40	78	89	79	93	77	86	74	84	73	84	75	83
Monaco	4	3	...	...	...	...	...	...	...	...	...	...	...	87	...	90
Netherlands	3	3	1 384	1 083	117	139	120	143	114	136	89	...	87	...	90	...
Norway	3	3	399	318	97	116	95	119	100	113	86	94	84	94	88	94
Poland	.	4	2 004	2 556	78	96	76	95	81	96	73	83	70	79	76	86
Portugal	3	3	1 013	921	57	102	53	98	62	106	...	78	...	74	...	83
Republic of Moldova	♦5	2	548	552	86	80	83	78	89	81	...	...	...	...	...	...
Romania	♦4	4	1 636	2 853	84	78	87	77	81	78	...	73	...	72	...	74
Russian Federation	5	2	13 789	15 778	97	87	96	84	98	91	...	...	...	...	...	...
San Marino	3	5	...	...	...	...	...	...	...	...	...	...	...	...	...	...
Slovakia	4	4	...	730	...	91	...	89	...	93	...	...	...	...	...	...
Slovenia	4	4	...	233	...	91	...	90	...	92	...	...	...	...	...	...
Spain	3	4	4 626	4 029	98	118	95	112	102	123	...	94	...	91	...	97
Sweden	3	3	683	601	90	132	89	130	92	133	...	96	...	96	...	97
Switzerland	3	4	659	553	88	91	92	94	83	88	78	...	82	...	74	...
The FYR of Macedonia	.	4	137	142	56	57	...	56	...	57	...	51	...	50	...	51
Ukraine	♦5	2	3 531	5 207	96	91	...	88	...	94	...	...	...	...	...	...
United Kingdom	3	4	5 826	4 992	84	134	82	123	86	145	80	92	78	91	82	93
Yugoslavia	4	4	...	1 273	...	65	...	64	...	67	...	...	...	...	...	...
Oceania																
Australia	4	2	1 597	1 488	80	147	79	147	81	146	78	89	77	89	79	90
Cook Islands	3	3	...	...	...	...	...	...	...	...	...	...	...	...	...	...
Fiji	.	6	88	104	51	64	51	64	51	65	...	...	...	...	...	...
Kiribati	.	5	...	...	...	...	...	...	...	...	...	...	...	...	...	...
New Zealand	4	3	415	358	85	117	84	118	87	116	84	93	83	93	85	94
Papua New Guinea	4	2	502	561	12	14	14	17	9	11	...	...	...	...	...	...
Samoa	.	5	31	28	66	47	62	44	71	50	...	45	...	42	...	48
Solomon Islands	3	2	33	45	19	17	...	21	...	14	...	...	...	...	...	...
Tonga	.	7	...	...	...	...	...	...	...	...	...	...	...	...	...	...
Tuvalu	.	4	...	...	...	...	...	...	...	...	...	...	...	...	...	...
Vanuatu	4	3	...	24	...	20	...	23	...	18	...	...	...	...	...	...

Table 7
Teaching staff in pre-primary, primary and secondary education

| Country or territory | Pupil-teacher ratio | | | | | | Percentage of female teachers | | | | | | Teachers (all levels) per 1,000 non-agricultural labour force | |
| | Pre-primary | | Primary | | Secondary general | | Pre-primary | | Primary | | Secondary general | | | |
	1985	1995	1985	1995	1985	1995	1985	1995	1985	1995	1985	1995	1985	1995
Africa														
Algeria	...	26	28	27	22	17	...	89	40	44	37	45	53	52
Angola	44	...	31	...	38	...	...	...	...	...	...	...	45	...
Benin	21	23	33	49	36	29	55	61	24	24	17	...	28	19
Botswana	...	...	32	26	25	18	...	...	78	76	42	44	42	47
Burkina Faso	40	22	62	58	25	35	91	...	25	24	...	18	24	45
Burundi	55	44	56	65	17	25	94	...	47	47	23	...	46	37
Cameroon	30	24	51	46	34	31	100	99	27	32	21	25	41	39
Cape Verde	32	33	38	29	34	27	100	...	61	59	74	36	26	34
Central African Republic	40	...	66	...	74	...	100	...	23	...	10	...	28	...
Chad	29	28	71	62	38	40	100	100	4	8	...	4	18	20
Comoros	29	29	35	42	32	25	...	...	21	...	...	...	83	55
Congo	10	7	61	70	41	33	100	100	30	36	8	15	41	28
Côte d'Ivoire	37	21	37	45	19	21	100	93	18	18	...	...	36	32
Dem. Rep. of the Congo	...	43	37	45	...	...	...	53	...	22	...	...	40	33
Djibouti	59	41	44	36	23	23	...	100	...	33	...	19	...	...
Egypt	40	28	30	24	21	20	99	99	49	53	38	41	49	51
Equatorial Guinea	...	28	...	55	...	31	...	100	...	27	...	12	...	51
Eritrea	...	35	...	41	...	39	...	99	...	35	...	13	...	25
Ethiopia	46	37	48	33	43	33	...	96	26	27	11	10	31	32
Gabon	26	26	46	52	21	25	...	...	35	44	25	19	40	30
Gambia	32	32	23	30	28	29	...	...	35	34	23	...	61	53
Ghana	19	21	23	28	20	19	97	...	40	...	26	...	50	42
Guinea	...	34	36	49	23	30	...	80	19	25	7	12	49	35
Guinea-Bissau	28	...	25	...	10	...	87	...	23	...	11	...	69	...
Kenya	37	34	34	31	20	16	100	97	34	40	37	33	100	91
Lesotho	...	...	55	49	21	24	...	...	77	79	52	51	20	22
Liberia	...	...	...	...	...	...	...	...	...	...	...	...	...	...
Libyan Arab Jamahiriya	14	...	16	...	14	...	100	...	56	...	21	...	84	...
Madagascar	...	...	38	40	29	20	...	...	53	56	...	...	57	38
Malawi	...	...	61	62	22	...	...	...	33	38	...	...	36	77
Mali	...	32	34	66	12	25	...	89	22	23	16	18	31	19
Mauritania	...	...	51	52	24	24	...	100	15	20	...	10	15	16
Mauritius	...	19	22	22	20	21	...	...	43	50	41	44	37	31
Morocco	21	21	28	28	19	16	10	30	33	38	27	32	48	41
Mozambique	...	...	64	58	40	38	...	...	22	23	24	19	21	18
Namibia	...	25	...	32	...	21	...	100	...	65	...	46	...	50
Niger	35	22	37	37	26	28	100	100	33	34	17	23	32	35
Nigeria	...	...	40	37	38	...	...	...	41	46	...	...	25	23
Rwanda	52	...	57	...	...	...	79	...	46	...	...	...	75	...
Sao Tome and Principe	...	...	39	...	21	...	...	...	46	...	...	...	...	...
Senegal	23	21	46	58	24	24	...	65	27	26	17	15	32	27
Seychelles	29	18	22	17	13	14	100	100	85	88	28	51	...	...
Sierra Leone	18	...	39	...	33	...	100	...	22	...	21	...	34	...
Somalia	12	...	19	...	18	...	94	...	45	...	11	...	17	...
South Africa	...	25	...	37	...	28	...	98	...	58	...	64	...	27
Sudan	42	...	35	36	25	...	41	41	44	60	33	...	35	37
Swaziland	...	20	34	33	19	18	...	...	80	77	46	43	52	55
Togo	27	27	46	51	22	34	100	100	20	14	13	11	36	34
Tunisia	29	...	32	25	...	...	100	...	39	49	...	36	43	45

Country or territory	Pupil-teacher ratio						Percentage of female teachers						Teachers (all levels) per 1,000 non-agricultural labour force	
	Pre-primary		Primary		Secondary general		Pre-primary		Primary		Secondary general			
	1985	1995	1985	1995	1985	1995	1985	1995	1985	1995	1985	1995	1985	1995
Uganda	...	...	34	35	21	17	...	...	31	32	...	...	68	62
United Rep. of Tanzania	...	...	34	37	19	18	...	100	39	43	25	25	60	46
Zambia	...	...	49	39	23	...	...	...	43	43	25	...	53	57
Zimbabwe	...	...	40	39	28	30	...	...	43	41	30	32	65	54
America, North														
Antigua and Barbuda	...	...	...	...	...	...	...	...	...	...	...	...	...	...
Bahamas	...	17	29	22	13	16	97	100	91	91	50	69	35	27
Barbados	...	...	21	...	20	...	...	...	74	...	53	...	33	...
Belize	16	17	26	26	13	14	...	99	72	71	43	47	70	66
British Virgin Islands	13	9	18	16	14	11	93	100	83	85	...	65	...	...
Canada	33	39	17	16	15	19	...	67	66	67	46	67	28	24
Costa Rica	28	23	31	31	19	21	...	...	...	...	...	...	37	35
Cuba	23	25	14	14	12	10	100	100	77	81	53	61	61	45
Dominica	29	23	25	29	...	...	100	99	73	80	...	...	...	...
Dominican Republic	...	...	44	35	37	22	...	...	...	71	...	50	28	29
El Salvador	45	26	42	28	...	...	97	...	66	...	...	...	32	39
Grenada	21	...	21	23	27	27	99	99	70	70	48	52	...	...
Guatemala	30	25	37	34	...	...	...	...	62	...	36	...	40	43
Haiti	22	...	38	...	20	...	100	...	50	...	12	...	39	...
Honduras	35	29	38	35	...	...	100	100	74	73	...	...	43	35
Jamaica	37	...	35	37	22	...	...	...	88	89	46	...	32	28
Mexico	30	24	34	29	18	17	100	98	57	...	...	...	57	47
Netherlands Antilles	...	...	...	...	...	...	...	...	...	...	...	...	...	...
Nicaragua	32	29	33	38	30	38	96	97	75	84	58	56	37	29
Panama	25	23	25	...	19	...	99	...	78	...	56	...	49	...
Saint Kitts and Nevis	33	17	22	21	15	15	98	100	82	79	54	59	...	...
Saint Lucia	18	15	30	27	19	18	100	100	79	83	58	61	...	...
Saint Vincent and the Grenadines	13	14	18	20	24	25	...	99	64	67	52	51	...	...
Trinidad and Tobago	14	...	22	25	20	20	96	...	70	74	52	56	34	29
United States	...	...	14	16	...	15	...	...	...	86	...	56	...	31
America, South														
Argentina	19	16	20	...	8	...	100	94	92	...	74	...	57	...
Bolivia	44	...	25	...	25	...	...	...	...	...	...	...	56	...
Brazil	24	21	24	23	...	11	...	...	...	...	...	...	39	38
Chile	24	30	29	27	...	...	100	97	75	72	...	...	35	37
Colombia	26	21	30	25	21	22	60	96	79	80	43	...	39	37
Ecuador	24	21	32	26	15	13	95	90	65	68	41	44	61	53
Guyana	18	19	36	29	26	41	99	99	70	80	50	44	38	27
Paraguay	...	21	25	24	...	12	...	90	...	55	...	65	49	56
Peru	31	23	35	28	21	19	99	98	60	58	...	39	54	56
Suriname	25	28	23	21	12	...	...	100	83	87	...	...	89	69
Uruguay	27	26	25	20	...	...	95	100	93	...	...	...	32	...
Venezuela	25	23	25	23	...	...	98	98	77	75	...	...	42	39
Asia														
Afghanistan	19	...	37	58	18	28	100	100	53	38	33	34	14	18
Armenia	11	8	...	22	...	10	...	...	...	97	...	85	...	44
Azerbaijan	8	7	...	20	...	...	100	100	...	83	...	...	...	76
Bahrain	30	27	21	18	16	14	100	100	50	67	62	61	35	40

Table 7 (continued)

| Country or territory | Pupil-teacher ratio | | | | | | Percentage of female teachers | | | | | | Teachers (all levels) per 1,000 non-agricultural labour force | |
| | Pre-primary | | Primary | | Secondary general | | Pre-primary | | Primary | | Secondary general | | | |
	1985	1995	1985	1995	1985	1995	1985	1995	1985	1995	1985	1995	1985	1995
Bangladesh	...	...	47	...	28	...	...	...	8	...	9	...	24	...
Bhutan	...	...	37	30	...	...	...	...	...	...	...	...	44	57
Brunei Darussalam	22	21	16	15	12	14	89	92	55	60	34	48	56	50
Cambodia	23	25	38	45	39	18	100	100	25	37	28	28	50	45
China	27	31	25	24	18	16	96	95	40	47	28	36	57	53
Cyprus	24	20	22	19	13	12	99	99	49	65	50	55	...	...
Dem. People's Rep. of Korea	21	...	26	...	...	...	100	...	90	...	38	...	...	...
Georgia	...	8	...	16	...	...	...	100	...	94	...	...	...	54
Hong Kong	30	21	27	24	23	20	98	99	74	76	52	51	19	19
India	62	62	47	63	26	25	93	...	27	32	31	35	36	32
Indonesia	22	17	25	23	15	14	...	...	49	52	33	39	65	58
Iran, Islamic Republic of	18	23	22	32	16	32	100	100	52	55	39	46	65	47
Iraq	17	19	24	22	30	20	100	100	67	68	55	55	56	45
Israel	...	30	14	16	...	7	...	97	81	83	...	...	70	62
Japan	19	17	24	18	...	...	88	89	56	60	...	34	26	27
Jordan	21	23	31	21	18	20	100	100	66	61	46	48	...	...
Kazakhstan	...	6	26	20	15	10	...	...	96	97	71	74	53	52
Kuwait	17	16	18	15	13	11	100	100	68	71	52	54	50	52
Kyrgyzstan	...	9	19	20	17	13	...	...	82	83	63	71	75	57
Lao People's Dem. Rep.	16	16	25	30	12	13	100	100	32	42	38	39	86	74
Lebanon	25	...	16	12	...	...	...	...	...	...	...	...	...	...
Macau	...	...	...	...	...	...	...	...	...	...	...	...	...	...
Malaysia	32	23	24	20	22	19	98	99	50	59	48	54	42	41
Maldives	...	...	...	...	...	...	...	...	...	...	...	...	...	...
Mongolia	28	12	30	25	22	18	...	100	...	91	...	67	42	33
Myanmar	...	...	54	48	23	16	...	...	59	67	69	74	30	37
Nepal	23	...	35	39	...	...	61	...	10	16	...	...	151	174
Oman	23	20	27	26	13	17	100	100	44	50	33	48	52	73
Pakistan	...	...	41	...	18	...	...	...	32	...	31	...	23	...
Palestinian Auton. Territories	.	31	.	42	.	7	.	98	.	48	.	41	.	...
Gaza Strip	39	.	42	.	28	.	...	.	...	.	...	.	...	...
West Bank	26	.	35	.	20	.	94	.	50	.	39	.	...	...
Philippines	41	...	31	35	32	36	...	...	95	...	95	...	40	34
Qatar	20	22	13	9	9	10	100	100	66	79	55	60	36	37
Republic of Korea	34	21	38	32	37	24	90	94	43	59	32	41	24	24
Saudi Arabia	17	13	16	13	14	11	98	100	42	51	42	49	51	60
Singapore	23	...	27	...	22	...	100	...	69	...	58	...	19	...
Sri Lanka	...	...	35	28	22	22	...	...	...	83	...	62	51	47
Syrian Arab Republic	31	22	26	24	18	17	100	94	61	65	27	44	74	70
Tajikistan	...	9	...	23	...	10	...	...	...	51	...	34	...	84
Thailand	20	...	19	20	18	20	...	...	...	...	...	...	62	46
Turkey	20	16	31	28	24	27	99	99	42	44	36	40	40	37
Turkmenistan	...	...	...	...	...	...	...	...	...	...	...	...	...	...
United Arab Emirates	22	16	18	17	13	13	100	100	54	69	...	55	20	33
Uzbekistan	16	11	24	21	13	9	...	...	78	82	49	49	88	96
Viet Nam	26	25	34	34	23	25	100	...	70	...	63	...	63	52
Yemen	...	18	...	...	...	...	...	...	...	...	...	...	...	...
Europe														
Albania	23	19	20	18	29	17	100	100	52	60	57	51	66	57
Austria	22	18	10	12	10	8	99	98	79	84	57	61	41	45

Country or territory	Pupil-teacher ratio						Percentage of female teachers						Teachers (all levels) per 1,000 non-agricultural labour force	
	Pre-primary		Primary		Secondary general		Pre-primary		Primary		Secondary general			
	1985	1995	1985	1995	1985	1995	1985	1995	1985	1995	1985	1995	1985	1995
Belarus	8	7	17	20	...	...	...	...	...	...	...	...	46	47
Belgium	20	17	17	12	...	...	99	99	65	72	...	...	47	61
Bosnia and Herzegovina	...	...	...	...	...	...	...	...	...	...	...	...	...	...
Bulgaria	12	11	18	17	17	11	100	100	75	89	67	75	34	37
Croatia	...	12	19	20	...	15	...	100	73	89	...	67	26	29
Czech Republic	...	11	28	20	...	12	...	100	...	93	...	72	34	37
Denmark	16	13	12	10	9	9	57	92	57	58	...	49	36	40
Estonia	...	9	...	17	...	10	...	100	...	89	...	83	...	42
Finland	...	...	15	...	14	...	...	...	...	...	...	...	35	34
France	25	24	17	19	...	...	78	80	76	78	...	...	36	38
Germany	...	20	...	18	...	14	...	97	...	85	...	48	...	30
Greece	21	16	23	16	17	12	100	100	49	55	56	56	38	42
Hungary	13	11	15	11	13	12	100	100	82	84	64	67	40	47
Iceland	...	...	...	...	...	...	...	...	...	...	...	...	...	...
Ireland	29	25	27	23	...	...	76	78	76	78	...	...	44	44
Italy	15	13	14	11	10	8	...	100	89	93	67	71	47	42
Latvia	...	7	...	14	10	8	...	99	...	97	...	81	...	44
Lithuania	7	8	25	17	16	10	...	100	97	98	78	82	43	44
Luxembourg	17	19	13	...	10	...	...	...	49	...	...	...	30	...
Malta	24	15	22	20	12	11	100	100	67	83	38	47	38	49
Monaco	...	22	...	19	...	12	...	...	...	...	...	71	...	...
Netherlands	17	16	17	19	15	12	100	100	53	54	27	30	39	34
Norway	4	4	10	9	...	7	98	96	70	...	...	...	63	61
Poland	17	13	18	16	16	22	98	99	...	...	...	...	38	43
Portugal	20	20	17	12	14	...	99	...	83	...	63	...	37	45
Republic of Moldova	9	7	26	23	...	...	100	100	96	97	...	...	55	51
Romania	26	18	21	20	14	12	100	100	70	84	53	65	32	36
Russian Federation	10	9	27	20	15	12	...	...	98	98	77	79	34	39
San Marino	7	9	9	5	7	...	100	100	88	88	61	...	...	...
Slovakia	14	12	...	24	...	16	...	100	...	91	...	75	...	33
Slovenia	...	11	...	14	...	17	...	98	...	92	...	76	...	32
Spain	28	22	25	18	21	...	93	95	69	71	48	...	35	37
Sweden	...	4	10	11	...	11	...	97	77	72	...	64	44	42
Switzerland	...	21	...	12	...	...	...	99	...	69	...	...	...	...
The FYR of Macedonia	...	11	21	20	...	17	...	99	...	53	...	52	36	29
Ukraine	8	8	23	20	10	11	...	...	98	98	...	...	41	41
United Kingdom	26	35	18	19	14	13	100	100	80	82	50	57	27	31
Yugoslavia	...	11	...	22	...	...	...	95	...	75	...	...	...	28
Oceania														
Australia	...	...	17	16	12	12	100	...	70	76	48	52	32	38
Cook Islands	26		...	...	...	...	...	...	...	...	...	...	...	...
Fiji	21	...	28	...	17	...	99	...	58	56	44	47	64	...
Kiribati	...	...	29	27	16	18	...	...	51	59	50	44	...	...
New Zealand	27	18	19	18	19	14	96	95	70	81	46	56	37	40
Papua New Guinea	...	32	30	33	25	24	...	66	30	37	35	35	46	40
Samoa	...	...	26	24	24	19	...	...	74	71	46	45	...	...
Solomon Islands	...	...	26	24	19	...	...	...	34	...	22	...	64	83
Tonga	...	...	23	22	19	18	...	...	62	66	45	31	...	...
Tuvalu	...	...	22	...	...	...	...	...	70	...	...	...	...	...
Vanuatu	...	...	21	31	...	19	...	...	...	41	...	36	...	...

Table 8
Tertiary education: enrolment and breakdown by ISCED level

Country or territory	Number of students per 100,000 inhabitants		Gross enrolment ratio (%) Total		Male		Female		Percentage of students by ISCED level 1995 Level 5	Level 6	Level 7	Percentage of female students in each ISCED level 1995 Level 5	Level 6	Level 7
	1985	1995	1985	1995	1985	1995	1985	1995						
Africa														
Algeria	798	1 126	7.9	10.9	10.7	12.8	5.0	8.9	♦ 15	80	6	37	47	27
Angola	63	...	0.7	...	...	...	...	...	...	...	...	...	...	...
Benin	225	208	2.4	2.6	4.4	4.2	0.7	0.9	...	...	...	...	...	...
Botswana	180	403	1.8	4.1	2.0	4.4	1.6	3.7	♦ 22	74	5	66	45	50
Burkina Faso	52	96	0.6	1.1	0.9	1.6	0.3	0.5	4	96	./.	34	22	./.
Burundi	59	74	0.6	0.9	0.9	1.3	0.3	0.4	...	...	...	...	...	...
Cameroon	190	...	2.2	...	...	...	...	...	...	...	...	...	...	...
Cape Verde	–	–	–	–	–	–	–	–	–	–	–	...	...	...
Central African Republic	102	...	1.2	...	2.2	...	0.2	...	...	...	...	...	...	...
Chad	...	70	...	0.8	...	1.5	...	0.1	♦ –	74	26	–	...	...
Comoros	...	41	...	0.5	...	0.6	...	0.3	...	...	...	...	...	...
Congo	555	...	6.3	...	10.9	...	1.9	...	13	68	19	...	...	...
Côte d'Ivoire	219	396	2.6	4.4	4.2	6.7	1.0	2.1	16	80	3	33	21	20
Dem. Rep. of the Congo	129	212	1.4	2.3	...	...	...	...	...	...	...	...	...	...
Djibouti	...	22	...	0.2	...	0.2	...	0.2	100	–	–	47	–	–
Egypt	1 718	1 674	18.1	18.1	24.5	22.1	11.2	13.7	♦ –	86	14	–	40	32
Equatorial Guinea	...	...	...	...	...	...	...	...	...	...	...	...	...	...
Eritrea	...	102	...	1.1	...	1.9	...	0.3	10	90	–	21	13	–
Ethiopia	66	60	0.7	0.7	1.2	1.1	0.3	0.3	53	45	2	24	16	9
Gabon	...	...	...	...	...	...	...	...	...	...	...	...	...	...
Gambia	...	148	...	1.7	...	2.3	...	1.2	...	...	...	...	...	...
Ghana	132	...	1.4	...	...	...	...	...	...	...	...	...	...	...
Guinea	176	...	2.1	...	3.5	...	0.6	...	...	...	...	...	...	...
Guinea-Bissau	...	...	...	...	...	...	...	...	...	...	...	...	...	...
Kenya	109	...	1.2	...	1.8	...	0.7	...	...	...	...	...	...	...
Lesotho	113	221	1.3	2.4	1.2	2.2	1.3	2.7	58	40	2	56	53	48
Liberia	216	...	2.5	...	3.7	...	1.2	...	...	...	...	...	...	...
Libyan Arab Jamahiriya	792	...	9.2	...	...	...	...	...	...	...	...	...	...	...
Madagascar	366	316	3.8	3.4	...	3.8	...	3.0	62	36	2	30	44	39
Malawi	54	76	0.6	0.8	0.9	1.2	0.3	0.5	65	34	0	37	21	18
Mali	86	...	0.9	...	1.6	...	0.2	...	...	...	...	...	...	...
Mauritania	256	393	2.8	4.1	...	6.8	...	1.4	10	90	–	34	16	–
Mauritius	114	564	1.1	6.3	1.3	...	0.8	...	...	...	...	...	...	...
Morocco	837	1 153	8.7	11.3	11.9	13.0	5.5	9.4	11	83	6	36	42	30
Mozambique	11	41	0.1	0.5	0.2	...	0.1	...	./.	100	–	./.	26	–
Namibia	...	738	...	8.1	...	6.3	...	9.9	...	...	...	...	...	...
Niger	43	...	0.6	...	0.9	...	0.2	...	...	...	...	...	...	...
Nigeria	321	367	3.3	4.1	4.9	...	1.8	...	♦ –	100	–	–	...	–
Rwanda	33	...	0.4	...	0.7	...	0.1	...	...	...	...	...	...	...
Sao Tome and Principe	–	–	–	–	–	–	–	–	–	–	–	–	–	–
Senegal	209	290	2.4	3.4	3.8	...	1.0	...	...	...	...	...	...	...
Seychelles	...	...	...	...	...	...	...	...	...	...	...	...	...	...
Sierra Leone	159	...	1.8	...	...	...	...	...	...	...	...	...	...	...
Somalia	174	...	2.1	...	3.4	...	0.8	...	...	...	...	...	...	...
South Africa	...	1 524	...	15.9	...	16.6	...	15.2	47	46	8	48	52	43
Sudan	174	...	2.0	...	2.4	...	1.4	...	...	...	...	...	...	...
Swaziland	421	543	4.4	5.1	...	5.7	...	4.5	64	31	4	42	50	52
Togo	173	281	1.9	3.2	3.4	5.6	0.5	0.8	44	56	–	16	12	–
Tunisia	567	1 253	5.5	12.9	6.9	14.2	4.0	11.5	8	86	6	44	44	35

Country or territory	Number of students per 100,000 inhabitants		Gross enrolment ratio (%)						Percentage of students by ISCED level 1995			Percentage of female students in each ISCED level 1995		
			Total		Male		Female		Level 5	Level 6	Level 7	Level 5	Level 6	Level 7
	1985	1995	1985	1995	1985	1995	1985	1995						
Uganda	68	142	0.8	1.5	1.2	2.2	0.4	0.9	63	32	5	32	33	24
United Rep. of Tanzania	22	43	0.3	0.5	0.4	0.8	0.1	0.1	32	64	5	19	15	16
Zambia	181	241	2.0	2.5	3.6	3.6	0.6	1.4	...	...	...	...	...	...
Zimbabwe	368	679	3.9	6.9	...	10.1	..	3.8	69	28	3	41	20	25
America, North														
Antigua and Barbuda	–	–	–	–	–	–	–	–	–	–	–	–	–	–
Bahamas	1 956	2 331	17.7	...	...	...	...	...	...	...	...	...	...	...
Barbados	...	2 501	...	28.1	...	22.4	...	33.9	♦ –	90	10	–	64	49
Belize	–	–	–	–	–	–	–	–	...	...	...	...	...	...
British Virgin Islands	–	–	–	–	–	–	–	–	–	–	–	–	–	–
Canada	6 320	6 984	69.6	102.9	62.0	95.7	77.7	110.2	49	45	6	50	57	46
Costa Rica	2 414	2 919	22.0	31.9	...	...	...	...	♦ –	100	–	–	...	–
Cuba	2 325	1 116	20.1	12.7	18.3	10.1	22.1	15.5	–	100	–	–	60	–
Dominica	86	...	...	...	...	...	...	...	100	–	–	47	–	–
Dominican Republic	1 941	...	18.0	...	...	...	...	...	...	...	...	...	...	...
El Salvador	...	2 031	...	17.7	...	17.5	...	17.9	20	80	./.	61	48	./.
Grenada	...	...	...	...	...	...	...	...	...	...	...	...	...	...
Guatemala	741	755	8.1	8.1	...	...	...	...	...	...	...	...	...	...
Haiti	107	...	1.1	...	1.6	...	0.6	...	...	...	...	...	...	...
Honduras	875	985	8.8	10.0	10.9	11.0	6.7	8.8	2	98	0	43	44	38
Jamaica	475	667	4.4	6.0	5.0	6.8	3.8	5.2						
Mexico	1 600	1 586	15.9	14.3	20.4	15.3	11.5	13.3	♦ –	96	4	–	46	37
Netherlands Antilles	–	–	–	–	–	–	–	–	–	–	–	–	–	–
Nicaragua	905	1 029	9.3	9.4	8.2	9.4	10.4	9.3	...	...	...	...	...	...
Panama	2 552	2 686	24.6	27.2	20.6	21.9	28.6	32.6	♦ 9	90	1	33	62	60
Saint Kitts and Nevis	493	1 024	...	...	...	...	...	...	100	–	–	55	–	–
Saint Lucia	290	725	...	...	...	...	...	...	...	...	...	...	...	...
Saint Vincent and the Grenadines	722	...	...	...	...	...	...	...	...	...	...	...	...	...
Trinidad and Tobago	559	715	5.3	7.7	6.5	8.4	4.1	6.8	9	74	18	69	52	45
United States	5 064	5 395	60.2	81.1	56.3	71.0	64.3	91.7	39	47	14	58	54	53
America, South														
Argentina	2 792	3 083	35.7	36.2	33.6	...	37.8	...	...	...	...	...	...	...
Bolivia	2 068	...	22.5	...	...	...	...	...	...	...	...	...	...	...
Brazil	1 079	1 094	10.3	11.3	...	10.4	...	12.2	–	100	./.	–	55	./.
Chile	1 639	2 412	15.6	28.2	17.6	30.2	13.7	26.0	26	71	2	44	46	44
Colombia	1 331	1 643	11.3	17.2	11.6	16.8	11.0	17.6	20	74	6	51	52	51
Ecuador	...	...	...	...	...	...	...	...	...	...	...	...	...	...
Guyana	294	846	2.4	8.6	2.5	8.9	2.3	8.2	74	24	2	47	53	55
Paraguay	889	931	9.1	10.3	...	9.8	...	10.8	17	83	0	77	48	78
Peru	2 321	3 268	22.4	31.1	...	...	...	...	...	...	...	...	...	...
Suriname	730	...	...	...	...	...	...	...	...	...	...	...	...	...
Uruguay	...	2 223	...	27.3	...	...	...	...	...	...	...	...	...	...
Venezuela	2 585	...	25.3	...	29.3	...	21.1	...	...	...	...	...	...	...
Asia														
Afghanistan	...	...	...	...	...	...	...	...	...	...	...	...	...	...
Armenia	3 076	...	32.3	...	...	...	...	...	...	...	...	...	...	...
Azerbaijan	2 730	1 751	24.4	19.8	...	21.9	...	17.6	25	75	./.	55	...	./.
Bahrain	1 011	...	12.8	...	9.7	...	16.4	...	...	...	...	...	...	...

World education report

Table 8 (continued)

Country or territory	Number of students per 100,000 inhabitants		Gross enrolment ratio (%)						Percentage of students by ISCED level 1995			Percentage of female students in each ISCED level 1995		
			Total		Male		Female		Level 5	Level 6	Level 7	Level 5	Level 6	Level 7
	1985	1995	1985	1995	1985	1995	1985	1995						
Bangladesh	464	...	4.8	...	7.4	...	1.9	...	...	...	...	...	...	...
Bhutan	...	...	...	...	...	...	...	...	...	...	...	...	...	...
Brunei Darussalam	271	514	2.9	6.6	2.1	5.3	3.9	8.0	37	61	2	64	53	38
Cambodia	...	119	...	1.6	...	2.7	...	0.5	...	...	...	...	...	...
China	328	478	2.9	5.7	3.9	7.3	1.7	4.0	62	35	2	...	...	...
Cyprus	484	1 191	7.0	20.0	7.0	16.0	7.0	24.0	76	22	2	54	82	28
Dem. People's Rep. of Korea	...	...	...	...	...	...	...	...	...	...	...	...	...	...
Georgia	2 697	2 845	32.7	38.1	...	35.2	...	41.1	19	80	1	53	52	55
Hong Kong	1 448	1 635	13.3	21.9	16.9	23.9	9.4	19.7	30	58	12	43	45	32
India	582	601	6.0	6.4	8.1	7.9	3.8	4.8	...	...	...	...	...	...
Indonesia	586	1 146	6.3	11.1	8.5	13.5	4.1	8.6	29	71	./.	42	32	./.
Iran, Islamic Republic of	377	1 364	4.1	14.8	5.7	18.7	2.4	10.7	♦ 14	80	7	28	34	21
Iraq	1 108	...	11.5	...	14.4	...	8.6	...	...	...	...	...	...	...
Israel	2 742	3 598	33.1	41.1	33.9	...	32.2	...	41	41	18	47	54	53
Japan	1 943	3 139	27.8	40.3	35.5	44.0	19.8	36.3	34	63	3	68	32	19
Jordan	...	...	...	...	...	...	...	...	23	71	6	65	42	25
Kazakhstan	3 481	2 807	36.7	32.7	...	28.7	...	36.8	44	55	0	58	53	...
Kuwait	1 377	2 247	16.6	25.4	15.3	22.4	17.9	28.3	28	71	2	47	68	49
Kyrgyzstan	1 777	1 115	18.3	12.2	...	11.6	...	12.8	...	...	...	...	...	...
Lao People's Dem. Rep.	150	134	1.6	1.5	2.0	2.2	1.1	0.8	33	67	−	6	37	−
Lebanon	...	2 712	...	27.0	...	27.2	...	26.8	1	99	./.	61	49	./.
Macau	...	1 872	...	26.4	...	34.9	...	20.0	...	...	...	...	...	...
Malaysia	595	971	5.9	10.6	6.6	...	5.2	...	...	...	...	...	...	...
Maldives	−	−	−	−	−	−	−	−	−	−	−	−	−	−
Mongolia	2 101	1 569	21.6	15.2	...	9.1	...	21.3	14	83	2	80	68	54
Myanmar	478	564	4.5	5.4	4.2	4.2	4.8	6.7	14	83	2	80	68	54
Nepal	424	501	4.4	5.2	...	...	...	...	53	36	11	...	...	...
Oman	69	495	0.8	4.7	1.0	4.7	0.6	4.6	...	...	...	...	...	...
Pakistan	265	...	2.5	...	3.5	...	1.4	...	...	...	...	...	...	...
Palestinian Auton. Territories	.	...	.	...	.	...	.	...	...	...	...	...	...	...
Gaza Strip	...	...	...	...	...	...	...	...	21	79	0	44	35	27
West Bank	...	...	...	...	...	...	...	...	13	87	0	60	54	35
Philippines	2 565	2 701	24.9	27.4	...	23.4	...	31.5	14	82	4	64	55	67
Qatar	1 494	1 422	20.7	27.4	12.7	14.7	33.8	42.1	6	91	3	65	72	81
Republic of Korea	3 568	4 955	34.0	52.0	45.8	65.5	21.2	37.6	28	67	5	38	36	28
Saudi Arabia	898	1 280	10.6	15.3	11.8	15.9	9.2	14.7	8	89	3	52	47	51
Singapore	1 474	2 522	13.6	33.7	16.6	36.7	10.4	30.7	...	...	...	...	...	...
Sri Lanka	370	474	3.7	5.1	4.4	6.0	3.0	4.2	28	60	13	38	46	47
Syrian Arab Republic	1 726	1 690	17.1	17.9	21.5	21.4	12.3	14.3	...	...	...	...	...	...
Tajikistan	2 086	1 857	20.1	20.3	23.1	27.0	16.9	13.4	32	68	3	39	38	39
Thailand	2 009	2 096	19.0	20.1	...	...	...	...	♦ 0	94	6	...	...	...
Turkey	934	1 930	8.9	18.2	11.6	21.9	6.0	14.3	25	69	6	45	36	36
Turkmenistan	2 347	...	22.4	...	...	...	...	...	...	...	...	...	...	...
United Arab Emirates	501	493	6.8	8.8	4.8	4.7	9.5	14.1	...	...	...	...	...	...
Uzbekistan	3 121	2 960	30.0	31.7	...	...	...	...	...	...	...	...	...	...
Viet Nam	255	404	1.9	4.1	...	...	...	...	...	...	...	...	...	...
Yemen	...	...	...	...	...	...	...	...	...	...	...	...	...	...
Europe														
Albania	1 080	899	10.5	9.6	10.3	8.8	10.7	10.5	...	...	...	...	...	...
Austria	2 292	2 933	26.4	44.8	28.4	45.3	24.3	44.3	7	86	8	68	45	36

Country or territory	Number of students per 100,000 inhabitants 1985	1995	Gross enrolment ratio (%) Total 1985	1995	Male 1985	1995	Female 1985	1995	Percentage of students by ISCED level 1995 Level 5	Level 6	Level 7	Percentage of female students in each ISCED level 1995 Level 5	Level 6	Level 7
Belarus	3 425	3 031	44.8	42.6	...	39.1	...	46.0	–	99	1	...	52	...
Belgium	2 511	3 206	32.2	49.1	34.3	48.9	30.0	49.4	49	45	6	55	45	38
Bosnia and Herzegovina	...	...	...	...	...	...	...	...	...	...	...	...	...	...
Bulgaria	1 270	2 942	18.9	39.4	16.8	29.3	21.2	49.9	10	89	0	75	61	38
Croatia	1 250	1 917	17.7	28.3	...	28.3	...	28.3	# 24	76	–	33	54	–
Czech Republic	1 060	1 739	16.2	20.8	...	21.2	...	20.4	17	78	4	64	44	27
Denmark	2 275	3 272	29.1	45.0	28.8	42.1	29.5	48.2	10	50	40	44	59	45
Estonia	1 625	2 670	24.1	38.1	19.6	35.1	29.0	41.2	31	60	8	54	52	51
Finland	2 611	4 033	34.1	66.9	34.2	61.7	34.0	72.3	23	68	8	66	50	43
France	2 318	3 617	29.8	49.6	29.2	44.2	30.3	55.4	22	68	10	53	57	46
Germany	...	2 649	...	42.7	...	46.6	...	38.5	# 13	87	–	60	41	–
Greece	1 831	2 858	24.2	38.1	23.6	37.5	24.8	38.7	# 28	72	–	47	50	–
Hungary	939	1 514	15.4	19.1	13.9	17.6	16.9	20.7	45	55	./.	56	50	./.
Iceland	1 957	2 808	21.1	35.2	18.4	29.9	23.8	40.5	...	...	...	...	...	...
Ireland	1 979	3 455	22.3	37.0	24.8	36.7	19.8	37.3	27	46	5	45	52	44
Italy	2 088	3 135	25.5	40.6	27.0	37.8	23.8	43.6	0	97	2	68	51	48
Latvia	1 692	1 737	22.7	25.7	18.0	21.8	27.5	29.6	–	99	1	...	56	48
Lithuania	2 713	2 023	32.5	28.2	23.5	22.5	41.8	34.1	29	61	11	68	58	47
Luxembourg	...	...	...	...	...	...	...	...	...	...	...	...	...	...
Malta	428	1 595	5.8	21.8	7.6	22.0	3.9	21.7	24	66	10	47	49	42
Monaco	–	–	–	–	–	–	–	–	–	–	–	–	–	–
Netherlands	2 794	3 485	31.8	48.9	36.8	51.7	26.6	46.0	./.	59	41	./.	49	45
Norway	2 279	4 009	29.6	54.5	27.8	48.4	31.6	60.9	31	44	25	53	59	46
Poland	1 221	1 946	17.1	27.4	14.8	23.2	19.5	31.8	15	75	10	74	53	57
Portugal	1 046	2 812	12.3	34.0	11.3	29.0	13.3	39.2	–	97	3	–	57	51
Republic of Moldova	2 700	1 976	32.8	25.0	...	22.1	...	27.9	35	64	1	58	54	...
Romania	703	1 483	10.0	18.3	10.7	...	9.1	...	...	...	...	...	...	...
Russian Federation	3 799	2 998	54.2	42.9	45.9	37.4	62.8	48.5	42	57	1	60	53	...
San Marino	–	–	–	–	–	–	–	–	–	–	–	–	–	–
Slovakia	...	1 715	...	20.2	...	20.0	...	20.5	3	93	4	75	49	38
Slovenia	...	2 387	...	31.9	...	26.8	...	37.3	25	75	./.	49	60	./.
Spain	2 431	3 858	28.5	46.1	28.5	42.7	28.6	49.8	1	95	4	49	51	47
Sweden	2 115	2 810	30.0	42.5	28.1	37.6	32.1	47.7	./.	93	7	./.	56	36
Switzerland	1 685	2 085	21.0	31.8	28.1	39.1	13.7	24.2	41	49	10	32	42	32
The FYR of Macedonia	1 979	1 372	22.6	17.5	...	15.5	...	19.7	# 12	88	–	61	53	–
Ukraine	3 263	2 812	46.8	40.6	...	35.0	...	46.4	...	...	...	...	...	...
United Kingdom	1 824	3 126	21.7	48.3	23.1	46.0	20.1	50.8	28	57	15	54	50	44
Yugoslavia	...	1 556	...	21.1	...	19.1	...	23.2	# 18	82	–	50	55	–
Oceania														
Australia	2 366	5 401	27.7	71.7	28.3	70.0	27.0	73.5	40	47	13	44	55	50
Cook Islands	...	...	...	...	...	...	...	...	...	...	...	...	...	...
Fiji	331	...	3.2	...	3.9	...	2.4	...	...	...	...	...	...	...
Kiribati	...	...	...	...	...	...	...	...	...	...	...	...	...	...
New Zealand	2 950	4 603	33.1	58.2	35.3	50.9	30.8	65.8	30	59	11	55	57	50
Papua New Guinea	147	318	1.6	3.2	2.2	4.2	0.8	2.1	51	49	0	39	25	24
Samoa	...	...	...	...	...	...	...	...	...	...	...	...	...	...
Solomon Islands	...	...	...	...	...	...	...	...	...	...	...	...	...	...
Tonga	...	...	...	...	...	...	...	...	...	...	...	...	...	...
Tuvalu	...	...	...	...	...	...	...	...	...	...	...	...	...	...
Vanuatu	–	–	–	–	–	–	–	–	–	–	–	–	–	–

Table 9
Tertiary education: students and graduates by broad field of study, 1995

Country or territory	Percentage of students (and graduates) by field of study					Percentage of female students in each field of study						Gender segregation index (%)
	Education	Humanities	Law and social sciences	Natural sciences, engin. & agric.	Medical sciences	All fields	Education	Humanities	Law and social sciences	Natural sciences, engin. & agric.	Medical sciences	
Africa												
Algeria	♦ 0 (1)	13 (16)	23 (25)	52 (52)	10 (6)	43	27	62	45	35	52	8
Angola	... (...)	... (...)	... (...)	... (...)	... (...)	...	...	...	...	...	...	...
Benin	21 (...)	./. (...)	56 (...)	19 (...)	4 (...)	18	20	./.	20	11	23	3
Botswana	♦ 13 (...)	29 (...)	30 (...)	24 (...)	– (...)	50	61	53	59	26	–	11
Burkina Faso	7 (...)	31 (...)	35 (...)	18 (...)	8 (...)	22	14	32	22	8	24	7
Burundi	... (...)	... (...)	... (...)	... (...)	... (...)	...	...	...	...	...	...	...
Cameroon	... (...)	... (...)	... (...)	... (...)	... (...)	...	...	...	...	...	...	...
Cape Verde	– (–)	– (–)	– (–)	– (–)	– (–)	–	–	–	–	–	–	...
Central African Republic	... (...)	... (...)	... (...)	... (...)	... (...)	...	...	...	...	...	...	...
Chad	9 (...)	42 (...)	30 (...)	14 (...)	3 (...)	11	7	13	11	3	8	3
Comoros	... (...)	... (...)	... (...)	... (...)	... (...)	...	...	...	...	...	...	...
Congo	6 (...)	5 (...)	53 (...)	11 (...)	2 (...)	...	...	...	...	...	...	...
Côte d'Ivoire	♦ 3 (...)	20 (...)	36 (...)	26 (...)	14 (...)	23	10	29	31	10	23	8
Dem. Rep. of the Congo	... (...)	... (...)	... (...)	... (...)	... (...)	...	...	...	...	...	...	...
Djibouti	28 (...)	– (...)	72 (...)	– (...)	– (...)	47	61	–	41	–	–	8
Egypt	♦ 17 (24)	18 (17)	40 (32)	15 (15)	8 (10)	39	52	51	33	27	42	9
Equatorial Guinea	... (...)	... (...)	... (...)	... (...)	... (...)	...	...	...	...	...	...	...
Eritrea	... (...)	... (...)	... (...)	... (...)	... (...)	...	...	...	...	...	...	...
Ethiopia	22 (19)	4 (3)	32 (36)	36 (35)	6 (8)	20	22	25	28	11	17	7
Gabon	... (...)	... (...)	... (...)	... (...)	... (...)	...	...	...	...	...	...	...
Gambia	... (...)	... (...)	... (...)	... (...)	... (...)	...	...	...	...	...	...	...
Ghana	... (...)	... (...)	... (...)	... (...)	... (...)	...	...	...	...	...	...	...
Guinea	... (...)	... (...)	... (...)	... (...)	... (...)	...	...	...	...	...	...	...
Guinea-Bissau	... (...)	... (...)	... (...)	... (...)	... (...)	...	...	...	...	...	...	...
Kenya	... (...)	... (...)	... (...)	... (...)	... (...)	...	...	...	...	...	...	...
Lesotho	19 (35)	7 (5)	50 (30)	25 (30)	– (–)	55	68	52	67	21	–	17
Liberia	... (...)	... (...)	... (...)	... (...)	... (...)	...	...	...	...	...	...	...
Libyan Arab Jamahiriya	... (...)	... (...)	... (...)	... (...)	... (...)	...	...	...	...	...	...	...
Madagascar	2 (...)	14 (...)	49 (...)	23 (...)	13 (...)	35	36	66	25	31	46	12
Malawi	56 (73)	2 (0)	20 (11)	18 (12)	4 (4)	31	38	40	18	15	79	11
Mali	... (...)	... (...)	... (...)	... (...)	... (...)	...	...	...	...	...	...	...
Mauritania	11 (52)	26 (13)	55 (27)	8 (9)	– (–)	17	30	18	15	15	–	3
Mauritius	... (...)	... (...)	... (...)	... (...)	... (...)	...	...	...	...	...	...	...
Morocco	0 (0)	30 (33)	37 (28)	29 (33)	3 (3)	41	31	51	42	28	49	7
Mozambique	3 (7)	13 (17)	26 (19)	50 (49)	8 (9)	26	35	33	22	21	55	7
Namibia	22 (23)	16 (17)	12 (10)	5 (3)	23 (36)	61	55	56	40	31	85	12
Niger	... (...)	... (...)	... (...)	... (...)	... (...)	...	...	...	...	...	...	...
Nigeria	♦ 15 (...)	11 (...)	22 (...)	41 (...)	11 (...)	...	...	...	...	...	...	...
Rwanda	... (...)	... (...)	... (...)	... (...)	... (...)	...	...	...	...	...	...	...
Sao Tome and Principe	– (–)	– (–)	– (–)	– (–)	– (–)	–	–	–	–	–	–	–
Senegal	... (...)	... (...)	... (...)	... (...)	... (...)	...	...	...	...	...	...	...
Seychelles	... (...)	... (...)	... (...)	... (...)	... (...)	...	...	...	...	...	...	...
Sierra Leone	... (...)	... (...)	... (...)	... (...)	... (...)	...	...	...	...	...	...	...
Somalia	... (...)	... (...)	... (...)	... (...)	... (...)	...	...	...	...	...	...	...
South Africa	21 (43)	12 (7)	44 (31)	18 (14)	4 (4)	49	64	61	46	29	61	10
Sudan	... (...)	... (...)	... (...)	... (...)	... (...)	...	...	...	...	...	...	...
Swaziland	34 (18)	8 (5)	26 (37)	22 (33)	5 (5)	45	51	67	52	16	43	13
Togo	1 (–)	37 (48)	38 (37)	16 (8)	8 (7)	13	10	16	13	5	18	3
Tunisia	3 (9)	25 (17)	39 (36)	24 (25)	9 (10)	44	46	58	42	28	54	9

Country or territory	Percentage of students (and graduates) by field of study												Percentage of female students in each field of study							Gender segregation index (%)
	Education		Humani-ties		Law and social sciences		Natural sciences, engin. & agric.		Medical sciences				All fields	Edu-cation	Humani-ties	Law and social sciences	Natural sciences, engin. & agric.	Medical sciences		
Uganda	39	(51)	6	(7)	38	(25)	13	(15)	3	(2)			32	29	28	40	17	29		7
United Rep. of Tanzania	14	(4)	–	(–)	41	(56)	39	(26)	3	(15)			16	18	–	20	9	28		6
Zambia	...	(...)	...	(...)	...	(...)	...	(...)	...	(...)			...	...	...	...	...	...		...
Zimbabwe	47	(...)	7	(...)	20	(...)	23	(...)	3	(...)			35	41	33	44	14	35		10
America, North																				
Antigua and Barbuda	–	(–)	–	(–)	–	(–)	–	(–)	–	(–)			–	–	–	–	–	–		–
Bahamas	...	(...)	...	(...)	...	(...)	...	(...)	...	(...)			...	...	...	...	...	...		...
Barbados	♦ 2	(...)	23	(...)	54	(...)	19	(...)	2	(...)			63	57	77	64	44	46		8
Belize	–	(–)	–	(–)	–	(–)	–	(–)	–	(–)			–	–	–	–	–	–		–
British Virgin Islands	–	(–)	–	(–)	–	(–)	–	(–)	–	(–)			–	–	–	–	–	–		–
Canada	...	(...)	...	(...)	...	(...)	...	(...)	...	(...)			...	...	...	...	...	...		...
Costa Rica	12	(19)	4	(4)	39	(46)	18	(13)	4	(16)			...	...	...	...	...	...		...
Cuba	34	(34)	2	(1)	7	(9)	23	(25)	25	(22)			58	72	60	62	35	71		16
Dominica	–	(–)	11	(12)	31	(21)	58	(67)	–	(–)			47	–	77	72	28	–		22
Dominican Republic	...	(...)	...	(...)	...	(...)	...	(...)	...	(...)			...	...	...	...	...	...		...
El Salvador	15	(50)	2	(2)	40	(25)	25	(12)	17	(10)			51	66	53	53	28	65		11
Grenada	...	(...)	...	(...)	...	(...)	...	(...)	...	(...)			...	...	...	...	...	...		...
Guatemala	...	(...)	...	(...)	...	(...)	...	(...)	...	(...)			...	...	...	...	...	...		...
Haiti	...	(...)	...	(...)	...	(...)	...	(...)	...	(...)			...	...	...	...	...	...		...
Honduras	13	(5)	2	(1)	41	(35)	26	(21)	12	(38)			44	68	47	43	26	58		10
Jamaica	...	(...)	...	(...)	...	(...)	...	(...)	...	(...)			...	...	...	...	...	...		...
Mexico	♦ 11	(3)	3	(3)	45	(51)	33	(33)	8	(10)			46	65	57	54	26	55		13
Netherlands Antilles	–	(–)	–	(–)	–	(–)	–	(–)	–	(–)			–	–	–	–	–	–		–
Nicaragua	...	(...)	...	(...)	...	(...)	...	(...)	...	(...)			...	...	...	...	...	...		...
Panama	♦ 12	(22)	11	(6)	46	(35)	26	(27)	4	(10)			60	77	65	66	36	75		13
Saint Kitts and Nevis	15	(16)	5	(5)	12	(16)	57	(57)	11	(5)			55	83	50	55	38	100		19
Saint Lucia	...	(...)	...	(...)	...	(...)	...	(...)	...	(...)			...	...	...	...	...	...		...
Saint Vincent and the Grenadines	...	(...)	...	(...)	...	(...)	...	(...)	...	(...)			...	...	...	...	...	...		...
Trinidad and Tobago	♦ 5	(13)	15	(15)	25	(31)	45	(37)	10	(4)			49	68	73	58	34	43		14
United States	...	(10)	...	(17)	...	(38)	...	(19)	...	(11)			...	...	...	...	...	...		...
America, South																				
Argentina	♦ 2	(...)	11	(...)	42	(...)	30	(...)	14	(...)			52	80	74	53	36	62		10
Bolivia	...	(...)	...	(...)	...	(...)	...	(...)	...	(...)			...	...	...	...	...	...		...
Brazil	12	(18)	9	(10)	44	(42)	22	(17)	9	(10)			55	81	73	51	34	66		12
Chile	8	(13)	6	(4)	38	(42)	42	(33)	6	(8)			45	79	69	51	29	66		14
Colombia	15	(20)	4	(3)	42	(42)	31	(26)	9	(9)			51	68	55	55	32	67		12
Ecuador	...	(...)	...	(...)	...	(...)	...	(...)	...	(...)			...	...	...	...	...	...		...
Guyana	19	(28)	2	(2)	25	(27)	43	(33)	5	(5)			48	81	58	71	24	55		25
Paraguay	19	(33)	2	(4)	40	(35)	25	(19)	6	(9)			53	77	41	48	42	64		10
Peru	...	(...)	...	(...)	...	(...)	...	(...)	...	(...)			...	...	...	...	...	...		...
Suriname	...	(...)	...	(...)	...	(...)	...	(...)	...	(...)			...	...	...	...	...	...		...
Uruguay	...	(...)	...	(...)	...	(...)	...	(...)	...	(...)			...	...	...	...	...	...		...
Venezuela	...	(...)	...	(...)	...	(...)	...	(...)	...	(...)			...	...	...	...	...	...		...
Asia																				
Afghanistan	...	(...)	...	(...)	...	(...)	...	(...)	...	(...)			...	...	...	...	...	...		...
Armenia	...	(...)	...	(...)	...	(...)	...	(...)	...	(...)			...	...	...	...	...	...		...
Azerbaijan	32	(24)	5	(5)	12	(12)	38	(47)	11	(10)			...	...	...	...	...	...		...
Bahrain	26	(23)	./.	(8)	22	(27)	39	(25)	13	(17)			58	68	./.	71	42	64		12

Table 9 (continued)

Country or territory	Percentage of students (and graduates) by field of study					Percentage of female students in each field of study						Gender segregation index (%)
	Education	Humanities	Law and social sciences	Natural sciences, engin. & agric.	Medical sciences	All fields	Education	Humanities	Law and social sciences	Natural sciences, engin. & agric.	Medical sciences	
Bangladesh	... (...)	... (...)	... (...)	... (...)	... (...)	...	...	...	...	...	...	...
Bhutan	... (...)	... (...)	... (...)	... (...)	... (...)	...	...	...	...	...	...	...
Brunei Darussalam	♦ 62 (80)	1 (3)	19 (13)	6 (4)	– (–)	59	74	56	53	36	–	18
Cambodia	... (...)	... (...)	... (...)	... (...)	... (...)	...	...	...	...	...	...	...
China	23 (28)	8 (8)	25 (22)	37 (35)	7 (6)	...	...	...	...	...	...	...
Cyprus	14 (9)	6 (3)	50 (59)	19 (22)	11 (7)	59	93	76	56	28	74	15
Dem. People's Rep. of Korea	... (...)	... (...)	... (...)	... (...)	... (...)	...	...	...	...	...	...	...
Georgia	11 (6)	14 (13)	16 (18)	48 (51)	10 (12)	53	74	77	47	40	66	14
Hong Kong	7 (9)	8 (9)	25 (34)	36 (42)	4 (4)	43	66	75	59	19	47	17
India	... (...)	... (...)	... (...)	... (...)	... (...)	...	...	...	...	...	...	...
Indonesia	17 (14)	6 (7)	46 (50)	28 (27)	2 (2)	35	43	41	37	23	48	6
Iran, Islamic Republic of	♦ 13 (15)	12 (10)	21 (14)	37 (35)	18 (26)	33	39	48	27	20	50	12
Iraq	... (...)	... (...)	... (...)	... (...)	... (...)	...	...	...	...	...	...	...
Israel	41 (25)	./. (./.)	25 (35)	27 (30)	6 (10)	51	61	./.	50	32	69	11
Japan	8 (8)	18 (18)	38 (38)	23 (24)	8 (8)	44	71	72	39	13	64	18
Jordan	10 (14)	17 (20)	32 (28)	28 (24)	12 (11)	46	64	65	37	35	54	12
Kazakhstan	16 (19)	12 (9)	15 (15)	42 (40)	10 (14)	...	...	...	...	...	...	...
Kuwait	31 (...)	8 (...)	34 (...)	23 (...)	4 (...)	62	74	70	60	43	72	10
Kyrgyzstan	32 (...)	4 (...)	4 (...)	28 (...)	8 (...)	52	75	52	39	38	67	17
Lao People's Dem. Rep.	23 (28)	11 (7)	8 (13)	45 (38)	13 (11)	27	38	40	35	11	50	15
Lebanon	0 (1)	26 (23)	52 (52)	17 (18)	3 (6)	49	38	54	50	37	53	4
Macau	... (...)	... (...)	... (...)	... (...)	... (...)	...	...	...	...	...	...	...
Malaysia	... (...)	... (...)	... (...)	... (...)	... (...)	...	...	...	...	...	...	...
Maldives	... (...)	... (...)	... (...)	... (...)	... (...)	...	...	...	...	...	...	...
Mongolia	19 (20)	20 (19)	22 (16)	24 (23)	12 (18)	70	85	73	67	53	88	12
Myanmar	0 (–)	41 (60)	21 (8)	36 (30)	2 (2)	61	69	64	59	61	42	2
Nepal	12 (...)	37 (...)	33 (...)	17 (...)	1 (...)	...	...	...	...	...	...	...
Oman	... (...)	... (...)	... (...)	... (...)	... (...)	...	...	...	...	...	...	...
Pakistan	... (...)	... (...)	... (...)	... (...)	... (...)	...	...	...	...	...	...	...
Palestinian Auton. Territories	... (...)	... (...)	... (...)	... (...)	... (...)	...	...	...	...	...	...	...
Gaza Strip	28 (20)	29 (11)	15 (10)	19 (8)	5 (8)	37	43	38	31	38	39	5
West Bank	9 (15)	30 (26)	27 (26)	28 (19)	6 (12)	54	69	63	48	43	72	10
Philippines	12 (15)	7 (6)	33 (30)	31 (28)	15 (19)	57	79	56	71	27	75	20
Qatar	... (37)	... (29)	... (8)	... (18)	... (–)	72	89	80	43	44	–	...
Republic of Korea	7 (8)	18 (18)	29 (29)	39 (36)	6 (7)	35	72	57	37	16	53	15
Saudi Arabia	47 (57)	27 (18)	7 (4)	14 (15)	4 (2)	47	60	39	38	26	38	12
Singapore	... (7)	... (8)	... (24)	... (58)	... (2)	...	...	...	...	...	...	...
Sri Lanka	10 (6)	18 (29)	33 (28)	29 (29)	10 (7)	44	60	57	43	31	45	8
Syrian Arab Republic	2 (4)	21 (15)	35 (25)	29 (36)	11 (19)	38	55	61	32	30	34	10
Tajikistan	38 (...)	1 (...)	5 (...)	23 (...)	14 (...)	33	39	21	21	13	67	14
Thailand	12 (15)	14 (17)	50 (38)	19 (24)	5 (6)	53	60	68	56	23	77	11
Turkey	9 (13)	5 (6)	53 (32)	21 (30)	10 (18)	38	43	47	37	28	61	7
Turkmenistan	... (...)	... (...)	... (...)	... (...)	... (...)	...	...	...	...	...	...	...
United Arab Emirates	... (...)	... (...)	... (...)	... (...)	... (...)	...	...	...	...	...	...	...
Uzbekistan	... (...)	... (...)	... (...)	... (...)	... (...)	...	...	...	...	...	...	...
Viet Nam	... (...)	... (...)	... (...)	... (...)	... (...)	...	...	...	...	...	...	...
Yemen	... (...)	... (...)	... (...)	... (...)	... (...)	...	...	...	...	...	...	...
Europe												
Albania	30 (25)	16 (12)	21 (12)	24 (37)	7 (11)	53	66	63	47	40	52	10
Austria	7 (17)	16 (13)	40 (32)	29 (25)	8 (11)	46	74	62	47	26	60	12

Country or territory	Percentage of students (and graduates) by field of study					Percentage of female students in each field of study						Gender segregation index (%)
	Education	Humanities	Law and social sciences	Natural sciences, engin. & agric.	Medical sciences	All fields	Education	Humanities	Law and social sciences	Natural sciences, engin. & agric.	Medical sciences	
Belarus	♦ 18 (15)	27 (16)	13 (10)	35 (47)	6 (10)	...	...	...	...	...	...	...
Belgium	10 (22)	10 (6)	37 (17)	25 (36)	13 (13)	49	72	59	51	24	65	13
Bosnia and Herzegovina	... (...)	... (...)	... (...)	... (...)	... (...)	...	...	...	...	...	...	...
Bulgaria	14 (19)	8 (7)	41 (25)	25 (32)	8 (14)	62	80	75	66	45	69	12
Croatia	# 10 (10)	8 (5)	30 (27)	38 (40)	7 (12)	49	80	68	63	27	69	20
Czech Republic	16 (16)	8 (3)	28 (35)	36 (37)	10 (8)	47	70	57	52	25	67	16
Denmark	13 (15)	19 (12)	30 (30)	24 (30)	11 (13)	52	75	68	41	28	80	19
Estonia	9 (12)	12 (13)	34 (30)	34 (27)	7 (13)	53	86	69	60	25	83	19
Finland	9 (13)	14 (6)	22 (15)	37 (36)	18 (30)	53	76	70	58	23	84	22
France	4 (14)	25 (16)	29 (36)	24 (31)	11 (3)	55	74	71	58	30	63	13
Germany	# 5 (3)	15 (8)	30 (23)	35 (38)	10 (19)	43	72	62	44	21	62	15
Greece	# 17 (26)	4 (4)	35 (25)	30 (26)	11 (16)	49	73	51	54	27	60	13
Hungary	37 (42)	6 (5)	17 (16)	29 (26)	8 (9)	53	71	55	57	28	60	16
Iceland	... (...)	... (...)	... (...)	... (...)	... (...)	...	...	...	...	...	...	...
Ireland	2 (5)	6 (5)	39 (46)	31 (40)	4 (4)	49	75	62	58	33	60	11
Italy	3 (2)	15 (10)	41 (24)	28 (16)	9 (15)	52	89	78	53	33	53	11
Latvia	23 (19)	11 (8)	26 (28)	34 (37)	5 (5)	56	81	78	59	28	69	19
Lithuania	... (...)	... (...)	... (...)	... (...)	... (...)	...	...	...	...	...	...	...
Luxembourg	... (...)	... (...)	... (...)	... (...)	... (...)	...	...	...	...	...	...	...
Malta	19 (23)	23 (17)	24 (37)	13 (11)	18 (11)	48	64	52	44	21	56	10
Monaco	– (–)	– (–)	– (–)	– (–)	– (–)	–	–	–	–	–	–	–
Netherlands	13 (13)	9 (8)	48 (39)	20 (23)	10 (14)	47	65	62	47	17	70	12
Norway	15 (21)	12 (17)	31 (36)	19 (11)	10 (7)	54	71	63	50	27	80	13
Poland	14 (17)	12 (8)	32 (26)	29 (22)	10 (25)	57	82	70	61	31	68	16
Portugal	13 (22)	8 (13)	41 (31)	30 (20)	6 (11)	57	78	72	59	38	73	11
Republic of Moldova	29 (27)	4 (7)	16 (14)	34 (35)	11 (15)	...	...	...	...	...	...	...
Romania	2 (2)	10 (8)	25 (16)	51 (63)	10 (10)	47	32	60	58	38	62	11
Russian Federation	10 (12)	7 (6)	22 (22)	49 (45)	8 (13)	55	88	75	72	34	78	21
San Marino	– (–)	– (–)	– (–)	– (–)	– (–)	–	–	–	–	–	–	–
Slovakia	18 (22)	8 (10)	21 (21)	45 (38)	9 (9)	50	74	56	55	33	67	15
Slovenia	13 (11)	8 (6)	40 (38)	30 (32)	6 (9)	57	80	71	63	31	77	16
Spain	7 (10)	9 (11)	46 (43)	29 (20)	8 (11)	51	70	62	56	31	67	12
Sweden	16 (24)	15 (5)	26 (22)	29 (24)	14 (25)	55	77	64	56	27	74	16
Switzerland	5 (...)	14 (...)	41 (...)	32 (...)	8 (...)	37	70	58	39	15	54	14
The FYR of Macedonia	# 4 (13)	11 (8)	30 (25)	41 (38)	11 (12)	54	86	72	60	38	70	13
Ukraine	... (...)	... (...)	... (...)	... (...)	... (...)	...	...	...	...	...	...	...
United Kingdom	9 (6)	14 (13)	32 (32)	31 (28)	14 (13)	50	73	61	51	24	77	16
Yugoslavia	# 6 (14)	14 (10)	26 (21)	44 (42)	10 (12)	53	70	76	62	37	67	15
Oceania												
Australia	8 (19)	13 (14)	37 (29)	29 (22)	11 (14)	50	73	67	51	25	73	15
Cook Islands	... (...)	... (...)	... (...)	... (...)	... (...)	...	...	...	...	...	...	...
Fiji	... (...)	... (...)	... (...)	... (...)	... (...)	...	...	...	...	...	...	...
Kiribati	... (...)	... (...)	... (...)	... (...)	... (...)	...	...	...	...	...	...	...
New Zealand	13 (15)	20 (17)	34 (36)	20 (18)	7 (10)	55	81	64	52	31	76	13
Papua New Guinea	... (...)	... (...)	... (...)	... (...)	... (...)	...	...	...	...	...	...	...
Samoa	... (...)	... (...)	... (...)	... (...)	... (...)	...	...	...	...	...	...	...
Solomon Islands	... (...)	... (...)	... (...)	... (...)	... (...)	...	...	...	...	...	...	...
Tonga	... (...)	... (...)	... (...)	... (...)	... (...)	...	...	...	...	...	...	...
Tuvalu	... (...)	... (...)	... (...)	... (...)	... (...)	...	...	...	...	...	...	...
Vanuatu	– (–)	– (–)	– (–)	– (–)	– (–)	–	–	–	–	–	–	–

Table 10
Private enrolment and public expenditure on education

| Country or territory | Private enrolment as percentage of total enrolment | | | | | | Public expenditure on education | | | | | | |
| | Pre-primary | | Primary | | Secondary general | | As percentage of GNP | | As percentage of government expenditure | | Average annual growth rate (%) | Current expenditure as percentage of total | |
	1985	1995	1985	1995	1985	1995	1985	1995	1985	1995	1985–95	1985	1995
Africa													
Algeria	–	–	–	–	–	–	8.5	...	20.7	...	...	69.3	...
Angola	–	...	–	–	–	–	5.1	...	10.8	...	...	97.7	...
Benin	–	...	...	...	0	...	...	3.1	...	15.2	...	...	85.6
Botswana	–	...	6	6	50	74	6.8	9.6	15.4	20.5	12.6	79.3	73.4
Burkina Faso	46	...	9	8	48	35	...	3.6	...	11.1	...	...	82.7
Burundi	26	...	1	1	13	11	2.5	2.8	15.5	...	2.8	92.7	86.1
Cameroon	43	41	34	24	49	...	3.1	...	14.8	...	...	82.4	...
Cape Verde	...	...	–	–	–	–	3.6	...	...	...	...	95.3	...
Central African Republic	...	...	...	...	8	...	2.8	...	...	...	...	97.5	...
Chad	...	...	6	8	5	13	...	2.2	...	...	...	...	99.0
Comoros	–	...	–	9	0	37	4.1	3.9	23.1	21.1	0.7	...	...
Congo	–	4	–	2	–	0	5.1	5.9	9.8	14.7	4.0	92.3	97.6
Côte d'Ivoire	63	54	11	12	29	36	...	...	...	...	...	...	...
Dem. Rep. of the Congo	...	...	4	13	...	26	1.0	...	7.3	...	...	98.4	...
Djibouti	100	100	10	7	3	11	2.7	...	7.5	...	...	100.0	...
Egypt	93	69	5	7	8	7	6.3	5.6	...	13.8	1.8	94.5	89.4
Equatorial Guinea	...	...	...	9	...	...	...	1.8	...	5.6	...	...	98.2
Eritrea	...	95	...	13	...	11	...	...	...	...	...	...	...
Ethiopia	100	100	11	9	6	9	3.0	4.7	9.5	13.0	6.7	84.3	68.2
Gabon	...	...	33	29	39	40	4.5	...	9.4	...	...	68.3	...
Gambia	...	...	18	15	32	...	3.2	5.5	...	16.0	11.6	80.1	60.2
Ghana	20	...	6	...	5	...	2.6	...	19.0	...	...	...	...
Guinea	–	92	–	9	–	2	...	...	15.3	...	...	99.7	...
Guinea-Bissau	–	–	–	...	–	...	3.2	...	11.2	...	...	...	...
Kenya	81	...	...	...	38	...	6.4	7.4	...	...	3.3	93.8	94.3
Lesotho	–	...	100	100	...	...	4.3	5.9	...	...	8.2	...	88.6
Liberia	43	...	33	...	...	...	...	...	...	...	...	...	...
Libyan Arab Jamahiriya	–	–	–	–	–	–	7.1	...	19.8	...	...	79.6	...
Madagascar	...	...	13	21	42	45	2.9	...	...	...	...	95.4	...
Malawi	–	...	6	21	14	...	3.5	5.7	9.6	15.0	4.7	72.2	82.7
Mali	...	...	4	8	9	...	3.7	2.2	...	...	−0.1	99.2	97.7
Mauritania	...	...	0	0	–	4	...	5.0	...	16.1	...	...	73.5
Mauritius	...	90	23	24	78	79	3.8	4.3	9.8	17.3	8.8	92.8	85.8
Morocco	100	100	3	4	6	3	6.3	5.6	22.9	22.6	2.3	79.0	89.4
Mozambique	–	...	–	–	–	–	4.2	...	10.6	...	...	93.2	...
Namibia	...	...	...	4	...	4	...	9.4	...	21.3	...	...	93.3
Niger	44	29	3	3	11	10	...	...	...	...	...	...	...
Nigeria	...	...	...	...	...	...	...	...	...	...	...	...	...
Rwanda	100	...	0	...	26	...	3.1	...	25.1	...	...	97.8	...
Sao Tome and Principe	–	...	–	...	–	...	4.6	...	18.8	...	...	...	...
Senegal	57	62	9	10	29	22	...	3.6	...	33.1	...	...	98.5
Seychelles	...	2	–	3	–	2	10.7	7.5	21.3	16.3	2.8	96.4	81.6
Sierra Leone	...	...	...	...	...	...	1.9	...	12.4	...	...	94.9	...
Somalia	–	...	–	...	–	...	...	...	...	...	...	...	...
South Africa	...	8	0	1	1	2	6.0	6.8	...	20.5	3.5	84.4	94.0
Sudan	69	...	2	...	...	6	...	...	...	...	...	...	...
Swaziland	...	...	80	...	37	...	5.9	8.1	20.3	21.7	6.8	84.3	86.7
Togo	48	59	23	25	13	14	5.0	5.6	19.4	18.7	2.6	94.6	96.9
Tunisia	...	...	0	0	9	9	5.8	6.8	14.1	17.4	5.1	90.2	86.9

Country or territory	Private enrolment as percentage of total enrolment						Public expenditure on education						
	Pre-primary		Primary		Secondary general		As percentage of GNP		As percentage of government expenditure		Average annual growth rate (%)	Current expenditure as percentage of total	
	1985	1995	1985	1995	1985	1995	1985	1995	1985	1995	1985–95	1985	1995
Uganda	...	...	...	...	...	...	3.5	...	...	...	...	71.1	...
United Rep. of Tanzania	...	...	0	0	49	53	4.4	...	14.0	...	...	86.0	...
Zambia	...	...	0	...	20	...	4.7	1.8	13.4	...	−6.5	92.9	92.6
Zimbabwe	...	...	88	88	67	85	9.1	8.5	15.0	...	2.5	99.2	...
America, North													
Antigua and Barbuda	100	...	31	...	...	...	2.7	...	...	...	...	95.8	...
Bahamas	...	...	22	25	24	25	4.0	...	18.0	...	...	94.5	...
Barbados	...	...	8	...	15	...	6.1	7.2	...	19.0	3.4	88.2	96.8
Belize	...	88	...	...	...	...	...	6.1	...	21.3	...	...	87.9
British Virgin Islands	100	100	11	14	−	...	...	...	16.7	...	...	90.5	...
Canada	3	5	3	4	7	6	6.6	7.3	11.9	13.7	3.3	93.1	...
Costa Rica	11	9	3	5	9	10	4.5	4.5	22.7	19.9	5.4	95.2	96.0
Cuba	−	−	−	−	−	−	6.3	...	...	10.2	...	93.9	99.3
Dominica	72	100	4	5	4	4	5.9	...	16.7	...	...	95.9	...
Dominican Republic	79	55	24	22	30	33	1.8	1.9	14.0	13.2	5.5	...	...
El Salvador	26	31	8	15	51	64	3.1	2.2	12.5	...	7.6	87.3	99.3
Grenada	7	...	6	...	...	...	...	...	...	...	...	...	...
Guatemala	25	33	14	17	38	...	1.8	1.7	12.4	18.2	2.0	97.8	94.8
Haiti	63	...	58	...	84	...	1.2	...	16.5	...	...	99.8	...
Honduras	18	...	5	5	42	...	4.2	3.9	13.8	16.5	1.1	98.6	98.1
Jamaica	84	...	3	...	4	...	5.7	8.2	12.1	7.7	4.7	93.7	90.9
Mexico	6	8	5	6	12	12	3.9	5.3	...	26.0	7.8	...	...
Netherlands Antilles	...	...	...	...	...	...	...	...	...	...	...	...	...
Nicaragua	26	26	13	15	20	24	6.8	...	10.2	...	...	96.7	...
Panama	27	25	7	9	14	...	4.6	5.2	18.7	20.9	2.6	97.7	96.6
Saint Kitts and Nevis	75	73	13	...	4	3	5.8	3.3	18.5	...	−1.9	99.7	95.2
Saint Lucia	95	100	2	...	9	...	5.5	9.9	...	22.2	12.5	94.4	65.9
Saint Vincent and the Grenadines	100	100	2	3	54	46	5.8	...	11.6	...	...	93.4	...
Trinidad and Tobago	...	...	72	...	...	...	6.1	4.5	...	...	−6.5	87.5	90.7
United States	35	34	12	12	...	...	4.9	5.3	15.5	14.2	3.5	91.7	...
America, South													
Argentina	31	31	19	21	30	...	...	4.5	...	15.0	...	...	...
Bolivia	11	...	8	...	...	...	2.1	6.6	...	8.2	16.6	...	86.6
Brazil	34	23	12	12	...	...	3.8	...	...	...	...	...	...
Chile	44	49	32	40	39	44	4.4	2.9	15.3	14.0	4.0	...	94.7
Colombia	61	56	13	18	42	39	2.9	3.5	...	12.9	6.6	93.7	81.9
Ecuador	44	40	16	20	34	...	3.7	3.4	20.6	...	1.9	93.7	99.9
Guyana	−	−	−	−	−	−	9.8	4.1	10.4	8.1	−8.0	83.1	77.9
Paraguay	54	38	14	13	23	24	1.5	2.9	16.7	16.9	16.8	81.4	92.7
Peru	23	22	14	12	15	16	2.9	3.8	15.7	...	2.2	96.3	93.2
Suriname	49	...	50	...	38	...	9.4	3.5	...	...	−6.4	...	99.0
Uruguay	26	29	15	16	15	16	2.8	2.8	9.3	13.3	1.8	96.0	88.1
Venezuela	15	17	13	15	25	35	5.1	5.2	20.3	22.4	3.0	...	96.6
Asia													
Afghanistan	−	−	−	−	−	−	...	...	...	...	...	...	...
Armenia	−	...	−	...	−	...	...	...	...	...	...	...	...
Azerbaijan	−	...	−	...	−	...	5.7	3.0	26.7	17.5	...	...	91.1
Bahrain	100	100	11	17	12	15	4.1	4.8	10.4	12.8	4.3	94.2	91.9

Table 10 (continued)

Country or territory	Private enrolment as percentage of total enrolment						Public expenditure on education						
	Pre-primary		Primary		Secondary general		As percentage of GNP		As percentage of government expenditure		Average annual growth rate (%)	Current expenditure as percentage of total	
	1985	1995	1985	1995	1985	1995	1985	1995	1985	1995	1985–95	1985	1995
Bangladesh	...	...	11	...	93	...	♦1.9	♦2.3	♦9.7	♦8.7	5.9	77.2	79.7
Bhutan	...	...	...	...	...	...	...	...	...	...	...	...	...
Brunei Darussalam	52	64	29	30	17	12	2.1	...	...	...	...	89.9	...
Cambodia	...	...	...	...	...	...	...	...	...	...	...	...	...
China	–	–	–	–	–	–	2.5	2.3	12.2	...	8.3	87.9	88.2
Cyprus	58	66	4	4	13	11	3.7	4.4	12.2	13.8	8.0	95.4	91.2
Dem. People's Rep. of Korea	–	–	–	–	–	–	...	...	...	...	...	...	...
Georgia	–	...	–	...	–	...	...	5.2	...	6.9	...	...	82.8
Hong Kong	100	100	10	10	...	12	2.8	2.8	18.4	17.0	6.7	92.0	95.1
India	...	...	...	...	...	...	3.4	3.5	9.4	12.1	6.3	97.6	99.0
Indonesia	100	100	17	18	50	42	...	...	...	...	...	...	...
Iran, Islamic Republic of	–	...	–	2	–	3	3.6	4.0	17.2	17.8	5.4	88.6	82.9
Iraq	–	...	–	...	–	–	4.0	...	...	...	...	...	...
Israel	...	...	...	...	...	...	7.0	6.6	9.3	12.3	4.9	92.3	91.2
Japan	75	80	0	0	13	16	...	3.8	...	10.8	...	...	...
Jordan	98	100	8	25	19	8	5.5	6.3	13.0	16.6	0.0	87.1	93.8
Kazakhstan	–	...	–	0	–	0	...	4.5	18.9	17.6	...	...	99.9
Kuwait	37	25	28	33	14	27	4.9	5.6	12.6	...	...	95.4	93.1
Kyrgyzstan	–	...	–	0	–	0	7.9	6.8	22.4	23.1	...	92.6	96.8
Lao People's Dem. Rep.	–	11	–	2	–	0	...	2.4	...	...	...	...	75.8
Lebanon	79	85	68	71	50	61	...	♦2.0	♦16.8	...	...	...	75.8
Macau	...	...	...	...	...	...	...	...	...	8.9	...	...	...
Malaysia	45	42	...	...	8	5	6.6	♦5.3	16.3	♦15.5	6.5	85.4	83.5
Maldives	...	93	...	...	...	38	4.4	8.4	7.2	13.6	...	82.4	72.3
Mongolia	–	–	–	–	–	–	7.8	5.6	...	...	–4.3	...	99.2
Myanmar	–	–	–	–	–	–	...	♦1.3	...	♦14.4	...	...	78.0
Nepal	100	...	1	6	...	...	2.6	2.9	12.7	13.2	6.5	...	...
Oman	100	100	1	3	0	0	4.0	4.6	...	15.2	4.5	62.7	89.1
Pakistan	...	...	...	...	...	...	2.5	...	...	...	...	74.3	...
Palestinian Auton. Territories	.	100	.	6	.	8	...	...	...	...	...	...	...
Gaza Strip	100	...	0	...	3	...	...	...	...	...	...	...	...
West Bank	100	...	5	...	6	...	...	...	...	...	...	...	...
Philippines	61	53	6	7	41	31	1.4	♦2.2	7.4	...	10.0	93.4	86.9
Qatar	100	100	22	34	11	19	4.1	3.4	...	...	...	75.7	91.8
Republic of Korea	54	78	1	2	39	37	4.5	3.7	...	17.4	9.1	79.7	...
Saudi Arabia	78	76	3	6	3	4	6.7	5.5	12.0	...	0.0	81.9	95.5
Singapore	69	...	24	...	28	...	4.4	3.0	...	23.4	4.8	78.2	76.0
Sri Lanka	...	...	1	2	2	2	2.6	3.1	6.9	8.1	5.8	84.4	80.3
Syrian Arab Republic	62	95	4	4	6	6	6.1	...	11.8	...	...	...	...
Tajikistan	–	...	–	...	–	...	...	8.6	29.5	17.9	...	94.1	90.2
Thailand	41	26	9	12	12	6	3.8	4.2	18.5	20.1	11.5	85.9	80.1
Turkey	4	5	0	0	3	3	1.8	3.4	...	...	3.5	83.4	93.3
Turkmenistan	–	...	–	...	–	...	...	...	28.0	...	...	...	...
United Arab Emirates	62	66	26	41	15	28	1.7	1.8	10.4	16.3	...	94.2	92.3
Uzbekistan	–	...	–	...	–	...	...	9.5	25.1	24.4	...	84.1	97.8
Viet Nam	–	–	–	–	–	...	...	2.7	...	7.4	...	...	92.7
Yemen	...	...	...	...	...	...	...	7.5	...	20.8	...	...	90.5
Europe													
Albania	–	...	–	...	–	...	...	3.4	...	...	...	...	90.8
Austria	27	26	4	4	7	8	5.9	5.5	7.9	10.2	1.9	90.1	91.2

Country or territory	Private enrolment as percentage of total enrolment						Public expenditure on education						
	Pre-primary		Primary		Secondary general		As percentage of GNP		As percentage of government expenditure		Average annual growth rate (%)	Current expenditure as percentage of total	
	1985	1995	1985	1995	1985	1995	1985	1995	1985	1995	1985–95	1985	1995
Belarus	–	–	–	–	–	–	...	5.6	...	17.1	...	84.3	95.5
Belgium	58	57	55	56	64	69	6.2	5.7	15.2	10.2	2.2	94.9	99.1
Bosnia and Herzegovina	–	...	–	...	–	...	...	...	...	...	...	...	...
Bulgaria	–	0	–	0	–	0	5.5	4.2	...	...	–5.0	89.6	93.9
Croatia	–	3	–	0	–	...	...	5.3	...	...	...	...	...
Czech Republic	–	2	–	0	–	2	...	6.1	...	16.9	...	...	88.1
Denmark	...	3	9	11	14	15	7.2	8.3	...	12.6	3.1	...	94.3
Estonia	–	0	–	1	–	0	...	6.9	...	25.5	...	...	88.7
Finland	...	6	...	0	...	5	5.4	7.6	11.8	11.9	5.2	92.5	94.4
France	13	12	15	14	22	21	5.8	5.9	...	10.8	2.7	94.5	91.4
Germany	...	52	...	2	...	7	...	4.7	...	9.4	...	...	90.6
Greece	4	4	6	6	3	4	2.9	3.7	7.5	9.9	4.0	95.2	...
Hungary	–	1	–	3	–	...	5.5	6.6	6.4	6.9	1.7	89.0	94.5
Iceland	...	...	...	...	...	...	4.9	5.0	13.8	12.0	2.1	...	89.2
Ireland	100	100	100	100	...	...	6.4	6.3	8.9	13.2	4.3	91.0	95.1
Italy	32	30	7	8	6	6	5.0	4.9	8.3	8.8	1.8	90.9	95.8
Latvia	–	0	–	0	–	0	3.4	6.3	12.4	16.8	–0.2	95.4	99.1
Lithuania	–	0	–	0	–	0	5.3	6.1	12.9	21.8	–4.7	90.3	93.5
Luxembourg	0	1	0	...	8	7	3.8	...	...	...	...	87.3	...
Malta	56	39	27	33	31	28	3.4	5.2	7.7	11.8	11.7	98.2	94.9
Monaco	...	28	34	33	...	30	...	...	...	...	...	...	...
Netherlands	68	68	68	69	72	76	6.4	5.3	...	9.5	1.1	93.9	96.1
Norway	37	36	0	1	3	0	5.9	8.3	14.6	15.0	5.8	88.3	93.1
Poland	0	2	–	0	–	4	4.9	4.6	12.2	...	1.3	81.5	93.3
Portugal	58	58	7	8	9	...	4.0	5.4	...	...	7.9	88.7	93.7
Republic of Moldova	–	18	–	0	–	...	...	6.1	...	22.9	...	84.3	95.2
Romania	–	0	–	–	–	0	2.2	3.2	...	9.1	1.6	96.7	95.2
Russian Federation	–	7	–	...	–	0	3.2	4.1	...	9.6	–0.4	...	95.5
San Marino	–	–	–	...	–	...	...	...	10.7	...	...	91.3	98.3
Slovakia	–	0	–	4	–	5	...	5.1	...	...	...	...	78.5
Slovenia	–	0	–	0	–	0	...	5.8	...	12.6	...	...	93.4
Spain	38	34	34	35	35	29	3.3	5.0	...	12.6	8.2	89.5	92.1
Sweden	...	10	0	2	0	...	7.7	8.0	12.6	11.0	2.0	88.8	...
Switzerland	3	7	2	3	6	8	4.8	5.5	18.6	15.6	3.3	91.0	89.5
The FYR of Macedonia	–	–	–	–	–	–	5.5	5.5	18.7	18.7	...	95.6	95.6
Ukraine	–	–	–	...	–	–	5.2	7.7	21.2	...	...	84.9	87.5
United Kingdom	5	...	4	5	8	8	4.9	5.5	...	11.4	3.3	95.8	...
Yugoslavia	–	–	–	–	–	–	...	...	...	...	...	...	92.2
Oceania													
Australia	26	27	23	26	29	34	5.6	5.6	12.8	13.6	3.0	91.7	95.8
Cook Islands	...	...	16	...	7	...	...	...	9.5	12.4	...	99.1	99.9
Fiji	100	100	96	96	88	87	6.0	5.4	...	18.6	2.0	98.0	96.9
Kiribati	...	...	0	–	68	77	6.0	6.3	18.5	17.6	5.9	100.0	100.0
New Zealand	...	...	2	2	5	5	4.7	6.7	18.4	17.2	6.5	91.2	95.4
Papua New Guinea	100	41	1	2	4	3	...	...	...	...	...	...	...
Samoa	...	...	...	13	25	43	...	...	...	...	...	...	...
Solomon Islands	...	9	9	11	...	17	4.7	...	12.4	...	...	...	...
Tonga	...	...	7	7	86	80	4.1	4.7	16.1	17.3	2.6	100.0	...
Tuvalu	...	...	3	2	...	...	...	...	...	...	...	...	...
Vanuatu	...	...	...	...	...	...	...	4.9	...	...	...	...	100.0

Table 11
Public current expenditure on education

Country or territory	Teachers' emoluments as percentage of total current expenditure 1995	Percentage distribution of current expenditure by level						Current expenditure per pupil as a percentage of GNP per capita					
		1985			1995			1985			1995		
		Pre-prim. + prim.	Sec.	Tert.	Pre-prim. + prim.	Sec.	Tert.	Pre-prim. + prim.	Sec.	Tert.	Pre-prim. + prim.	Sec.	Tert.
Africa													
Algeria	...	...	...	...	...	...	...	...	...	...	...	...	...
Angola	...	86.8	./.	5.0	...	...	...	25	./.	402	...	...	...
Benin	♦78.6	...	...	...	59.1	21.7	18.8	...	...	...	11	22	240
Botswana	...	36.3	40.7	17.2	...	...	...	9	65	515	...	...	...
Burkina Faso	♦61.5	38.1	20.3	30.7	...	...	...	16	57	1 137	...	...	...
Burundi	56.1	45.0	32.3	19.8	41.5	30.4	28.1	13	139	796	13	69	941
Cameroon	...	72.6	./.	27.4	...	...	...	9	./.	362	...	...	...
Cape Verde	...	61.5	15.9	–	...	...	...	11	32	–	...	...	...
Central African Republic	...	55.2	17.6	18.8	...	...	...	13	23	503	...	...	...
Chad	64.7	...	...	...	42.1	21.7	7.6	...	...	...	10	33	234
Comoros	70.3	...	...	...	36.6	35.1	17.2	...	...	...	8	39	1 168
Congo	♦83.7	65.6	./.	34.4	62.0	./.	28.0	9	./.	290	13	./.	224
Côte d'Ivoire	...	40.2	42.7	17.1	...	...	...	21	94	495	...	...	...
Dem. Rep. of the Congo	...	71.3	./.	28.7	...	...	...	4	./.	218	...	...	...
Djibouti	...	63.7	23.5	–	...	...	...	26	35	–	...	...	...
Egypt	♦79.1	...	...	...	64.3	./.	35.7	...	...	...	13	./.	108
Equatorial Guinea	...	...	...	...	...	...	...	...	...	...	...	...	...
Eritrea	...	...	...	...	...	...	...	...	...	...	...	...	...
Ethiopia	...	51.5	28.3	14.4	53.6	27.7	10.5	21	42	538	37	62	592
Gabon	...	...	...	...	...	...	...	...	...	...	...	...	...
Gambia	♦51.1	49.0	21.3	13.8	45.4	25.0	10.9	12	26	...	12	28	235
Ghana	...	24.5	29.5	12.5	...	...	...	3	7	135	...	...	...
Guinea	55.6	30.8	36.9	23.5	35.0	29.1	18.4	5	18	106	11	38	498
Guinea-Bissau	...	...	...	...	...	...	...	...	...	...	...	...	...
Kenya	...	59.9	17.7	12.4	62.4	19.2	13.7	13	46	677	15	47	540
Lesotho	65.2	39.1	32.7	22.3	50.8	30.9	17.0	6	44	766	14	51	399
Liberia	...	...	...	...	...	...	...	...	...	...	...	...	...
Libyan Arab Jamahiriya	...	...	...	...	...	...	...	...	...	...	...	...	...
Madagascar	...	42.3	26.5	27.2	...	...	...	8	17	209	...	...	...
Malawi	...	41.3	15.2	23.3	59.4	16.4	16.9	8	107	1 076	9	145	979
Mali	♦57.1	48.4	22.6	13.4	45.9	21.6	17.7	38	86	589	17	35	522
Mauritania	51.9	25.1	30.3	17.5	40.4	35.5	20.4	26	122	559	12	59	157
Mauritius	...	45.2	37.6	5.6	...	...	...	10	18	171	...	...	...
Morocco	...	35.3	47.6	17.1	33.0	50.7	16.3	13	41	102	12	51	74
Mozambique	...	...	...	...	...	...	...	...	...	...	...	...	...
Namibia	...	...	...	...	48.0	33.4	7.2	...	...	...	17	44	86
Niger	...	...	...	...	...	...	...	...	...	...	...	...	...
Nigeria	...	...	...	...	...	...	...	...	...	...	...	...	...
Rwanda	...	67.6	15.3	11.5	...	...	...	16	67	1 210	...	...	...
Sao Tome and Principe	...	55.6	27.0	–	...	...	...	...	...	...	...	...	...
Senegal	♦66.8	50.1	25.1	19.0	...	...	...	23	52	384	...	...	...
Seychelles	♦61.5	29.5	54.3	–	37.9	30.9	13.1	11	92	–	13	15	.
Sierra Leone	...	40.7	32.3	15.1	...	...	...	6	22	172	...	...	...
Somalia	...	...	...	...	...	...	...	...	...	...	...	...	...
South Africa	74.4	73.1	./.	24.8	81.8	./.	15.4	15	./.	132	18	./.	59
Sudan	...	...	...	...	...	...	...	...	...	...	...	...	...
Swaziland	70.6	37.3	26.6	21.0	36.6	26.4	27.5	9	30	296	10	29	302
Togo	59.5	34.0	29.1	22.8	35.2	30.3	27.1	9	43	527	10	42	521
Tunisia	77.0	44.0	37.0	18.2	42.6	36.8	18.8	13	31	167	15	23	89

Country or territory	Teachers' emoluments as percentage of total current expenditure 1995	Percentage distribution of current expenditure by level						Current expenditure per pupil as a percentage of GNP per capita					
		1985			1995			1985			1995		
		Pre-prim. + prim.	Sec.	Tert.	Pre-prim. + prim.	Sec.	Tert.	Pre-prim. + prim.	Sec.	Tert.	Pre-prim. + prim.	Sec.	Tert.
Uganda	...	44.5	33.4	13.2	...	...	...	8	61	499	...	...	...
United Rep. of Tanzania	...	57.5	20.5	12.7	...	...	...	15	180	2 131	...	...	...
Zambia	...	43.9	26.9	18.3	41.5	18.4	23.2	9	53	441	4	9	160
Zimbabwe	...	58.4	28.3	9.0	51.7	26.4	17.3	20	41	193	22	39	234
America, North													
Antigua and Barbuda	...	36.6	30.6	12.7	...	...	...	...	...	...	...	...	...
Bahamas	...	...	...	...	...	...	...	...	...	...	...	...	...
Barbados	...	31.0	32.5	22.3	...	...	...	13	15	58	...	...	...
Belize	...	65.7	31.0	3.4	57.1	26.1	7.5	10	28	105	11	29	367
British Virgin Islands	...	38.9	35.8	9.7	27.8	31.3	24.7	11	17	...	10	27	...
Canada	♦80.2	63.6	./.	28.7	65.5	./.	34.6	22	./.	30	26	./.	36
Costa Rica	♦95.6	35.1	22.3	41.4	38.3	23.3	30.9	10	22	73	10	19	44
Cuba	♦60.2	26.3	42.0	12.9	31.3	34.9	15.7	13	22	33	...	...	...
Dominica	...	62.4	26.2	2.6	...	...	...	17	17	163	...	...	...
Dominican Republic	...	47.3	19.7	20.8	53.5	13.3	9.0	4	4	17	4	5	5
El Salvador	...	...	...	...	63.5	6.5	7.2	...	...	...	6	5	8
Grenada	...	...	...	...	...	...	...	...	...	...	...	...	...
Guatemala	62.8	...	...	...	58.9	11.5	15.5	...	...	...	6	5	33
Haiti	...	51.0	18.1	10.8	...	...	...	4	9	119	...	...	...
Honduras	67.8	49.1	16.7	21.3	52.5	21.5	16.6	10	16	100	10	22	59
Jamaica	66.4	31.9	34.0	19.4	31.5	37.7	23.1	9	18	221	10	25	193
Mexico	♦97.9	...	...	...	48.5	32.1	19.3	...	...	...	12	20	61
Netherlands Antilles	...	...	...	...	45.1	44.8	4.2	...	...	...	10	18	...
Nicaragua	...	45.7	16.7	23.2	...	...	...	15	27	170	...	...	...
Panama	♦57.7	38.3	25.2	20.4	30.3	20.7	24.8	10	13	36	10	13	47
Saint Kitts and Nevis	70.6	50.3	40.1	2.1	37.6	43.0	11.6	13	24	25	6	14	40
Saint Lucia	...	50.9	26.8	4.5	44.9	24.4	12.5	9	25	82	11	18	114
Saint Vincent and the Grenadines	...	73.1	26.6	0.2	...	...	...	16	17	2	...	...	...
Trinidad and Tobago	♦66.7	47.5	36.8	8.9	40.5	33.1	13.3	17	24	84	11	17	77
United States	52.9	44.7	30.3	25.1	40.2	36.6	23.3	18	16	22	19	24	23
America, South													
Argentina	...	37.7	27.4	19.2	50.5	26.1	17.6	5	12	20	9	12	17
Bolivia	42.8	...	...	...	53.0	./.	28.7	...	...	...	10	18	67
Brazil	...	...	...	...	...	...	...	...	...	...	...	...	...
Chile	...	57.0	19.5	20.3	62.7	16.2	18.1	13	15	54	10	9	21
Colombia	...	39.2	30.8	22.2	38.8	33.1	16.8	8	14	48	7	11	29
Ecuador	...	45.5	35.8	17.8	29.0	30.9	21.5	8	15	20	6	15	34
Guyana	...	38.7	23.8	17.8	71.3	./.	7.7	...	...	...	...	...	...
Paraguay	...	36.6	29.7	23.8	47.9	19.8	17.5	3	9	33	7	11	52
Peru	...	...	...	...	...	...	...	...	...	...	...	...	...
Suriname	...	63.7	13.5	7.7	60.4	14.8	7.6	31	15	88	8	7	21
Uruguay	44.5	37.7	28.4	22.4	29.8	26.7	27.0	8	11	28	6	8	28
Venezuela	...	...	...	...	...	...	...	...	...	...	...	...	...
Asia													
Afghanistan	..	...	...	...	...	...	...	...	...	...	...	...	...
Armenia	...	...	...	...	77.5	./.	22.6	...	...	...	14	./.	19
Azerbaijan	♦63.1	...	...	...	79.0	./.	7.8	...	...	...	10	./.	13
Bahrain	62.7	...	...	...	...	...	...	...	...	...	...	...	...

Table 11 (continued)

Country or territory	Teachers' emoluments as percentage of total current expenditure 1995	Percentage distribution of current expenditure by level						Current expenditure per pupil as a percentage of GNP per capita					
		1985			1995			1985			1995		
		Pre-prim. + prim.	Sec.	Tert.	Pre-prim. + prim.	Sec.	Tert.	Pre-prim. + prim.	Sec.	Tert.	Pre-prim. + prim.	Sec.	Tert.
Bangladesh	....	46.1	34.7	10.4	44.2	43.3	7.9	6	16	33	6	23	30
Bhutan	53.2	...	...	...	...	...	...	...	...	...	...	...	...
Brunei Darussalam	...	...	...	...	...	...	...	...	...	...	...	...	...
Cambodia	...	...	...	...	...	...	...	...	...	...	...	...	...
China	...	29.5	33.2	21.8	36.9	31.5	16.5	4	14	136	6	14	81
Cyprus	80.2	37.7	50.7	4.2	36.8	50.8	6.5	13	25	31	12	26	22
Dem. People's Rep. of Korea	...	...	...	...	...	...	...	...	...	...	...	...	...
Georgia	♦52.6	...	...	...	67.1	./.	18.5	...	...	...	19	./.	28
Hong Kong	...	31.5	37.9	25.1	21.9	35.0	37.1	5	11	43	6	12	52
India	...	37.1	25.2	15.5	38.4	26.1	13.6	11	14	87	11	13	78
Indonesia	...	...	...	...	...	...	...	...	...	...	...	...	...
Iran, Islamic Republic of	...	42.0	37.9	10.7	27.7	36.1	22.0	10	18	91	7	12	62
Iraq	...	46.5	19.5	25.0	...	...	...	10	10	90	...	...	...
Israel	♦73.1	42.8	30.8	18.9	42.2	31.7	17.2	12	33	44	12	29	31
Japan	♦77.6	...	...	...	38.2	42.2	13.5	...	...	...	17	19	16
Jordan	...	63.7	./.	32.0	57.5	./.	34.4	13	./.	109	14	./.	111
Kazakhstan	...	...	...	...	74.5	./.	12.5	...	...	...	16	./.	20
Kuwait	...	77.1	./.	16.7	...	...	...	14	./.	58	...	...	...
Kyrgyzstan	♦54.1	71.3	./.	8.8	80.2	./.	8.3	19	./.	36	23	./.	49
Lao People's Dem. Rep.	65.0	...	...	...	42.2	43.5	3.9	...	...	...	5	25	55
Lebanon	...	...	...	...	...	...	...	...	...	...	...	...	...
Macau	...	...	...	...	...	...	...	...	...	...	...	...	...
Malaysia	♦62.1	37.8	37.1	14.6	35.4	41.2	16.8	13	25	138	9	22	77
Maldives	...	...	...	...	66.7	31.9	–	...	...	...	17	24	–
Mongolia	...	79.9	./.	20.1	82.1	./.	17.8	10	34	74	14	34	74
Myanmar	♦56.8	...	...	...	47.7	40.3	11.7	...	...	...	4	10	21
Nepal	...	35.7	19.9	33.4	44.5	17.7	28.1	8	17	207	8	12	156
Oman	♦84.8	50.9	32.1	15.3	47.8	45.3	5.8	14	32	...	13	23	...
Pakistan	...	36.0	33.3	18.2	...	...	...	9	21	126	...	...	...
Palestinian Auton. Territories	...	.	.	.	...	...	...	.	.	.	...	...	...
Gaza Strip	...	...	...	...	...	...	...	...	...	...	...	...	...
West Bank	...	...	...	...	...	...	...	...	...	...	...	...	...
Philippines	...	63.9	10.1	22.5	...	...	...	5	2	11	...	...	...
Qatar	♦79.5	...	...	...	...	...	...	...	...	...	...	...	...
Republic of Korea	♦73.5	47.0	36.7	10.9	45.5	34.4	7.9	13	11	11	16	12	6
Saudi Arabia	♦84.6	...	...	...	82.2	./.	17.8	...	...	...	21	./.	63
Singapore	...	30.5	36.9	27.9	25.7	34.6	34.8	10	17	65	7	13	32
Sri Lanka	...	90.2	./.	9.8	72.7	./.	12.2	8	./.	58	7	./.	64
Syrian Arab Republic	...	38.4	25.3	33.6	...	...	...	10	15	99	8	17	...
Tajikistan	♦63.4	64.9	./.	7.7	85.0	./.	9.7	18	./.	30	27	./.	39
Thailand	61.6	58.4	21.1	13.2	52.8	21.5	16.5	12	16	21	11	11	25
Turkey	♦86.7	45.9	22.4	23.9	45.4	23.0	31.7	5	6	38	13	9	51
Turkmenistan	...	...	...	...	...	...	...	...	...	...	...	...	...
United Arab Emirates	♦73.6	...	...	...	...	...	...	...	...	...	...	...	...
Uzbekistan	♦58.4	...	...	...	86.7	./.	9.7	...	...	...	28	./.	28
Viet Nam	...	...	...	...	...	...	...	...	...	...	...	...	...
Yemen	...	...	...	...	...	...	...	...	...	...	...	...	...
Europe													
Albania	♦75.2	...	...	...	63.9	20.6	10.3	...	...	...	11	23	36
Austria	♦70.3	23.1	46.9	16.6	29.8	48.1	19.4	18	22	38	19	25	32

Country or territory	Teachers' emoluments as percentage of total current expenditure 1995	Percentage distribution of current expenditure by level						Current expenditure per pupil as a percentage of GNP per capita					
		1985			1995			1985			1995		
		Pre-prim. + prim.	Sec.	Tert.	Pre-prim. + prim.	Sec.	Tert.	Pre-prim. + prim.	Sec.	Tert.	Pre-prim. + prim.	Sec.	Tert.
Belarus	...	74.8	./.	14.0	87.0	./.	11.0	16	./.	17	24	./.	20
Belgium	76.9	24.7	46.4	16.7	29.8	46.9	20.3	13	32	39	15	25	35
Bosnia and Herzegovina	...	...	...	...	...	...	...	...	...	...	...	...	...
Bulgaria	...	65.3	./.	12.4	75.1	./.	15.8	16	./.	48	17	./.	21
Croatia	...	...	...	...	...	...	...	...	...	...	...	...	...
Czech Republic	37.1	...	...	...	29.2	53.5	14.7	...	...	...	18	25	41
Denmark	49.3	66.5	./.	21.9	72.4	./.	22.8	24	./.	63	30	./.	55
Estonia	♦50.1	...	...	...	73.8	./.	17.6	...	...	...	23	./.	40
Finland	53.2	30.8	41.6	18.7	34.3	37.7	26.1	18	26	39	26	30	46
France	♦77.1	29.5	40.8	12.9	32.1	50.0	16.5	13	23	30	15	26	24
Germany	♦83.1	...	...	...	73.0	./.	21.8	...	...	...	18	./.	35
Greece	♦91.2	37.7	41.3	20.1	35.9	40.9	22.6	10	14	30	16	19	29
Hungary	♦45.7	51.1	19.9	16.9	54.1	23.0	17.8	15	24	88	25	28	73
Iceland	♦72.9	...	...	...	34.0	41.5	20.8	...	...	...	14	16	34
Ireland	75.9	39.3	39.7	17.7	32.7	41.6	23.3	14	24	52	15	23	38
Italy	65.7	30.0	35.5	10.2	30.4	48.5	15.7	15	17	22	19	26	23
Latvia	...	72.0	./.	10.3	81.0	./.	12.2	12	./.	20	29	./.	45
Lithuania	♦68.1	...	...	...	66.2	./.	18.0	...	...	...	21	./.	51
Luxembourg	...	43.5	42.7	3.3	...	...	...	17	21	55	...	...	...
Malta	38.7	31.0	43.3	8.2	22.5	40.4	17.9	8	18	63	8	19	62
Monaco	68.2	...	...	...	17.3	45.6	−	...	...	...	...	...	...
Netherlands	♦76.9	22.6	35.9	26.4	30.1	39.0	31.0	13	19	55	15	20	44
Norway	♦78.6	73.5	./.	13.5	65.3	./.	26.0	19	./.	31	25	./.	50
Poland	...	44.2	17.9	18.2	49.7	20.5	16.0	11	17	60	16	19	42
Portugal	♦92.5	51.0	30.6	12.7	37.1	38.8	14.9	13	19	43	16	20	25
Republic of Moldova	♦71.1	...	...	...	...	...	...	...	...	...	...	...	...
Romania	♦56.6	...	...	...	44.9	23.8	15.9	...	...	...	17	7	40
Russian Federation	...	...	...	...	...	...	...	...	...	...	...	...	...
San Marino	...	52.9	33.3	4.2	48.2	32.1	14.0	...	...	...	...	...	...
Slovakia	♦52.1	...	...	...	47.0	12.8	16.7	...	...	...	20	4	39
Slovenia	62.2	...	...	...	30.0	48.4	16.9	...	...	...	20	24	38
Spain	♦81.7	...	...	...	30.0	53.2	14.7	...	...	...	16	21	18
Sweden	♦62.8	68.1	./.	13.1	73.3	./.	26.7	27	./.	42	30	./.	76
Switzerland	♦84.3	76.7	./.	18.1	77.8	./.	20.0	19	./.	47	23	./.	48
The FYR of Macedonia	♦82.5	...	...	...	54.9	22.8	22.2	...	...	...	...	...	...
Ukraine	...	74.1	./.	13.5	73.5	./.	10.7	19	./.	18	13	./.	20
United Kingdom	48.6	26.7	45.9	19.8	32.6	44.4	23.0	14	25	51	19	22	44
Yugoslavia	♦40.6	...	...	...	65.6	./.	21.8	...	...	...	...	...	...
Oceania													
Australia	♦76.3	61.9	./.	30.5	70.5	./.	29.5	17	./.	66	17	./.	30
Cook Islands	...	37.8	35.8	6.0	...	...	...	...	...	...	...	...	...
Fiji	♦73.5	...	...	...	...	...	...	...	...	...	...	...	...
Kiribati	♦55.1	...	...	...	...	...	...	...	...	...	...	...	...
New Zealand	...	38.4	28.5	28.3	27.9	40.7	29.4	13	11	41	14	23	39
Papua New Guinea	...	...	...	...	...	...	...	...	...	...	...	...	...
Samoa	...	...	...	...	...	...	...	...	...	...	...	...	...
Solomon Islands	...	...	...	...	...	...	...	...	...	...	...	...	...
Tonga	♦70.7	44.7	30.9	17.9	38.8	24.2	7.3	9	8	94	...	...	...
Tuvalu	...	...	...	...	...	...	...	...	...	...	...	...	...
Vanuatu	68.3	...	...	...	57.9	33.0	6.4	...	...	...	14	49	...

IV. National reports and UNESCO reports, publications and periodicals concerning education, 1995–97

THIS APPENDIX is in four parts: 1. National reports on education presented by Member States and Observers at the 45th session of the International Conference on Education (Geneva, 30 September– 5 October 1996); 2. Reports of UNESCO meetings concerning education; 3. UNESCO publications on education; and 4. UNESCO periodicals relating to education. The period covered by this listing is June 1995 to mid-1997.

National reports are listed by country in alphabetical order. UNESCO reports, publications and periodicals are listed alphabetically by title.

For each title, the English version of the publication is given. When a title is not published in English, it is presented in its original language of publication. Besides English, some titles are published in other languages. An indication of the different language versions is given in parentheses: for example (F, S) indicates that the title is also published in French and in Spanish. The abbreviations for the different languages are as follows: Ar: Arabic; Cat: Catalan; Ch: Chinese; E: English; F: French; G: German; Port.: Portuguese; R: Russian, S: Spanish; Ukr: Ukrainian.

For periodicals which present each issue with a special theme, this is indicated.

National reports presented at the 45th session of the International Conference on Education (Geneva, 30 September–5 October 1996)

ANGOLA. *Développement de l'éducation: rapport national de la République d'Angola*. Luanda, Ministère de l'Éducation, 1996. 44 pp.

ARGENTINA. *Fortalecimiento de la función del personal docente en un mundo cambiante. Propuesta argentina/Strengthening the Work of the Teaching Staff in a Changing World. Argentine Proposal*. Buenos Aires, Ministerio de Cultura y Educación de la Nación, 1996. Bilingual: Spanish/English. 103 pp.

AUSTRALIA. *National Report on the Development of Education in Australia*. Canberra, 1996. 112 pp.

AUSTRIA. *Austria: Development of Education, 1994– 1996*. Vienna, Federal Ministry of Education and Cultural Affairs, 1996. 143 pp.

BAHRAIN. *Development of Education in Bahrain,* *1994/95–1995/96*. Manama, Ministry of Education, 1996. Bilingual: English (213 pp.)/Arabic (243 pp.).

BELGIUM. *Educational Developments in Flanders, 1994–1996*. Brussels, Ministry of the Flemish Community, Department for Education, 1996. 117 pp.

   Le système éducatif en Communauté française de Belgique. Brussels, Ministère de l'Éducation, de la Recherche et de la Formation, 1996. 147 pp.

BELIZE. *A National Report on the Development of Education, 1994–1996*. Belmopan, Ministry of Education, 1996. 39 pp.

BENIN. *Développement de l'éducation: rapport national de la République du Bénin*. Porto-Novo, Ministère de l'Éducation Nationale, Institut National pour la Formation et la Recherche en Éducation, 1996. 103 pp.

BRAZIL. *Development of Education in Brazil*. Brasilia, Ministry of Education and Sports, 1996. 72 pp. (F)

BULGARIA. *Development of Education in 1994–1996. National Report of the Republic of Bulgaria*. Sofia, Ministry of Education, Science and Technologies, Institute for Education and Science, 1996. 67 pp.

BURUNDI. *Développement de l'éducation: rapport national du Burundi*. Bujumbura, Ministère de l'Éducation, de l'Enseignement de Base et de l'Alphabétisation des Adultes/Ministère de l'Enseignement Secondaire, Supérieur et de la Recherche Scientifique, 1996. 52 pp.

CAMEROON. *Développement de l'éducation. Rapport national du Cameroun*. Yaoundé, Commission Nationale de la République du Cameroun pour l'UNESCO, 1996. 98 pp.

CANADA. *The Development of Education/Le développement de l'éducation*. Toronto, Council of Ministers of Education/Conseil des Ministres de l'Éducation, 1996. Bilingual: English (60 pp., annexes)/French (73 pp., annexes).

   Enhancing the Role of Teachers in a Changing World/Renforcement du rôle des enseignants dans un monde en changement. Toronto, Council of Ministers of Education/Conseil des Ministres de l'Éducation, 1996. Bilingual: English (46 pp., annexes)/ French (51 pp., annexes).

CHAD. *Rapport national sur le développement de l'éducation*. N'Djamena, Commission Nationale Tchadienne pour l'UNESCO, Ministère de l'Éducation Nationale, 1996. 46 pp., annexes.

CHINA. *The Development and Reform of Education in China, 1995–1996*. Beijing, State Education Commission, 1996. 69 pp.

CROATIA. *The Development of Education*. Zagreb, Ministry of Education and Sports, 1996. 32 pp.

CUBA. *Cuba: Organization of Education, 1994–1996*. Havana, Ministry of Education, 1996. 41 pp. (S)

CYPRUS. *Development of Education, 1994–1996: National Report of Cyprus*. Nicosia, Ministry of Education and Culture, 1996. 74 pp.

CZECH REPUBLIC. *National Report on the Development of Education*. Prague, Ministry of Education, Youth and Sports, 1996. 212 pp.

DEMOCRATIC PEOPLE'S REPUBLIC OF KOREA. *Strengthening Teacher Training and Role of Teachers*. Pyongyang, State Education Commission, 1996. 11 pp.

DEMOCRATIC REPUBLIC OF THE CONGO (FORMER ZAIRE). *Développement de l'éducation. Rapport national du Zaïre*. Kinshasa, Commission Nationale Zaïroise pour l'UNESCO, 1996. 67 pp.

DENMARK. *Development of Education, 1994–1996: National Report of Denmark*. Copenhagen, Danish National Commission for UNESCO, Ministry of Education, 1996. 8 pp.

EGYPT. *Development of Education in Arab Republic of Egypt, 1994/95–1995/96*. Cairo, National Centre for Educational Research and Development, 1996. 114 pp.

   Reinforcement of Teachers' Role in a Changing World. Cairo, National Centre for Educational Research and Development, 1996. 45 pp.

ESTONIA. *Education in Estonia: Present Situation and Developments*. Tallinn, Ministry of Education, 1996. 22 pp.

ETHIOPIA. *The Federal Democratic Republic of Ethiopia: Educational Development, 1994–1995*. Addis Ababa, Ministry of Education, 1996. 16 pp.

FINLAND. *The Development of Education, 1994–1996*. Helsinki, National Board of Education, 1996. 66 pp.

FRANCE. *Rapport de la France*. Paris, Ministère de l'Éducation Nationale, de l'Enseignement Supérieur et de la Recherche, 1996. 66 pp.

GAMBIA. *Country Paper of the Republic of The Gambia*. Banjul, Ministry of Education, 1996. 15 pp.

GERMANY. *Bericht über die Entwicklung des Bildungswesens: 1994–1996/Report on the Development of Education: 1994–1996*. Bonn, Sekretariat der Ständigen Konferenz der Kultusminister der Länder in der Bundesrepublik Deutschland/Secretariat of the Standing Conference of the Ministers of Education and Cultural Affairs of the Länder in the Federal Republic of Germany, 1996. Bilingual: German (124 pp.)/English (140 pp.).

   Stärkung der Lehrerrolle in einer Welt im Umbruch/Enhancing the Role of Teachers in a Changing World. Bonn, Sekretariat der Ständigen Konferenz der Kultusminister der Länder in der Bundesrepublik Deutschland/Secretariat of the Standing Conference of the Ministers of Education and Cultural Affairs of the Länder in the Federal Republic of Germany, 1996. Bilingual: German (101 pp.)/English (98 pp.).

GHANA. *The Development of Education, 1994–1996: National Report from Ghana*. Accra, Ministry of Education, 1996. 49 pp.

GUINEA. *Développement de l'éducation, 1994–1996: rapport national de la République de Guinée*. Conakry, Ministère de l'Éducation Nationale et de la Recherche Scientifique, 1996. 25 pp.

HUNGARY. *The Development of Education. National Report of Hungary*. Budapest, Elemér Kelemen, 1996. 51 pp.

INDIA. *Development of Education in India, 1995–1996 with Special Reference to Teacher Education*. New Delhi, Department of Education, Ministry of Human Resource Development, 1996. 59 pp.

INDONESIA. *Education Development in Indonesia: A Country Report*. Jakarta, Ministry of Education and Culture, 1996. 133 pp.

IRAN (Islamic Republic of). *The Development of Education: National Report of the Islamic Republic of Iran*. Tehran, Ministry of Education, 1996. 223 pp.

IRAQ. *Development of Education in Iraq: 1993/1994–1994/1995*. Baghdad, Ministry of Education, 1996. Bilingual: English (51 pp.)/Arabic (41 pp.).

ISRAEL. *The Development of Education. National Report of Israel*. Jerusalem, Ministry of Education, Culture and Sport, 1996. 136 pp.

JAPAN. *Development of Education in Japan 1994–1996*. Tokyo, Ministry of Education, Science, Sports and Culture, 1996. 107 pp.

JORDAN. *The Development of Education in the Hashemite Kingdom of Jordan, 1995/1996*. Amman,

The General Directorate of Planning, Research and Development, Ministry of Education, 1996. 59 pp.

KENYA. *Development of Education, 1995 to 1996: National Report from Kenya.* Nairobi, Ministry of Education, 1996. 84 pp., appendices.

KUWAIT. *National Report on the Development of Education, State of Kuwait, 94/95–95/1996.* Kuwait, Ministry of Education, 1996. 195 pp. (Ar)

LEBANON. *La restructuration du système éducatif libanais. Dossier II.* Beirut, Ministère de l'Éducation Nationale, de la Jeunesse et des Sports, Centre National de Recherche et de Développement Pédagogiques, 1996. 82 pp.

LESOTHO. *The Development of Education, 1996–1998.* Maseru, Ministry of Education, 1996. 49 pp., annexes.

LIBYAN ARAB JAMAHIRIYA. *Development of Education. National Report of the Great Socialist People's Libyan Arab Jamahiriya during the Period 1994–1995–1996.* Tripoli, Secretariat of Education and Scientific Research, National Commission for Education, Culture and Science, 1996. Bilingual: English (113 pp.)/Arabic (206 pp.).

LUXEMBOURG. *Développement de l'éducation. Rapport national.* Luxembourg, Ministère de l'Éducation Nationale et de la Formation Professionnelle, 1995. 84 pp.

MADAGASCAR. *Rapport national sur le développement de l'éducation: 1994–1996.* Antananarivo, Unité d'Étude et de Recherches Pédagogiques, Ministère de l'Éducation Nationale, 1996. 74 pp.

MALAWI. *The Development of Education in Malawi, 1994–1996.* Lilongwe, Ministry of Education, Malawi National Commission for UNESCO, 1996. 31 pp.

MALAYSIA. *Strengthening the Role of Teachers in a Changing World. Country Paper.* Kuala Lumpur, Ministry of Education, 1996. 23 pp.

MALDIVES. *Developments in Education: 1994–1996.* Male', Ministry of Education, 1996. 34 pp.

MALI. *Développement de l'éducation au Mali, 1995–1996.* Bamako, Ministère de l'Éducation de Base, Ministère des Enseignements Secondaire, Supérieur et de la Recherche Scientifique, Commission Nationale Malienne pour l'UNESCO, 1996. 40 pp.

MALTA. *The Development of Education, 1995–96: National Report of Malta.* Floriana, Ministry of Education and Human Resources, 1996. 61 pp.

MAURITANIA. *Développement de l'éducation. Rapport national de la République islamique de Mauritanie.* Nouakchott, Ministère de l'Éducation Nationale, 1996. 40 pp.

MEXICO. *Education Development. National Report of Mexico, 1995–1996.* Mexico City, Secretary of Public Education, 1996. 39 pp., annexes. (S)

MOZAMBIQUE. *The Development of Education. National Report of Mozambique.* Maputo, Ministry of Education, 1996. 72 pp.

NETHERLANDS. *The Development of Education: Education Policy in the Netherlands: 1994–1996.* Zoetermeer, Ministry of Education, Culture and Science, 1996. 63 pp.

NICARAGUA. *Desarrollo de la educación, 1994–1996: Informe nacional de la República de Nicaragua.* Managua, Ministerio de Educación, Dirección General de Educación, 1996. 15 pp.

NIGER. *Rapport national sur le développement de l'éducation au Niger, 1994–1996.* Niamey, Commission Nationale Nigérienne pour l'Éducation, la Science et la Culture, Ministère de l'Éducation Nationale, 1996. 86 pp., annexes.

NIGERIA. *The Development of Education 1994–1996.* Lagos, Federal Ministry of Education, 1996. 59 pp.

NORWAY. *The Development of Education, 1994–96. National Report.* Oslo, Royal Ministry of Education, Research and Church Affairs, 1996. 49 pp.

OMAN. *Development of Education. The National Report of the Sultanate of Oman 1994–1996.* Muscat, Ministry of Education, 1996. 91 pp.

PARAGUAY. *Desarrollo de la educación: Informe nacional.* Asunción, Ministerio de Educación y Culto, 1996. 117 pp.

PERU. *Developments in Peru Education, Executive Summary.* Lima, Ministry of Education, 1996. 12 pp.

PHILIPPINES. *The Development of Education. A National Report on the Philippines.* Manila, Department of Education, Culture and Sports, 1996. 19 pp.

POLAND. *Development of Education in Poland.* Warsaw, Ministry of National Education, 1996. 171 pp.

PORTUGAL. *Développement de l'éducation. Rapport national du Portugal.* Lisbon, Ministère de l'Éducation, Bureau des Affaires Européennes et des Relations Internationales, 1996. 395 pp.

QATAR. *National Report on the Development of Education in the State of Qatar.* Doha, Ministry of Education, Qatar National Commission for Education, 1996. Bilingual: English (51 pp.)/Arabic (90 pp.).

REPUBLIC OF KOREA. *The Development of Education, National Report of the Republic of Korea.* Seoul, Ministry of Education, 1996. 96 pp.

ROMANIA. *Rapport concernant le système d'éducation en Roumanie.* Bucharest, Ministère de l'Éducation, 1996. 26 pp.

RUSSIAN FEDERATION. *Russia's Educational System: National Report of the Russian Federation.* Moscow, Ministry of Education, 1996. 89 pp., annexes.

SAUDI ARABIA. *Development of Education in the Kingdom of Saudi Arabia: National Report.* Riyadh, Ministry of Education, Centre for Statistical Data and Educational Documentation, 1996. Bilingual: English (121 pp.)/Arabic (125 pp.).

SENEGAL. *Rapport national sur le développement de l'éducation au Sénégal.* Dakar, Ministère de l'Éducation Nationale, 1996. 19 pp.

SIERRA LEONE. *The Development of Education: National Report from Sierra Leone.* Freetown, Ministry of Education, 1996. 7 pp.

SLOVAKIA. *Development of Education.* Bratislava, Institute of Information and Prognoses of Education, 1996. 131 pp.

SLOVENIA. *White Paper on Education in the Republic of Slovenia.* Ljubljana, Ministry of Education and Sport, 1996. 331 pp.

SPAIN. *Informe nacional de educación 1996/Education National Report 1996.* Madrid, Ministerio de Educación y Cultura/Ministry of Education and Culture, 1996. Bilingual: Spanish (83 pp.)/English (83 pp.).

SUDAN. *Sudan's Report to the International Conference on Education.* Khartoum, Ministry of General Education, General Directorate of Educational Planning, 1996. 81 pp. (Ar)

SWAZILAND. *The Development of Education: National Report of Swaziland.* Mbabane, Ministry of Education, 1996. 43 pp.

SWEDEN. *The Development of Education: National Report of Sweden.* Stockholm, Ministry of Education and Science, 1996. 36 pp.

SWITZERLAND. *Développement de l'éducation: rapport national de la Suisse.* Bern, Secrétariat Général de la Conférence Suisse des Directeurs Cantonaux de l'Instruction Publique, 1996. 74 pp.

SYRIAN ARAB REPUBLIC. *National Report on Development of Education in the Syrian Arab Republic.* Damascus, Ministry of Education, 1996. 44 pp.

TAJIKISTAN. *National Report on the Development of Education.* Dushanbe, Ministry of Education, State Pedagogical University of Dushanbe, 1996. 55 pp.

THAILAND. *Development of Education.* Bangkok, Ministry of Education, 1996. 50 pp.

New Aspirations for Education in Thailand towards Educational Excellence by the Year 2007. Bangkok, Ministry of Education, 1996. 34 pp.

THE FORMER YUGOSLAV REPUBLIC OF MACEDONIA. *National Report on Education for 1994–1996.* Skopje, Ministry of Education and Physical Culture, 1996. Bilingual: English (52 pp., annexes)/Macedonian (52 pp., annexes).

TOGO. *Développement de l'éducation: rapport national du Togo.* Lomé, Ministère de l'Éducation Nationale et de la Recherche Scientifique, Commission Nationale pour l'UNESCO, 1996. 61 pp.

TUNISIA. *Développement de l'éducation en Tunisie, 1994–1996.* Tunis, Ministère de l'Éducation, Commission Nationale Tunisienne pour l'Éducation, la Science et la Culture, 1996. 115 pp. (Ar)

TURKEY. *The Development of Education: Turkey.* Ankara, Ministry of National Education, 1996. 110 pp.

UNITED ARAB EMIRATES. *National Report of the United Arab Emirates on the Development of Education from 1993/1994–1995/1996.* Abu Dhabi, Ministry of Education, Planning and Evaluation Sector, 1996. Bilingual: English (120 pp.)/Arabic (110 pp.).

UNITED REPUBLIC OF TANZANIA. *The Development of Education: 1995–1996. National Report of the United Republic of Tanzania.* Dar es Salaam, Ministry of Education and Culture (Tanzania Mainland), Ministry of Education (Zanzibar), 1996. 90 pp., annexes.

UNITED STATES OF AMERICA. *Education in States and Nations. Indicators Comparing U.S. States with Other Industrialized Countries in 1991.* Washington, D.C., United States Department of Education, National Center for Education Statistics, 1996. 359 pp.

The Condition of Education 1996. Washington, D.C., National Center for Education Statistics, United States Department of Education, 1996. 387 pp.

URUGUAY. *Desarrollo de la educación. Informe nacional de Uruguay/Development in Education. National Report of Uruguay.* Montevideo, Ministerio de Educación y Cultura/Ministry of Education and Culture, 1996. Bilingual: Spanish (125 pp.)/English (119 pp.).

VANUATU. *Rapport national sur le développement de l'éducation: 1994–1996. République de Vanuatu.* Port-Vila, Ministère de l'Éducation, Bureau International de l'Éducation, 1995. 61 pp., annexes.

YUGOSLAVIA. *Development of Education in the FR Yugoslavia 1994–1995.* Belgrade, Yugoslav Commission for UNESCO, 1996. 91 pp.

ZAMBIA. *The Development of Education, 1994–1996: A National Report of Zambia.* Lusaka, Ministry of Education, 1996. 29 pp.

ZIMBABWE. *Development of Education: National Report of Zimbabwe.* Harare, Ministry of Education, Ministry of Higher Education, 1996. 46 pp.

Reports of UNESCO meetings

Advisory Committee of the Regional Programme for the Universalization and Renewal of Primary Education and the Eradication of Adult Illiteracy in the Arab States (ARABUPEAL). Cairo, Egypt, 23–24 February 1997. Final Report. Beirut, UNESCO/UNEDBAS, 1997. 92 pp. (Arabic with French summary)

APEID in Action: Educational Innovation for Development through Networks and Partnerships. Report to the First Meeting of the Intergovernmental Regional Committee on Education in Asia and the Pacific. Bangkok, Thailand, 24–26 June 1996. Bangkok, APEID/UNESCO/PROAP, 1996. 36 pp. ISBN 974-680-036-1.

Arab Regional Preparatory Conference on the Fifth International Conference on Adult Education. Cairo, Egypt, 25–27 February 1997. Final Report. Beirut, UNESCO/UNEDBAS, 1997. 154 pp. (Ar, F)

Asia-Pacific Programme of Education for All: Report to the First Meeting of the Intergovernmental Regional Committee on Education in Asia and the Pacific (EDCOM). Bangkok, Thailand, 24–26 June 1996. Bangkok, APPEAL/UNESCO/PROAP, 1996. 42 pp. ISBN 974-680-019-1.

Asia Regional Study Directors' Meeting for Project

INT/92/P78: Sociocultural Factors Affecting Demographic Behaviour and Implications for the Formulation and Execution of Population Policies and Programmes. Bangkok, Thailand, 27–29 March 1996. Final Report. Bangkok, UNESCO/PROAP, 1996. 41 pp. ISBN 974-680-025-6.

Case Studies on Technical and Vocational Education in Asia and the Pacific: Conference Report. UNESCO/UNEVOC Regional Meeting. Kuala Lumpur, Malaysia, 12–15 December 1994. By A. R. Haas. Bangkok, UNESCO/PROAP, 1996. 23 pp. ISBN 974-680-058-2.

Case Studies to Accompany Guide Book for Curriculum Development and Adaptation. Technical Working Group Meeting on Technical and Vocational Education. Bhopal, India, 29 November–6 December 1994. Bangkok, UNESCO/Adelaide Institute/Tafe Sa, 1995. 108 pp.

Design of Basic Education Programmes and Project: Report of Subregional Meeting. Genting Highlands, Malaysia, 1–17 November 1993. By A. Magnen, L. Mählck and J. Sequeira. Paris, UNESCO-IIEP, 1995. 143 pp.

Developments after Jomtien: EFA in the South-East Asia and Pacific Region. Report of a Seminar on 'Education for All: Developments after Jomtien'. Yangon, Myanmar, 28–31 March 1995. By A. De Grauwe and D. Bernard (eds). Paris, UNESCO-IIEP/UNICEF, 1995. 152 pp.

Development since Jomtien: EFA in the Middle East and North Africa. Report of a Seminar on 'Education for All: Developments after Jomtien'. Amman, Jordan, 19–22 October 1994. By R. Govinda and I. Lorfing (eds.). Paris, UNESCO-IIEP/UNICEF, 1995. 188 pp.

Education Aid Policies and Practices: A Report from the IWGE. Meeting of the International Working Group on Education (IWGE). Nice, France, 16–18 November 1994. Paris, UNESCO-IIEP, 1995. 81 pp.

Educational Challenges of the 21st Century: The Vision of Quality. SEAMEO/INNOTECH International Conference on Educational Challenges in the World Community of the 21st Century. Manila, Philippines, 5–7 December 1995. By J. Hallak. Paris, UNESCO-IIEP. 1996. 13 pp.

Environmental Issues and Environmental Education in the Mekong Region: Proceedings of a Regional Seminar on Environmental Education, March 1996.

By P. Bishop (ed.) and others. Bangkok, UNESCO, 1997. 129 pp.

ISBN 974-680-016-7.

Fifteenth APEID Regional Seminar on Special Education. Yokosuka, Japan, 16–23 October 1995. Final Report. Yokosuka, UNESCO/PROAP/APEID, 1996. 141 pp.

Fifth International Conference on Adult Education (CONFINTEA V). Hamburg, 14–18 July 1997. Final Report. Paris, UNESCO. In press. (ED-97/MD/101.)

Final Report of Regional Symposium on Linkage of TVE to the World of Work. Beirut, Lebanon, 18–21 November 1996. Beirut, UNESCO/UNEDBAS/ UNEVOC, 1996. 44 pp. (Ar)

Final Report on Round Table on Enhancing Access of Girls and Women to Science and Technology Education. Amman, Jordan, 2–4 March 1997. Beirut, UNESCO/UNEDBAS/UNEVOC, 1997. 60 pp. (Ar)

Final Report of Workshop on Enhancement of Learning and Training Opportunities for Youth. Amman, Jordan, 2–4 March 1997. Beirut, UNESCO/ UNEDBAS/UNEVOC, 1997. 72 pp. (Ar)

Financial Management in Higher Education Institutions for Eastern Mediterranean Countries: Report of a Sub-Regional Workshop. Patras, Greece, 29 May–2 June 1995. By J. Hallak and M. Martin. Paris, UNESCO-IIEP/University of Patras/Greek Ministry of National Education and Religious Affairs, 1995. 127 pp.

Financing of Education and Budget Programming Techniques: A Sub-Regional Workshop. Damascus, Syrian Arab Republic, 1–6 July 1995. Edited by H. Hajjar. Beirut, UNESCO, 1996. (Arabic (156 pp.) with executive summary in English (12 pp.))

First Meeting of the Intergovernmental Regional Committee on Education in Asia and the Pacific (EDCOM). Final Report. Bangkok, Thailand, 24–25 June 1996. Bangkok, UNESCO/PROAP, 1997. 58 pp.

ISBN 974-680-035-3.

Fourteenth APEID Regional Seminar on Special Education. Yokosuka, Japan, 6–11 November 1994. Final Report. Yokosuka, UNESCO/PROAP/APEID, 1995. 232 pp.

ISBN 974-680-066-3.

International Conference on Education, 45th Session. Geneva, 30 September–5 October 1996. Final Report. Paris, UNESCO-IBE, 1996. 26 pp., bibliog. (ED/MD/100.) (Ar, Ch, F, R, S)

International Expert Group Meeting on New Technologies of Training for Technical and Vocational Education. Manila, Philippines, 3–7 July 1995. Final Report. Paris/Turin/Manila, UNEVOC/ILO/ CPSC, 1995. 57 pp., appendices.

International Expert Meeting on the Promotion of Equal Access of Girls and Women to Technical and Vocational Education. Seoul, Republic of Korea, 10–15 July 1995. Final Report. Paris, UNESCO/ UNEVOC, 1996. 17 pp.

International Project on Technical and Vocational Education (UNEVOC). Expert Meeting on Teacher Education and Training for Technical and Vocational Education in the Arab States. Abu-Dhabi, United Arab Emirates, 24–27 March 1996. Final Report. Paris, UNESCO/UNEVOC, 1996. 44 pp., annexes.

International Project on Technical and Vocational Education (UNEVOC). International Advisory Committee. Third Session. Paris, France, 2–4 October 1995. Final Report. Paris, UNESCO/UNEVOC, 1995. 28 pp. (F)

International Project on Technical and Vocational Education (UNEVOC). Regional Symposium for Policy Makers in Technical and Vocational Education in Africa. Dakar, Senegal, 21–24 August 1995. Final Report. Dakar, UNESCO/BREDA/ UNEVOC, 1995. 21 pp.

International Project on Technical and Vocational Education (UNEVOC). The Challenge of the Future. Future Trends in Adult and Continuing Technical and Vocational Education. An International Symposium. Berlin, Germany, 16–20 October 1995. Berlin, UNESCO/UNEVOC, 1996. 107 pp.

Managing Schools for Better Quality: Multigrade Teaching and School Clusters. Report of a Joint UNICEF/UNESCO/SEAMES Workshop. Bangkok, Thailand, 28 November–2 December 1994. Bangkok, UNESCO/PROAP, 1995. 66 pp.

ISBN 974-680-018-3.

Mid-Decade Review of Education for All in East and South-East Asia and the Pacific: Report of a Policy Review Seminar. Hanoi, Viet Nam, 17 November 1995. Bangkok, UNESCO/PROAP, 1996. 44 pp.

ISBN 974-680-064-7.

Mid-Decade Review of Education for All in South Asia: Report of a Policy Review Seminar. Rawalpindi, Pakistan, 15–18 January 1996. Bangkok, UNESCO/PROAP, 1996, 62 pp.
ISBN 974-680-065-5.

Organizational Meeting to Form the Network of Regional Experts in Education for Peace, Human Rights and Democracy. Seoul, Republic of Korea, 29–31 March 1995. Final Report. Bangkok, UNESCO/PROAP, 1995. 43 pp.
ISBN 974-680-022-1.

Partnerships in Teacher Development for a New Asia. Report of An International Conference. Bangkok, Thailand, 6–8 December 1995. Bangkok, ACEID/UNESCO/PROAP, 1996. 476 pp.
ISBN 974-680-030-2.

Regional Convention on the Recognition Studies, Diplomas and Degrees in Higher Education in Asia and the Pacific. Third Session of the Regional Committee. Bangkok, Thailand, 14–16 December 1994. Final Report. Bangkok, UNESCO/PROAP, 1995. 40 pp.
ISBN 974-680-015-9.

Regional Workshop: Forging Integrated Partnership on Environment and Population Education and Information for Human Development (EPD). Final Report. Beijing, China, 19-23 June 1995. Bangkok, UNESCO/PROAP, 1995. 74 pp.
ISBN 974-680-024-8.

Report of the Consultative Meeting and Workshop: Planning Human Resource Development for Information Societies. Bangkok, Thailand, 3–7 March 1997. Bangkok, UNESCO/PROAP/Japanese Ministry of Education, Science, Sports and Culture, 1997. 109 pp.
ISBN 974-680-080-9.

Review of Innovative Pilot Project on Promotion of Primary Education for Girls and Disadvantaged Groups. Report of a Project Review Meeting. Ningxia, China, 15–19 May 1995. Bangkok, UNESCO/PROAP/APEID, 1995. 61 pp.
ISBN 974-680-061.

Seventh Conference of Ministers of Education of Latin America and the Caribbean. Kingston, Jamaica, 13–17 May 1996. Final Report. Santiago, UNESCO, 1996. 103 pp. (ED/MD/201.) (S)

Sub-regional Workshop: Alternative Strategies for Assessing Science Technology and Environment Literacy for Girls and Women. Final Report, SEAMEO/INNOTECH. Manila, Philippines, 7–9 December 1995. Bangkok, UNESCO/SEAMEO, 1995. 53 pp.
ISBN 974-680-034-5.

Virtual Learning Environments and the Role of the Teacher: UNESCO/Open University International Colloquium, Milton Keynes, August 1997. Report. By T. O'Shea and E. Scanlon, Paris/Milton Keynes, United Kingdom, UNESCO/Open University Institute of Educational Technology, 1997, 27 pp.

Publications

ALPHA 97: Basic Education and Institutional Environment. Edited by J.-P. Hautecoeur. Hamburg/Toronto, UNESCO-UIE/Culture Concepts Publishers, 1997. 372 pp. (F)
ISBN 92-829-1071-6.

ALPHA 96: Basic Education and Work. Edited by J.-P. Hautecoeur. Hamburg/Toronto, UNESCO-UIE/Culture Concepts Publishers, 1996. 348 pp. (F)
ISBN 92-820-1075-9.

Analfabetismo y mujer rural (Investigación). By M. Almeida-Duque, M. S. Leiva and G. de la Bastida. New York/Paris/Quito, UNICEF/UNESCO/FUNDELAM, 1995. 134 pp.
ISBN 9978-61-066-9.

Calidad de la educación en el istmo centroamericano. By J. B. Arrién et al. San José, UNESCO, 1996. 363 pp.
ISBN 92-9136-014-7.

Case Studies on Technical and Vocational Education in Asia and the Pacific: An Overview. By A. R. Haas. Bangkok, UNESCO/PROAP, 1996. 28 pp.
ISBN 974-680-057-4.

Challenges of Education for All in Asia and the Pacific and the APPEAL Response. Compiled by T. M. Sakya and G. Rex Meyer. Bangkok, UNESCO/PROAP, 1997. 176 pp.
ISBN 974-680-029-9.

Confronting Future Challenges: Educational Information, Research and Decision-Making. By F. Reimers, N. McGinn and K. Wild. Geneva, UNESCO-IBE, 1995. 185 pp. (Studies in Comparative Education.)
ISBN 92-9145-003-0.

Education and Human Resources Sector Analysis: A Training Manual. Bangkok, UNESCO/PROAP, 1996. 116 pp.
ISBN 974-680-081-7.

L'éducation dans les pays les moins avancés: améliorer dans l'adversité. By G.-C. Chang. Paris, UNESCO, 1996. 92 pp. (Études et documents d'éducation, 64.)
ISBN 92-3-203347-X.

Education, Democracy and Development. An International Perspective. Edited by R. Ryba. Hamburg/Dordrecht, UNESCO-UIE/Kluwer Academic Publishers, 1997. 118 pp. (IRE Library.)
ISBN 92-820-0009-5.

Education Planning and Management, and the Use of Geographical Information Systems. By J. M. Mendelsohn. Paris, UNESCO-IIEP, 1996. 78 pp.
ISBN 92-803-1158-1.

Education Policy-Planning Process: An Applied Framework. By W. D. Haddad and T. Demsky. Paris, UNESCO-IIEP, 1995. 94 pp. (Fundamentals of Educational Planning, 51.) (F)
ISBN 92-803-1155-7.

Enhancing the Skills of Early Childhood Trainers. By K. Torkington and C. Landers. The Hague/Paris, Bernard Van Leer Foundation/UNESCO, 1995. 5 Vols.
ISBN 92-3-103130-9.

La escuela global. La educación y la comunicación a lo largo de la historia de la UNESCO. By A. Monclús and C. Sabán. Paris/Madrid, UNESCO/Fondo de Cultura Económica, 1997. 374 pp.
ISBN 92-3-303366-X.

From Planning to Action: Government Initiatives for Improving School-level Practice. Edited by D. W. Chapman, L. O. Mählck and A. E. M. Smulders. Oxford/Paris, Pergamon/UNESCO-IIEP, 1997.
ISBN 92-803-1163-8.

Humanities and Culture Education in the South Pacific: Curriculum Reform Issues and Trends. By G. Withers. Bangkok, UNESCO/PROAP, 1995. 55 pp., illus.
ISBN 974-680-039-6.

Improving Education in Disadvantaged Contexts: The Joint Innovative Project in China. By Z. Tiedao and M. Lally. Bangkok, UNESCO/PROAP, 1995. 89 pp.
ISBN 974-680-063-9.

Information Technologies in Teacher Education: Issues and Experiences for Countries in Transition. By B. Collis, I. Nikolova and K. Martcheva. Paris, UNESCO, 1995. 317 pp. (The Teacher's Library.)
ISBN 92-3-103072-8.

Innovations in Science and Technology Education. Vol. VI. Edited by E. W. Jenkins and D. Layton. Paris, UNESCO, 1997. 285 pp.
ISBN 92-3-103278-X.

Innovations in University Management. By B. C. Sanyal. Paris, UNESCO-IIEP, 1995. 313 pp.
ISBN 92-803-1156-5.

Learning for a Sustainable Environment: An Agenda for Teacher Education in Asia and the Pacific. By J. Fien and D. Tillbury. Bangkok, UNESCO/PROAP, 1996. 84 pp.
ISBN 974-680-110-4.

Learning: The Treasure Within. Report to UNESCO of the International Commission on Education for the Twenty-first Century. By J. Delors et al. Paris, UNESCO, 1996. 266 pp. (Ar, Cat., F, G, Port., R, S and others)
ISBN 92-3-103274-7.

Management of Education Systems in Zones of Conflict-Relief Operations; A Case Study in Thailand. By Y. Suenobu. Bangkok, UNESCO/PROAP, 1995. 54 pp.
ISBN 974-680-082-5.

Mathematics Education Research: Past, Present and Future. By M. A. Clements and N. F. Ellerton. Bangkok, UNESCO/PROAP. 1996. 246 pp.
ISBN 974-680-032-9.

Modelos educativos en la historia de América Latina. By G. Weinberg. Paris/Buenos Aires, UNESCO/CEPAL/UNDP/A-Z Editora, 1995. 297 pp.
ISBN 950-534-310-8.

Multigrade Teaching in Primary School. By I. Birch and M. Lally. Bangkok, UNESCO/PROAP, 1995. 93 pp.
ISBN 974-680-038-8.

Population, Environment and Development Linkages. Bangkok, UNESCO/PROAP, 1996. 154 pp. (Abstract-Bibliography Series, 13.)
ISBN 974-680-078-7.

Quality Assurance for Higher Education: Developing and Managing Quality Assurance for Higher Education Systems and Institutions in Asia and the Pacific. By G. Harman. Bangkok, UNESCO/PROAP, 1996. 105 pp.
ISBN 974-680-026-4.

The Quality of Primary Schools in Different Develop-

ment Contexts. By G. Carron and T. N. Châu. Paris, UNESCO-IIEP, 1996. 306 pp.
ISBN 92-803-1159-9.

Report on the State of Education in Africa, 1995: Education Strategies for the 1990s. Orientations and Achievements. Dakar, UNESCO/BREDA, 1995. 189 pp. (F)
ISBN 92-9091-046-1.

Searching for Relevance: The Development of Work Orientation in Basic Education. By W. Hoppers. Paris, UNESCO-IIEP, 1996. 114 pp. (Fundamentals of Educational Planning, 52.)
ISBN 92-803-1157-3.

Study Abroad/Études à l'étranger/Estudios en el extranjero. Vol. XXX. Paris, UNESCO, 1997. 1,248 pp. (Trilingual: E/F/S)
ISBN 92-3-003401-0.

Teaching Primary School Mathematics. By D. Broomes et al., Kingston/Paris, Ian Randle Publishers/ UNESCO, 1995. 211 pp.
ISBN 92-3-102945-2.

Teaching Training and Multiculturalism: National Studies. Edited by R. Gagliardi. Paris/Geneva, UNESCO-IBE, 1995. 226 pp. (Studies in Comparative Education.)
ISBN 92-9145-002-2.

Tolerance – the Threshold of Peace. Unit 1: *Teacher-Training Resource Unit;* Unit 2: *Primary-School Resource Unit;* Unit 3: *Secondary-School Resource unit*. By B. A. Reardon. Paris, UNESCO, 1997. 136 pp. (Unit 1); 98 pp. (Unit 2); 114 pp. (Unit 3). (The Teachers Library.)
ISBN 92-3-103376-X (Unit 1);
ISBN 92-3-103377-8 (Unit 2);
ISBN 92-3-103378-6 (Unit 3).

To Live Together: Shaping New Attitudes to Peace Through Education. Edited by D. S. Halpérin. Paris, UNESCO-IBE, 1997. 186 pp. (Studies in Comparative Education.)
ISBN 92-3-185003-2.

UNESCO en el desarrollo y en las innovaciones de la educación en Centroamérica. By J. B. Arrién. San José, UNESCO, 1996. 355 pp.
ISBN 92-9136-024-4.

Women and the University Curriculum: Towards Equality, Democracy and Peace. Edited by M.-L. Kearney and A. H. Ronning. Paris/London, UNESCO/Jessica Kingsley Publishers, 1996. 270 pp.
ISBN 92-3-103243-7.

World Education Report 1995. Paris, UNESCO, 1995. 174 pp., figs., tables. (Ar, Ch, F, G, Port., R, S)
ISBN 92-3-103180-5.

World Guide to Higher Education. A Comparative Survey of Systems, Degrees and Qualifications (3rd ed.). Paris, UNESCO, 1996. 571 pp.
ISBN 92-3-102766-2.

Periodicals

Bulletin of the Major Project of Education in Latin America and the Caribbean (Santiago (Chile), UNESCO/OREALC). Bulletin published three times a year. (S).

Educación Superior y Sociedad (Caracas, UNESCO/ CRESALC). (Spanish only).

Higher Education in Europe (Bucharest, UNESCO/ CEPES). Quarterly review. (F, R).

International Review of Education/Internationale Zeitschrift für Erziehungswissenschaft/Revue internationale de l'éducation (Hamburg, UNESCO-UIE/ Kluwer Academic Publishers). Six issues a year. (Trilingual: E/G/F).

Prospects: Quarterly Review of Comparative Education (Geneva, UNESCO-IBE) (Ar, Ch, F, R, S).

UNESCO-AFRICA (Dakar, UNESCO/BREDA). Two issues a year. (F).